Bicycle Touring Interna

Bicycle Touring International

**The Complete Book on
Adventure Cycling**

Kameel Nasr

Bicycle Books
San Francisco

Printed in the United States of America

Published by:
Bicycle Books, Inc.
PO Box 2038, Mill Valley, CA 94942 (USA)

Distributed to the book trade by:
USA   National Book Network, Lanham, MD
Canada: Raincoast Book Distrib., Vancouver, BC
UK: Chris Lloyd Sales & Marketing Services
                 Poole, Dorset

Cover design: Lytle Design, Alameda, CA

Cover photo: Catharina Halter

Publisher's Cataloging in Publication Data:
Nasr, Kameel, 1949—. Bicycle Touring International
The Complete Book on Adventure Cycling.
1. Cycling, manuals and handbooks.
2. Bicycles
3. Travel, international
I. Authorship
II. Title

Library of Congress Catalog Card Number 92-75113

USA edition: ISBN 0-933201-53-2

UK edition only: ISBN 0-933201-51-6

To my mother and father

About the Author

Kameel Nasr was born in Lebanon and grew up in San Francisco. He has an MA in English and has taught writing at DePaul University. He also worked as a journalist for an English-language newspaper in Jeruzalem and has written articles on travel and Middle East politics.

In 1980 Kameel hopped on a bicycle and rode from Chicago to San Francisco. Since then, he has gone on two major cycling adventures that took him through Europe, Central and South America, Africa, the Middle East and Asia. He went alone, with a few dollars in his pocket, and panniers full of maps. He came back, not only with a host of stories, but also with a mind full of questions about the values of modern society.

Although delighted to grapple with heavy religious and social justice issues, Kameel is also ready to laugh. He lives in a rural house in Italy and encourages others, young and old, to tour foreign countries by bicycle.

Author's Preface

I didn't just want to see other places, I had to experience them. I had to find out for myself how the present-day Incas live, who the Masai are, what Hinduism is, why there is conflict in South Africa and the Middle East, what ancient Greek temples and Renaissance art look like, how people live in the Sahara. I had to confront life, to look over Kansas wheat fields, walk into the Louvre and the Great Pyramid, drink coffee with Turks, thumb my nose at Wall Street. I had to be there, see with my own eyes, feel with my own senses, move by my own power.

You too?

After the publication of my book *The World Up Close,* many people have asked me for practical information about touring: what to take, where to go, what to do about mechanical breakdowns, how to train, what and where to eat and sleep, keeping safe.

One of the beauties of traveling by bicycle is that you can get on your bicycle and go. Many aspects of distance bicycling can only be learned by experience; other aspects are common sense. But most bicyclists wish that they had a written guide with down-to-earth suggestions.

In the following pages, I hope to pass on not only my years of experience on the road, but the experience of dozens of other bicycle tourists I have met. I have tried to be practical and realistic, including the hard parts, the frustrating parts.

Good Riding!

Table of Contents

PART I.

THE BICYCLE TOURING EXPERIENCE

CHAPTER 1

The Experience that Can Change Your Life

The best way to see the world is by bicycle. On a bicycle you do not merely travel from one tourist place to another, skipping along the surface of different cultures; you become a true traveler, riding away from 'plastic' cities and interacting with people. You begin to see life in the raw, the underlying culture.

Anyone—young or mature, athletic or flabby, outgoing or shy—can read this book, train, and cycle through almost any part of the world. If the idea of riding through remote villages that rarely see foreigners excites you, and you think you may enjoy buying cheese from a dairy on a back road in Wisconsin, cruising by a medieval Austrian castle, or sitting in a Zulu chief's house, then you should consider taking a bicycle trip. Whether you have the desire for adventure or want to go with friends for a weekend cycling trek in the country, this could be one of the most rewarding experiences of your life. You need to take time out, simultaneously making a physical adventure and a mental retreat. The main ingredient is not muscles but desire. Make up your mind that this is what you want to do, and you will do it.

Dressed to kill: Bicycle touring through Bolivia's mountain region.

It Can Be Done

You will be safer on the road in most foreign countries than you will roaming about the streets of a big American city. Wild animals will not attack you, revolutionaries will not force you to fight for their cause, and cannibals will not throw you into a kettle of boiling water.

You will have the time of your life. The experience will give you more tranquillity and self-confidence, make you more open and understanding, and show you different customs and lifestyles.

However, bicycle touring is not always easy. You will see things that may disturb you. You will have mechanical breakdowns at the worst times, and you will probably get sick. You may meet unpleasant people. You will get tired, dirty, and sweaty. If you venture into the Third World you will find yourself crying out in the wilderness for social justice. You will see hunger, lack of sanitation, overcrowding, people treating each other badly, and people defecating near the road. This book will help you deal with these unpleasant elements, but you will face something even more challenging: you will meet aspects of yourself that you never wanted to see or acknowledge. At times you may find yourself becoming frustrated and angry, being selfish, petty or distrustful, even acting arrogant and hateful. A bicycle trip can be a profoundly emotional experience. Those negative feelings are temporary, however. They will eventually blow away, leaving you a more sensitive person from the experience.

Fantasy into Reality

Cycling is a wonderful form of travel: you are silent, non-polluting, surrounded by natural beauty, and not particularly slow. You do not waste half a day standing around an airport or a bus station. Travel, which comes from the French world *travail*, ceases to become a mundane or uncomfortable necessity to get you to another city. Some roads are smooth and a pleasure to cycle, winding through forests and quiet country towns. Other roads are rough. Remote areas can be reached by off-road or all-terrain bikes.

Some bicycle tourists spend months in one country, riding slowly from town to town. Other people breeze through, pedaling 100 miles a day or more. You ride quickly through places that do not interest you and more slowly where you find things exciting.

You may need to transport your bicycle. Mine has been shipped by plane over two dozen times and has been on trucks, trains, buses, and ships too often to count. Many people travel to various countries by plane or train and only cycle short distances. Others buy a bicycle in the country they visit.

Figuring Time and Money

Besides being the best way to travel and experience diverse cultures, bicycle touring is usually cheap. If you need to buy a new touring bike, plan on spending $500-1000. If you camp, you will need another $300–400 for one person ($400–500 for two) to buy a sleeping bag, tent, mattress, and accessories.

On the road, cyclists spend $8–15 per person per day. In India you might spend $4 a day, while in France you can spend $20 daily while being conservative. If you want to fly to your starting point and/or fly back, you need to include that expense in your estimation. Add a little for having a good time and include items you might want to buy during the trip. Bicyclists are rarely trinket collectors.

Before my first trip, when I was a poor student sharing a $90-a-month apartment, I went to Sears and bought a heavy $7.95 metal basket (I knew nothing about touring), attached it to my ailing 15-year-old street bike, and went on a 600-mile trip, spending $3 a day. It was Spartan but exciting. My last eight-month trip cost over $6,000. It is up to you how much to spend—just as it is where to go, what to see, or how long to stay.

Allot your time not only by how long a vacation you have, but by how much you have been touring. If it is your first trip it should definitely last no longer than a week, preferably three or four days. As you get used to touring, you can extend your trip a little at a time. You will probably ride between 40 and 100 miles a day. After your first trip, you will be better able to judge your daily distance.

Successful bicycle trips require planning. Not only do you need to plan when and where to go, but you need to get your equipment ready, read about the place or places you want to visit, perhaps obtain visas and vaccinations, and physically train for the ride. I know several couples who spent a year planning a summer tour of Europe. Without exaggeration, you can spend three times as long planning a trip as actually riding. Of course, anything can happen on the road. One cyclist who planned to take three months off from teaching to tour the Mediterranean wound up spending a year in North Africa. It did not matter that he ran out of money—the local people put him up.

This book gives you point-by-point suggestions on how to tour any area of the world by bicycle. It does not attempt to rob you of any excitement by telling you what to do from beginning to end. The book is divided into four sections. The first three present overall guidelines on the various aspects of long-distance bicycle touring in general, while the fourth, and longest, describes cycling in different areas of the world.

Although the book can be read cover-to-cover, each chapter is complete in itself and suitable to be read separately as well. Find out what you want to read from the contents, read those chapters, and set down a program to get your equipment, your legs, and your mind in shape for the expedition.

CHAPTER 2

Solo, with Friends, or in a Crowd

First you should consider whether to travel alone or with company. The options are: going solo, taking along one or two friends, or being part of a large group or commercially organized tour.

Traveling Alone

Riding solo, you are free to make your own decisions and do not need to sound out how your partner feels about doing something or worry about how much energy he or she has left. If you want to go, stay, change plans, or drop the whole idea, you can do so without concern or guilt.

Furthermore, soloists, especially in a foreign land, must depend on the local people. They cannot retreat into their own group and socialize among themselves, thus remaining outsiders to the place they are visiting. Soloists are forced to integrate, but they are also forced to rely on themselves on those long empty stretches, making them more self-confident and giving them a greater sense of accomplishment at the end.

With One or Two Friends

Being this alone does not appeal to most people whose idea of a bicycle trip is to have a good time with others. Two or more cyclists help each other break the

Two French touring cyclists on a two-year tour of the world, pictured here in Costa Rica.

wind, making riding physically easier. Wind is the hardest part of cycling. Another person can offer an alternative way to deal with a problem and provide moral support and encouragement, making a trip an enjoyable cooperative venture. With one or two friends you carry less gear, such as only one slightly larger tent for two people, only one set of tools, one camera, and one first aid kit. You can share tasks: one person washes clothes while another makes dinner. A trip with at least one other person is less intimidating and more merry.

Groups and Tours

Being part of a larger group of cyclists is usually a jolly experience. It puts less demand on each person, and the diversity of personalities offers more camaraderie. Groups provide greater moral support and make a trip easier. In a group someone knows bicycle mechanics. Many local bicycle clubs organize outings to nearby areas, usually for a weekend or a few days during summer. Except for the groups that are organized through professional tour operators, most cyclists on longer journeys either travel solo or in pairs. Three or more seems to be a crowd on a long trip.

commercial bicycle tour operators organize package vacations. They are convenient for beginning cyclists because they have an experienced leader and travel on safe, scenic routes, some providing a sag wagon for equipment and tired riders. You learn the tricks of touring with a crowd. Such tours are more expensive, and although some distance cyclists would consider a sag wagon cheating, such touring would be good for novices or those unsure of their cycling ability. Professional tours are offered to various parts of North America, East and West Europe, the Far East, Latin America, Australia, and New Zealand. A few tour operators are listed in Appendix 4; others advertise in cycling magazines.

You are probably not going to be able to put into words what you want to get out of a trip. Cyclists usually want a mixture of challenge, fun, exposure to other cultures, spiritual awakening, physical exercise, emotionally charged experiences, mixing with new people, and many other hard-to-define desires. Most people know instinctively whether they want to go alone, with another person, or in a group.

Choosing Partners

For those who are not interested in going solo or on a package tour, I offer these suggestions for choosing partners. First, make sure you are compatible. Riding, eating, and sleeping next to someone day after day is as close as a marriage. You must enjoy each other, not just be able to tolerate each other. You should both be capable of approximately the same physical stamina. Believe me, a few days of repeatedle waiting for some-one to catch up can create an unpleasant situation.

A person who wants to visit every religious shrine will not enjoy the company of one who wants to watch baseball games in different cities (I've met both). Some-one who wants to cycle many hours will have a hard time with a partner who considers the morning the only time to ride. Since pairs or groups cook and eat together, they should share gastronomic tastes.

Couples need special mention. Bicycle trips have been known to break up otherwise good marriages. A bicycle trip is no place to test the stability of a relation-ship. I have met many couples having a wonderful time on the road, and I have observed that their relaxed relationship is a result of both partners con-tributing to the success of the trip and making it a united effort.

If you want to take a trip with one or more persons, and you don't know anyone, you can advertise in cy-cling newsletters and local bicycle shops, stating when and where you want to go. When people respond to your ad, ask them about their interests, how many

American touring cyclist in Greece

miles a day they want to ride, how much riding experience they have had, what languages they speak (if that is important), and try to discover something of their temperament. Start the relationship on the right foot by revealing yourself and your aspirations. Local bicycle clubs are good places to meet potential partners.

CHAPTER 3

Personal Safety

Perhaps one of the first questions on your mind is whether you are going to make it through the experience alive. This seems to be a prime concern for many Americans whose first questions are, "Weren't you ever in danger?" and "Didn't people try to rob you?" They do not have a rational fear but a fear of the unknown, which they perceive as danger. Comparatively, America is a dangerous place to ride. If you can ride through the U.S. your chances of making it anywhere else are good.

Except in war zones, no one will harm you in rural areas around the world. However, in certain areas theft is, unfortunately, common, requiring common-sense precautions to make sure you are not a victim. If, for example, someone steals your air pump, and you are in the middle of nowhere, it can be a major problem. You need to establish a safe system of daily activity so you do not get obsessed with being robbed.

In rural Asia you can leave your bicycle and equipment and go into people's homes or a restaurant. The villagers will gather around and inspect the strange object, argue about the way everything works, look inside the handlebar bag, and put their feet in the toe clips, but no one would even think about stealing anything.

Holy week in Sevilla, Spain

On the other hand, do not be careless—don't let your equipment out of your sight for a second in a busy place. But do not become paranoid: either put your bicycle somewhere safe or simply keep it with you.

Distance cyclists seldom use locks, but you can take a light combination chain lock along. The Kryptonite or Citadel locks mandatory in U.S. cities are ridiculous to carry on the road. You will hardly be in a position to use a lock since you should never leave your bicycle out of your sight unless someone you trust is looking after it or it is in a house or hotel. At times this can restrict you. Ask someone—a storekeeper for example—to keep your bicycle while you run off. People are happy to accommodate.

Women and Bicycles

Although the risk is greater for women than for men, it is quite safe in most areas. Many women tour through Europe, and certainly East Asia is safe for women. I encourage women to cycle without necessarily being with men; I feel that women will usually be treated to even more hospitality and that the local people, men and women, will go out of their way to look after a woman's safety and 'honor.' Traveling in pairs or groups is usually safer than doing so alone.

In morally conservative countries, all cyclists, especially women, should dress modestly. If you look like an athlete you can get away with riding in shorts as long as you put on long pants as soon as you get off the bicycle. In Muslim countries I wear long pants (cycling tights) while riding, no matter how hot it gets.

Drugs and Alcohol

I have listened to many horror stories about people traveling in Colombia. I love riding in that country. After a while I began noticing a pattern to the ill-fated sequence of events, and every one involved drugs. Get your priorities straight: stay away from drug dealers, no matter how low the price of hashish is in Morocco. The possibility of a foreigner being double-crossed, robbed, or searched is too high.

While on the subject, we need to add that alcohol affects a hot body much more than a cool one. After a hard ride you will want a cool refreshing drink, and while a cold beer or other drink feels satisfying, drinking alcohol will make you sleepy and diminish your cycling energy. Also, your body cannot tolerate as much alcohol in high altitudes.

PART II.

_____ TOURING EQUIPMENT

CHAPTER 4

Choosing a Bicycle for Distance Touring

If you do not already own a touring bike, you will need to buy one that fits you and is right for touring. Bicycle touring has been given a new dimension with the introduction and popularity of the mountain or all-terrain bike (ATB), making almost every part of the globe accessible. However, ATBs are heavier, slower, and not as comfortable as the traditional bicycle. An ATB rider must hold the same arm position whereas a road bike rider can change body positions and discharge the strain on the back and shoulders.

Before you decide to buy a mountain bike, consider where you are going. Unless you plan to travel mainly on dirt, you best stick to the traditional touring bike. Mountain bikes are overused: they are not efficient on asphalt. You can select a durable road bike, put tough fat tires on it, and take it on plenty of rough, unpaved roads. I have taken my touring bike through thick mud, over mountain trails, and on thin snow. Only those who plan to ride off-road most of their trip should use a mountain bike.

Small-wheel folding bicycles are convenient since they can be easily carried or stored. One cyclist toured part of Central America using a folding bicycle, but much of his trip was by bus. Folding bicycles cannot take much equipment, are usually not strong, and are uncomfortable over long distances. However, those who want to integrate cycling with other forms of travel should consider a folding bike.

Tandems can be wonderful for pairs. They are tremendously efficient, providing twice the power while only splitting the wind once. I stayed at a California campground next to a tandem-touring pair. In the morning I got up early and began riding. I find the morning the best time for cycling, and that day I was full of energy and going strong. They got up later and effortlessly passed me on the road, stopped for breakfast, and passed me again, smiling and waving each time they passed.

Folding bicycles, though easy to transport, are not suitable for most distance touring.

However, tandems are not for every twosome. Both people need to be synchronized and not very different in height. Pairs have to try one out and see if they are suited and can develop a rhythm, before taking a tandem on a trip. Too many tandems end up in people's basements after only limited use. They are usually good for two women or two men.

Other bicycle styles such as recumbents have tremendous potential, and a few people have taken them touring. However, the traditional road bike remains the best choice for touring 90 percent of the time.

Bicycle Styles

Do not be put off by bicycle jargon. The mechanics and the language for this relatively simple sport are not difficult. If you choose not to learn technical terms, it will not prevent you from buying a good bicycle or touring. Buy a bicycle not only because it is technologically the best for you; buy it because you really like it. You will need to develop a working relationship with it. It must look nice and be painted the right color.

There are three types of so-called ten-speed bicycles: racing, touring, and junk. Junk bikes are the ones you buy in pedestrian department stores such as K-Mart or Sears. They are worthless for anything short of riding around the city. Do not use a junk bike for touring.

The parts of a bicycle frame

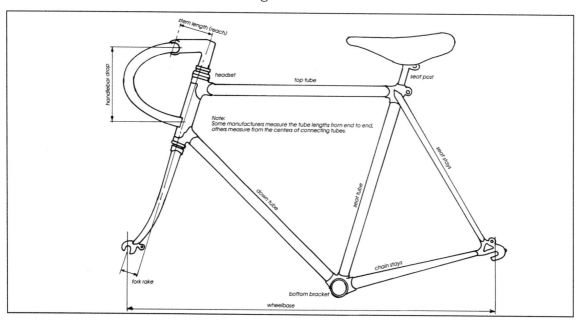

Although a racing bike looks similar to a touring bike, a racing bike's dimensions are sharper, and it cannot take on extra equipment. Racing bikes are lighter, shorter, lower, and more expensive. They are not designed for long, casual trips. Touring bikes have a longer wheelbase that allows more comfort, stability, and the ability to carry equipment. Its frame is made from a durable metal and is less rigid and more comfortable, but it is heavier by a few pounds. A decent touring bike will cost between $500 and $800.

Frame Materials

You can repair any mechanical problem on the road except for a cracked or bent frame, so pick out one that can take abuse. The frame needs to be hard and strong since it carries a heavy weight—rider and equipment—and is under tension, especially around curves. However, because the bicycle bounces along the road, the frame material has to be slightly elastic. A frame that is too rigid might crack, while a frame that is too elastic shakes and diminishes the efficiency of the ride. The metals that the major manufacturers use are all good, composed of steel tubes doctored with trace amounts of an alloy. These trace amounts, as well as the temperature to which the metal is heated and how it is cooled, radically change the nature of the steel.

Steel alloys popular for touring frames are those made by manufacturers like Columbus, Reynolds, and Tange. They are referred to as either chromemoly (chromium-molybendum) or manganese-molybdenum. Aluminum alloy frames were introduced in the early 1980s, but they have not found wide appeal for touring bikes. Modern aluminum frames are stiff, and especially with a loaded bicycle on a rough road, they may not only be uncomfortable, they may actually crack.

The way the tubes are joined is as important as the tubing material. Most road bikes have a crown or lug brazed on at the important joints. More expensive bicycles will be double butted. That is, the inside of the tubing will be thicker near the joints, the points that receive the greatest stress, making the bicycle stronger and better able to absorb shocks.

You can examine the design of the frame and put your finger inside it to see how well the joints are made, but unless you are knowledgeable in the complex science of frame making, you need to trust the advice of bicycle shops and experienced cyclists. Also check the major cycling magazines' annual test reports.

Fitting the Bicycle to You

If you shop around with tape measure in hand, you will find that frame makers use different angles and tube lengths. The primary dimensions—the height of the seat tube and the length of the top tube—and the secondary dimensions—the height of the bottom bracket above the ground, the amount of front fork rake, and the length of the wheelbase—determine the lengths and angles of all other tubes. Technical experts have devised formulas for choosing the dimensions of a bicycle based on the dimensions of your body. Bicycle stores can assist you. Make the final choice by what feels best, a quality too hard to define empirically.

Correct seat tube length involves striking a balance between a low center of gravity and the most efficient use of the legs. The higher you sit the more wind you hit. A high center of gravity makes sharp turns down mountain roads more difficult. The way you pack the bike also affects center of gravity, but body weight is the more significant factor. However, sitting too low will decrease the the push-pull power of the legs, and it may also hurt leg muscles and soft tissue in the knees.

For the leg muscles to push and pull at their maximum, the seat should be high enough to allow the knees to remain minimally bent when fully extended on the down stroke. I would say the biggest mistake in-

The saddle height is adjusted by loosening the binder bolt at the top of the seat tube.

Leg Length*	Frame Size**	Height of Bottom Bracket from Ground	Crank Arm Length	
28 in.	19 in.	10.1 in.	165 or less	*Measured from the crotch to the bottom of the bare feet.
30	20.5	10.25	165 or less	
31	21	10.25	165	
32	22	10.25	165	
33	22.5	10.5	170	**Measured from center of bottom bracket to the top of top tube.
34	23	10.5	170	
35	24	10.5	170	
36	24.5	10.75	170 or 175	
37	25	10.75	175	
38	26	10.75	175	

Torso and Arm Length*	Top Tube**	Stem Extension	
40 in.	19.5	85	*Measured from crotch to bone in bottom of the neck plus bone at the top of the shoulder to end of wrist.
41	20	90	
42	20.25	90	
43	20.5	90	
44	21	95	
45	21.25	95	
46	21.50	100	**Measured from center to center of connecting tubes.
47	22	100	
48	22.25	100	
49	22.5	105	
50	23	105	

Frame sizing table

experienced cyclists make is getting too tall a bike. It is better to keep your seat post extended 4–5 inches and get a slightly shorter bike. The seat can be raised or lowered where the stem meets the frame. A good way of judging proper saddle height is to get in a low gear on a downhill stretch and spin the cranks as fast as you can without bouncing up and down on the seat. Try spinning 150 rpm. This also builds endurance.

While the length of your legs controls the length of the seat tube, the size of the top part of your body determines the length of the top tube. Too long or too short a tube will give you an awkward and, over the miles, tiring ride. This dimension is also dependent on the handlebar stem. The horizontal part of the stem comes in different lengths. Adding a few centimeters to the stem makes the handlebar farther from the seat and is similar to using a longer top tube. The seat can be moved slightly forward or backward by adjustments under the seat.

People also use different size crank arms. The 170-mm standard suits the average size rider, but shorter people may find it better to pedal 165 mm, while taller people can go up to 180 mm. If your frame is under 22 inches, consider a crank length under 170 mm; if it is over 24 inches, try one over 170 mm; 175 mm is becoming standard for tall people.

Handlebars

Recent innovations in handlebars have given us diversity. However, many of the new handlebars or their attachments limit the possibility of using a handlebar bag. The traditional, or Maes, bar comes in three standard widths—38, 40, and 42 cm—depending on the width of the rider's shoulders. This is an often-overlooked dimension. I have narrow shoulders, and I remember how comfortable it felt when I changed to the narrower bars.

The handlebar height can be adjusted by loosening the long bolt in the center. For most people the top of the handlebar should be ½ to 1 inch lower than the bottom of the seat, and the flat part of the handlebar should be parallel to the ground.

Some people prefer a straight handlebar since it looks more comfortable. It is certainly more stable. However, before deciding against a dropped handlebar, try it. Over the long haul, a dropped handlebar is more comfortable since it offers the rider more hand positions and is better for fighting the wind.

Wheels and Tires

Some cyclists prefer sealed hubs because they hardly let dirt into the bearings. Dirt is the major cause of wear. Sealed hubs, standard on ATB's, need to be cleaned about every two years or after a long dirty trip. Regular hubs have to be cleaned four times as often. However, sealed hubs are a little heavier and have a bit more friction.

A loaded touring bike requires thicker spokes, especially on the rear wheel. Thick spokes are of course heavier and have more wind resistance (wind resistance for turning spokes is a subject that is often wrongly neglected). Heavy people should consider using 13-gauge spokes on the rear wheel and 14- or 15-gauge on the front (the lower the gauge, the thicker the spoke), depending on how much load the front wheel is holding. Butted spokes are a good alternative; they are thicker at the ends, the places most subject to stress.

Tubular tires, usually called sew-ups because they are sewn on the side that sits on the rim, give a much better ride. They are lighter and take the road more nicely. However, they are not for touring since they are expensive, hard to repair, not long-lasting, and not made for heavy loads. Sew-ups are a luxury that a tourist cannot afford except for short trips where speed is most important. Stick to regular wired-on tires, commonly referred to as clinchers.

Touring wheels come in two different diameters, an important consideration before buying a bicycle. The two sizes are close, but the frame is made around the wheels, and they cannot be interchanged. The European 700 mm standard tire is 14 mm smaller than the traditional British-American 27 inch tire, which is rapidly becoming extinct. Nowadays, virtually all bicycle shops in the U.S. and Britain stock the European size, but most European bicycle shops do not stock 27-inch tires. The inner tubes are interchangeable, but the tires are not. To complicate matters, many non-Western countries will more often than not have 27-inch tires. This is true for former British colonies and for most of the Americas. Former French colonies generally use 700-mm tires. Thus, you must either use a bicycle with the wheel size that is used in the place to which you travel or carry ample spare tires. The 700-mm size is becoming the standard, but at teh time of this writing, that trend had not hit the only bicycle shop for 100 miles in Broadus, Montana— nor the one in Luanshya, Zambia.

Pick up some culture along the way: studying a museum catalogue in Germany.

The rims on all good wheels are made of an aluminum alloy that is strong but lighter than steel. The width of the wheel will depend on where you are going: the rougher the road, the wider tires you will need. Rims over 30 mm wide will take good fat tires that can be used on rough dirt roads. Many cyclists have two sets of wheels: fat ones for trips and thin ones for training and city riding. The brakes need readjustment when changing wheels.

A good tire can last 3,000 miles on the front wheel and 2,000 miles on the rear wheel. The rear wheel wears faster since it takes more weight. When touring, expect the rear wheel to last even less, perhaps 1,000 miles (tires wear less on dirt roads). I have gotten the best tires for rough roads in Peru and Tanzania. I do not know what brand they were, but they were heavy and took the road well.

You usually need to carry at least one spare tire on the road. By twisting, it can be folded in thirds and packed up. I tape them on the luggage rack. Finally, the inner tube comes with two different valves called presta and shrader. Shrader valves are similar to car valves, while presta are longer and thinner. Most cyclists use presta. but will take along a small, 90-cent adapter that will allow them to fill up with air at a service station, since frame pumps cannot fill tires to their proper pressure.

Gearing

If the chain is on a front gear with 42 teeth, a common size for the smaller gear, and a rear freewheel gear with 15 teeth, every time you turn the cranks one revolution the wheels turn 2.8 times. If you have 27-inch wheels you would move about 20 feet for each spin of the pedals. If you shift to the higher gear in the front, say 52 teeth, another standard, and remain in the 15-tooth sprocket in the back, each crank turn would turn the wheels about 3.5 times, making you move almost 25 feet for the same spin of the crank. As you can see, your speed is directly controlled by the gears you use (except when you are rolling freely), and by how many revolutions per minute you turn the cranks.

Studies have shown that over a long distance, cyclists do better turning a lower gear faster than ap-plying pushing power in a higher gear. You should not exert force on the pedals unless you are going uphill, fighting a wind, accelerating, or sprinting. You should feel no pressure or strain when spinning the cranks. If you do, drop to a lower gear. This way you can go day after day without wearing yourself out.

The extra load touring cyclists carry requires spe-cial gearing considerations. You will need to pedal a heavy bicycle up steep hills, perhaps on dirt roads with poor traction. Many tourists add especially low gears for this purpose, using a third small chainring on the front crank arm with 28 to 34 teeth. Mountain bikes need this small chainring for hill climbing. In ad-dition, cycle tourists often use especially low gears, with big sprockets in the back and at least one small one in the front. Personally, I have never needed a third chainring in the front. On a steep hill I get out of the saddle and power the bicycle over the top. Such low gears are only required on grades over 12 percent. Luckily, those grades on roads are few, and they are usually not miles long. They do not, I believe, justify the extra weight, hassle, and potential mechanical problem of using a third chainring on a road bike. You can use a small chainring—as low as 38 teeth—and in the back a gear as low as 34 teeth. If you are fit you do not need a gear lower than that on asphalt.

Bicycle shops will generally put on whatever gears you request when you buy a bicycle, but if you want to change to a triple chainring in the front, you may also need to change the bottom bracket to give the new chainring clearance. First, determine your lowest and highest gear. Try taking a fully loaded bicycle up a long hill and see what gear should be your lowest. Unless you are going to tour an area that has few or no hills, I suggest that you should have your lowest gear in the front 40 or less, and 28 or more in the rear. Most tourists use a 50- or 52-tooth large chainring, and a 13- or 14-tooth smallest rear sprocket.

$$Gear = D_{wheel} \times T_{chainwheel} / T_{sprocket}$$

Where:

Gear　　　　　 = gear in inches

Rear cog	Front chain wheel								
	34	36	39	40	42	46	48	52	54
38	24	26	28	28	30	33	34	37	38
34	27	29	31	32	33	37	38	41	43
32	29	30	33	34	35	39	41	44	46
31	30	31	34	35	37	40	42	45	47
30	31	32	35	36	38	41	43	47	49
28	33	35	38	39	41	44	46	50	52
27	34	36	39	40	42	46	48	52	54
26	35	37	41	42	44	48	50	54	56
25	37	39	42	43	45	50	52	56	58
24	38	41	44	45	47	52	54	59	61
23	40	42	46	47	49	54	56	61	63
22	42	44	48	49	52	57	59	64	66
21	44	46	50	51	54	59	62	67	69
20	46	49	53	54	57	62	65	70	73
19	48	51	55	57	60	65	68	74	77
18	51	54	59	60	63	69	72	78	81
17	54	57	62	64	67	73	76	83	86
16	57	61	66	68	71	78	81	89	91
15	61	65	70	72	76	83	86	94	97
14	66	69	75	77	81	89	93	100	104
13	71	75	81	83	87	96	100	108	112

Gearing chart

D_{wheel} = diameter of rear wheel

$T_{chainring}$ = number of teeth on front chainring

$T_{sprocket}$ = number of teeth on rear sprocket

Devise the freewheel gears so there are two-, three-, or four-tooth differences between successive cogs. A common freewheel for six cogs would be 13-15-17-21-24-28 if you like high gears, or 14-16-20-24-28-32 if you favor lower gears. On the front you can use between 38 and 53. A 40-52 front combination is popular among cycle tourists. Chapter 17 discusses cadence and may help you decide on the best gear combination.

The Drivetrain

Good quality derailleurs are a must. There is nothing more maddening than a derailleur that shifts poorly because it has too much play in it. Fortunately, many Italian, French, Japanese, American, and British companies make quality derailleurs. Unfortunately, the quality ones are expensive. Shimano came out with a rear derailleur that shifts right into the gear without having to adjust, and many cyclists who otherwise use nothing but Campagnolo products are using the Japanese mechanism. It does not matter which you use as long as it is reliable and fits your gearing range.

The other components in the drive train—the crank, chain, bottom bracket, and pedals—also demand quality. Cheap chains, for example, stretch more than quality ones. I met someone in Europe who had stripped the threads on one of his bargain-brand crank arms and was walking his bike to the next town to try to buy another. My only suggestion is to consider the tools you will need to service these parts. Many are specialized tools, and the tools for one brand do not fit another. If you only have tools for Campagnolo, you might have to buy another set of tools if you buy a Shimano set. Also, buying each component separately is more expensive than buying all the components at one time, called a gruppo.

Saddles

The saddle should fit your bottom, and only you can judge the best fit. Men and women often require different saddles, a woman's being slightly wider. A good saddle often feels uncomfortable for a few days until your behind gets used to it. Over the long haul a comfortable touring saddle will be narrow and only slightly padded to absorb road bounce. The saddle should fit the hip and pelvic bone. Your buttocks will rest on three points that should match the two high points on the rear of the saddle and a point in the middle of the nose. You need to try a saddle for a few days before determining its fit. If you have not ridden for a while, your behind will need a day or two to readjust to the saddle.

Most cyclists tilt the saddle slightly down in line with the handlebar drops. There is a bolt under the seat that you can loosen to tilt the saddle. If you feel yourself gradually slipping forward as you ride, tilt it more horizontally. For greatest foot thrust, the front of the saddle should be 1.5–2.5 inches behind the center of the bottom bracket.

Brakes and Components

Because of the extra weight that touring cyclists carry, many people use larger brake shoes, the type used on tandems and ATBs. When coming down a hill you build up tremendous momentum, and it takes much more braking force to stop than does an unpacked bike. Stopping on a steep downhill in the rain is next to impossible with regular brake shoes. Longer brake shoes increase the area of friction and are safer. Invest the few dollars more for a decent set of brakes. Center pulls can get in the way of bike racks and bags. Side pulls with long brake shoes or cantilever brakes used on mountain bikes are the better choice.

Brake levers that you can reach from the top of the handlebar are not good for touring. You do not use brakes that often while touring country roads, and

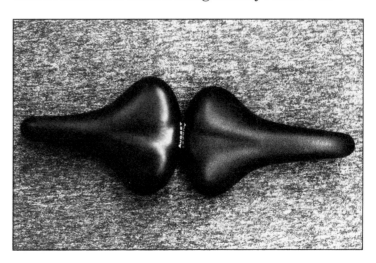

Some different saddle shapes and sizes. Make sure yours is comfortable before leaving on your grand tour.

studies have shown that top-mounted brake levers do not stop as quickly in an emergency because the levers bend, rather than carrying the brake force.

A kickstand is less convenient than it may seem. The main objection is not the extra weight, but the fact that they put too much stress on the chainstays. Especially with the extra load of packed panniers, a kickstand will hurt the frame. Instead, either find a wall or lay their bicycle gently on the ground. A Flickstand (made by Rhode Gear), a small mechanical device that steadies the front wheel and helps balance the bicycle when you lean it on a pole. It is best to leave gadgets such as horns and bells at home, except in countries where they are legally required.

Your bike is going to be under more stress than it would be if you took Sunday rides in the park. The few dollars you save on cheaper products will hurt if you are caught in the middle of nowhere with a brake that will not adjust or if you constantly have a hard time shifting gears. In the U.S. the most inexpensive way to buy bicycle parts is usually through the large catalog houses. Buy from them only if you know the product, not because the picture looks nice and the ad says it is wonderful. Find out about different products by asking other cyclists,. This is definitely one of the advantages of belonging to a local cycling club.

When and Where to Buy

I have found excellent prices on bicycles, parts, and especially clothing in bicycle stores at the end of the season. For those not knowledgeable in mechanics, the local bicycle store is the place to shop. They assemble the bike and after a month make other needed adjustments. Local stores are able to help their customers with problems, whereas dealing with a catalog house a thousand miles away can be frustrating. Sports stores that sell bicycles next to scuba equipment and tennis rackets are usually not knowledgeable enough for your needs.

Note: The large catalog houses will promptly deliver parts around the world. It is not a cheap service, and you need to have an address for them, but consider taking their phone number in case you are stuck in Bangladesh with a broken derailleur. You will not be able to buy another anywhere in the country.

CHAPTER 5

Mountain Bikes for Touring

They go by several names—mountain bikes, all-terrain bicycles or ATBs, off-road bikes, dirt bikes—and they have found tremendous popularity all over the world since the late 1970s. They are machines that can take abuse, jump curbs, and go over mud and snow and mountain trails. It is not surprising that many people are using them for touring, for there is hardly a road anywhere that they cannot tackle, from the dry hills around Los Angeles to the swamps in Malaysia. The rider sits in a stable position, often able to flip the quick-release and change seat height for bombing down rugged grades. Their fat knobby tires grab any piece of earth, and they can move.

Pros and Cons of Mountain Bikes

Mountain bikes are wonderful and fun and exciting and demanding. If you have not tried one on a trail you are missing a challenging riding experience. For touring they have as many drawbacks as advantages, so think where you are going before traveling with one. If you plan to cycle across the United States or through Europe and you are going to stay on secondary or farm roads, there is no sense taking a mountain bike. They are heavier by a good five pounds. Their fat tires cause considerably more rolling resistance, and although they are comfortable for one- or two-hour rides, over the long haul they are less comfortable than traditional or road bikes because they put a lot of stress on the shoulders and arms. Generally, for the same effort they go slower than road bikes. Their upright position increases wind resistance.

A surprising number of dirt roads can be tackled almost as well by road bikes with fat tires. I live half a mile down a dirt road, one that is full of rocks and sand, but I take my racing bike with its thin one-inch tires back and forth on it, keeping my toe straps loose. Since almost all my riding is on tar, it makes sense to use the efficiency that a traditional bicycle affords, but if much of your trip is going to be off-road or on trails, then a fat-tire bike is what you need. Bear in mind that cycling over dirt is much slower than on asphalt.

Choosing a Mountain Bike for Touring

If you shop for a mountain bike you will notice a much greater difference between them than you find between traditional touring bikes. The frame dimensions can vary greatly, up to two-inch differences, just in the length of the chainstays. Some bicycles have long straight handlebars. Others have narrow, curved, or bent bars. Their gearing combinations can be very low, with the lowest chainring smaller than the highest freewheel cog, or the gearing might be about the same as a road bike. That is because mountain bikes serve different purposes: some are for trail racing, others are for casual trail riding; some are designed for riding around the city, and others are specifically for touring.

Short chainstays, 16.7–17 inches, and steep head tube angles, 70–72 degrees, produce a short wheelbase, about 42 inches, which makes a bicycle much more responsive, just as sharp angles and a short wheelbase make a traditional bicycle more like a racing bike. Chainstay length is important to an ATB since a short wheelbase gives the rider more traction by putting the rear wheel closer under the rider's weight. Generally, touring ATBs have more relaxed dimensions, a 68–69-degree head tube angle, 17.5–18.5-inch chainstays, and a 43–44-inch wheelbase. Although this type of bicycle is less responsive, it is more comfortable for distance riding. A longer chainstay also gives the rider the option of fatter tires since on short bicycles the tires come close to the frame, allowing mud to build up around the brakes. A tighter frame gives you more control when descending in steep dirt, but most touring involves a rounded

Mountain bikes can be quite suitable for touring, providing you get one that has the more relaxed, or comfortable, geometry (left) rather than the racing geometry (right). (Photos courtesy Trek)

range of riding. Moreover, when using large rear panniers, riders with medium or large feet need long chainstays for heel clearance—try them out before buying either bicycle or pannier.

ATB seat tube sizes are about three or four inches shorter than those on a traditional bicycle. Touring riders make that up by raising the seat post, which is longer than that of a road bike. This gives the bicycle a lower center of gravity, essential for taking turns downhill in the dirt. When you straddle a traditional bicycle with your feet on the floor, your crotch should clear the top tube by an inch. With a mountain bike you should clear the top tube by about three inches. As with a road bike, the biggest mistake new cyclists make is getting too high a bicycle. There is no reason to carry enough spares to build an extra bicycle around. Raise the seat post to allow your legs the room to assert their maximum power.

Most manufacturers use chromoly frames because it is a tough metal, but aluminum frames with chromoly front forks are also common. The oversized tubes are generally not joined with lugs but welded and brazed together. Double-butted tubes provide much more durability and take the bounces better. For touring you want to have a hardy bicycle, one able to handle not only rough roads but the extra load of your equipment. Although you can buy clamps for luggage racks, it is much better to have braze-on mounts for the racks. Both racks sit lower, yielding more stability and control than you have on a road bike.

The crank arms on a mountain bike tend to be slightly longer to give the rider more torque when climbing hills. Most experts suggest 5 mm longer cranks than you would use on a traditional touring bike—175 mm is standard for people under 5-8" and 185 mm for taller people. In conjunction, the bottom bracket usually sits about an inch higher off the ground than that of a road bike to allow more clearance not only for the pedals but also for obstacles in the terrain.

Mountain Bike Components

Good off-road bikes use high-quality components: sturdy cantilever brakes; indexed thumb shifters that shift directly from one gear to the other; triple chainrings with the lowest gear about 26 teeth and large freewheel sprockets over 30 teeth, enabling the rider to

Suitable tire tread patterns for off-road touring.

get over any hill without walking; and sealed bearings (on the more expensive models every bearing is sealed, from headset to pedals), which protect the moving parts from dirt and reduce maintenance.

The tourist has the option of putting on toe clips, but not all pedals can take toe clips. If you are going to be rolling in the dirt, you want to be able to throw out your feet, but at other times toe clips give you much better pedaling action. For most of your touring needs you will want toeclips, so it is better to avoid the fat beartrap pedals and use the straight type.

When I said that most ATB riders have only one handlebar position, I was not telling the truth. Not only do you have a number of choices of straight or curved, but you can also use a variety of adapters, pieces of metal that attach to the handlebar and enable the rider to stretch out. There is an adapter that makes the handlebar a mixture of dropped and straight. Moreover, ATB handlebars come in a greater variety of widths than those of road bikes—from 20 to 30 inches. Some people like to spread their arms and take the trails, but most touring bikes use 22- to 24-inch bars; small 90-degree extensions attached to the ends are becoming popular.

For an 18- or 21-speed touring machine with quality components such as the Shimano Deore gruppo you can expect to pay about the same as for a road bike, between $500 and $800. The same suggestions apply to gearing off-road machines as road bikes, but tires are an entirely different story since the tire determines the characteristic of the bicycle. It is not smart to ride around town with knobby tires. Not only are knobby tires bumpy, like riding on cobblestones, but they wear much faster on pavement and take more effort to pedal.

The type of tire to use depends on the road. If you are going to tour the backwoods, then use 2.1-inch knobbies, but if you do not need the traction, then go with a 1.5-inch bald tire or one that has a smooth raised center ridge. Many off-road tires have a combination of treads, smooth down the middle and knobby on the edges. Such a tire is probably best for most types of touring. Some serious travelers take along extra tires for going on and off pavement. It is worth it to take 20 minuted and change to smooth tires if you are going to be spending all day on pavement.

CHAPTER 6

Bicycle Touring Clothing

A long-distance cyclist's clothing should be durable, visible, unobtrusive, easy to wash, lightweight, and comfortable. Furthermore, you should bring no more clothing than what you will need. Novice riders make the mistake of bringing too many inappropriate garments. Let us look at a cyclist's needs from the bottom up.

Shoes and Socks

Cycling shoes have a tremendous advantage over street shoes. They are long and thin, designed to fit in the toe clips, and they have a solid metal or plastic shank in the sole to spread the pressure against the pedal over the entire front part of the shoe. They are also light, an important consideration when you think how many times you lift each foot every hour. If each shoe is unnecessarily 4 ounces heavier than it need be, your feet may be lifting a wasted half ton per hour.

Cleated shoes provide the most efficient cycling since they grab the pedal and transfer the force of the legs directly to the drivetrain; however, they are terrible for walking. You can walk around a grocery store, but you cannot do much more. The same holds true for the shoes that are similar to ski bindings (which detach when the rider unintentionally twists a foot). A

Good bicycle touring shoes have stiff grippy soles and comfortable uppers. (Photo courtesy Bike Nashbar)

few touring cyclists use cleated shoes, then change into sandals or flip-flops when they're finished cycling, but it is a lot of trouble to have to sit down—often on the ground—to undo laces and change shoes.

Most touring cyclists wear non-cleated cycling shoes made by Avocet, Bata, Cannondale, Diadora, Ditto, Dueg, Look, Nike, REI, Sidi, Specialized, Tiger, Vittoria, and others. They look like running shoes, but they feel different because of the solid shank in the sole. In fact, they are not good for extended walking, and out of the question for running. They should have light leather or suede tops instead of hot nylon. Wear them tight, and trim the laces so they do not get caught in the moving parts. Touring shoes cost between $30 and $70.

Socks are an area of personal preference mandated by comfort and climate. Get durable material (not a synthetic) and something your feet enjoy. For the cold, make sure you have at least one extra warm pair should your first pair get wet. I know someone who takes along three identical socks and washes one a night, rotating them on his feet. Other people wear no socks except when it is cold. Short white socks are traditional, but they are hard to keep clean on a trip—try something a bit darker.

Shorts

Street shorts are not designed for cycling—most are downright uncomfortable on the saddle. In the cycling

The best shirts for bicycle touring are the cycling jerseys with large pockets in the back. Also note the special bicycle touring shorts. (Photo courtesy Cannondale)

position you stretch an entirely different way than do runners, basketball players, and tennis buffs. All clothing has to accommodate the riding position. Seams on standard walking shorts are stitched in awkward places for riding on the saddle. Bicycling shorts have a chamois or similar material in the crotch to pad the seat, making a long ride more pleasant. Black remains the traditional color of cycling shorts since it does not show dust and dirt, but in the past few years a rainbow of colors has been introduced.

Wool keeps its coolness and warmth even when wet from rain or perspiration, but many people find unlined wool uncomfortable. Lycra and polypropylene have become the most popular materials. Comfort is essential, but shorts should fit snugly.

Some companies such as Cannondale and Rhode Gear make touring shorts with large protruding pockets on the side, as opposed to the pocketless racing shorts. The pockets on these touring shorts are convenient, but they stick out, take more air, and cause a higher wind drag. They are good, comfortable shorts, but do not ride in shorts like that when you are fighting a wind. Shorts vary in price. A basic black Lycra or wool pair will cost $30–40. Those with someone's initials can be three times as expensive.

Pants

Even in the height of summer, if you are in the mountains and you ride down a steep grade in the early morning, your legs will get goose bumps from the cold air. You can feel the cold tighten your leg muscles. When you come to the bottom of the hill and start pedaling vigorously, you are in danger of straining the soft tissue in your legs.

The best long pants to use while riding are cycling tights, which are made by a dozen companies, traditionally black, but now in different, often bright, colors and various thicknesses. If you only need protection against wind, take a thin Lycra pair. Like shorts, they have crotch padding and stretch tight on the legs so they do not flap around in the wind and snag in the chain. Tights cost between $30 and $60 depending on their quality, but they look strange. I suggest taking a lightweight pair of non-iron cotton pants or a cotton dress for walking around and seeing the sights.

Jerseys

Cycling clothing, especially tops, is designed for the bicycle. Long or short sleeve, they fit tight around the body and have large pockets in the back, out of way from the cycling motion. You can choose from wool, cotton, or a blend—stay away from polyester. Bright colors are traditional, but they are also a good idea since they make you more visible on the road. White is too hard to keep clean. Jerseys come in a wide variety of cuts, thicknesses, and prices. Get long sleeves only if you need the warmth. Try the top on in the cycling position—bend at the hips with arms extended over the handlebar—and see if it is still comfortable.

A word of caution: the large pockets on the back of jerseys are easy for thieves to pick. Do not walk in a crowded area with your passport and wallet in your back pockets.

Many people cycle in T-shirts. I confess that on occasion I do, too. They pack up small and are convenient to carry. But T-shirts flap around and do not protect the lower back from the sun when you are lean-

A collection of suitable bicycle touring clothing from Cannondale.

ing over. Some men ride without a shirt. Besides possibly causing sunburn, it tends to allow the sun to rob you of more moisture. Wearing a top is better. A T-shirt or other light shirt is good to wear after cycling.

Rainwear

The perfect cycling raincoat has yet to be designed. It needs to fit tightly and cover the body. It needs to breath so it does not collect condensation and perspiration inside. It needs to be lightweight, bright, and visible. It needs to bend and cover well, especially on the back. It needs to take to the saddle and fit snugly over the head without blocking the rider's view. Finally, it needs to keep pedaling motion unrestricted.

Gore-tex, that breathable material, has become popular for rainwear, but many manufacturers still use ripstop nylon, sometimes in combination with rubber. A few decent rain suits are now offered by Cannondale, Rhode Gear, and others. Some of them only cover the top part of the body. Most cyclists feel that rain pants made from Gore-tex, nylon, or a similar plastic are uncomfortable, restricting, and unimportant unless traveling in a cold rain. Even in wet cold you might prefer wool tights. Cyclists also feel that Velcro closures are better than zippers.

Rainwear should be bright to stand out in poor visibility. Most people find that a lightweight but durable raincoat is better than a heavy one. In the event of cold rain, you can put warm clothes under it. Also, since most raincoats are loose, they blow in the

Women's Shoes					
American	5½	6½	7½	8 ½	9½
European	37	38	39	41	42
Men's Shoes					
American	7	8	9	10	11
European	41	42	43	44	45
Shirts					
American	14	15	16	17	
European	36	38	41	43	

Conversion table for American and European clothing sizes.

wind that often accompanies rain. A good cycling raincoat has straps that tighten it to the body. On most rainwear you should cover the seams with sealer every year, just as you do tents.

Also available are rain totes that fit over the cycling shoes or on the toe clips, and gaiters that keep the rain from flowing down your legs into your shoes. You should consider these in cold places as well, for although warm blood rushes down and keeps the legs warm, the feet are easily victimized by the cold, and there is nothing worse than cycling with cold, wet feet.

Hats and Gloves

The human hand has a sensitive nerve running down the middle, and after holding the handlebar for hours without properly insulating that nerve, you will lose the feeling in your hands for weeks. Whether you use handlebar padding or not, protect your hands with cycling gloves. They usually have leather or suede on the palm and a crocheted cotton or Lycra on the back. Cheap pairs cost under $10, while a specialty Italian pair may run $75.

Hats keep the sun out of your eyes and face. The only requirement is keeping your line of sight free. In the cycling position your head is tilted down, and a hat or helmet can mean that you have to unnaturally tilt your head back to see. Many cyclists use a green or yellow sun visor that they can see through; others use cycling caps that have a short lip. Baseball hats or hats with a long front lip are not for cycling. Helmets are discussed in the Safe Riding chapter.

Cold Weather Clothing

The ever-present wind chill makes cyclists especially vulnerable to cold weather. In high altitudes it can be chilly in any season. The cycling action, a rigorous exercise, warms the main part of the body. On a cold day you need to put on a sweater or jacket, but if you wear too much, your chest and underarms get hot and sweaty. The main part of the body needs to stay cool when exercising. Cyclists can use leggings of various thicknesses and sweaters or jackets, such as those sold in bike shops. In cool weather a cardigan is better than a pullover since it can be opened in the front if you get too hot, but in the cold the head, arms, and hands need special protection.

Since the hands are exposed to the wind and hold the cold handlebar, full-length gloves are essential for

When riding in a group, it is best to ride in a uniform formation. It helps minimize wind resistance and makes you more predictable to other road users.

cold-weather riding. Cold-weather cycling gloves, un-like regular gloves, are padded in the palm to protect the hand. In cold weather I wear a pair of knit mittens over my cycling gloves. Cyclists need to be careful not to use gloves that have a seam on the palm since it can hurt the hand. Padding the handlebar, either with thick handlebar tape or foam, also helps keep the hands warm.

To protect the neck and head, a cyclist can wear a scarf and a knit cap that extends to the ears and can take a helmet over it. A scarf can be moved up to the chin to protect the mouth and lower face. Scarves need to be tight so they do not get loose and waft into the wheels, and you must be sure they do not obstruct your rear vision over your shoulder.

Laundry

Cycling clothes become soiled rapidly from perspiration and dust. You need to carry a little laundry soap (a tube of concentrated soap is best) and wash something at least every other day. If you wash at night and hang it up, it probably will not be dry the next morning. However, you can put the wet clothes on top of your luggage racks, and the sun and wind will dry the clothing quickly during the ride the next day. If you pass through a city that has a coin-operated wash and dry, it is a good idea to take an hour off and wash everything you have.

CHAPTER 7

Loading the Bicycle

Before considering the saddlebags or panniers to carry equipment, let us talk about the racks that attach over the front and rear wheels. Major manufacturers, including Blackburn, Cannondale, Eclipse, Bruce Gordon, and Rhode Gear, offer a variety of standard bike racks made from a lightweight but strong aluminum alloy. They attach at the top to the brake stays or to the bolt on the center of the brake stays, and on the bottom they are bolted to the holes near the wheel hubs. Front racks are a bit shorter and usually hold smaller panniers. Racks come in different sizes. Get one that will not obstruct the movement of the brakes and fits horizontally when mounted on your bike.

Racks seem to cost considerably more than they should, $30–40 for this simple piece of metal. If you look carefully at the rack you will see brazing and sturdy workmanship, but it does not seem to justify the price. Touring ATBs come with brazed-on low riders so the front rack can be attached to the front fork. It is important to have a good part of the weight in the front when using ATBs on rough hills.

Packing a Touring Bicycle

Bicycles are designed to spread the weight of the rider over both wheels, the back wheel supporting most of the weight. As you move your hands from the top of the handlebar to the brakes, your torso moves forward, shifting your weight to the front wheel. When packing the bike you should preserve, roughly, the weight balance between the front and rear wheels. People who put too much weight in back and neglect the front will discover, much to their consternation, that when they go rapidly downhill they lose control of the steering. The front wheel jumps and shakes, requiring the rider to shift weight to the front by leaning forward and grabbing the handlebar drops.

To spread the weight over both wheels, put equipment directly over the front wheel, either with front panniers, a loaded front rack, or a heavy handlebar bag. Most cyclists believe that hill climbing is easier when most of the packed weight is in the front, pushing rather than pulling a load up hills. I have not

49

*Low-rider rack for front panniers
(Photo courtesy Cannondale)*

found scientific evidence to back the idea, but I put the heavy weight in the front when hill climbing.

A cyclist's center of gravity is already high since the body is well over the center of the hubs. When you add more weight to the bicycle, add it as low as you can. Pack heavy gear such as tools low, and light gear such as clothing on top. Water bottles should be mounted low on the frame. Whether you have brazed-on nipples for a water bottle cage or not, keep the full bottles low, even if it is a longer reach.

The touring bike is aerodynamically awful, and no manufacturer has come to our aid with an aerodynamically designed loaded touring bike. I too have no suggestions except to tough it out when the wind rages against you. The position of touring bags, instead of taking advantage of where a bicycle and rider already open the wind and following that space with equipment, take up a new area, forcing the rider to break much more wind. However, putting gear behind the rider's body would be impractical. Eventually, perhaps cyclists will be able to use shields or fairings to help break the wind and allow rider adn gear an easier ride. Perhaps someone reading this can devise an innovative design.

Neatness is next to beneficent winds. Have a set place for every item so you do not have to dump out your panniers searching for a screwdriver. Do not jam your clothing into the panniers or they will end up wrinkled and messy. Fold up clothes and put them into the panniers without stuffing them. Rolling your clothes will keep them wrinkle free.

Any bag you get to carry equipment should be examined for its size, the number of compartments, the quality of the material, its weather resistance, visibility, lightness, and attaching and detaching ease. Manufacturers exaggerate the cubic-inch capacity and rain resistance of their products.

Handlebar Bag

This often-used container attaches to the center of the handlebar either on a metal bracket that is prevented from bouncing by elastic straps stretching down to the bottom of the front fork, or on special clips that attach to the handlebar stem. The bracket or clip leaves room for the hands between the handlebar and the bag. For a long trip get the largest and best bag made. Without question, it should have a waterproof, clear plastic map case on top where maps can be easily visible while riding. It is also good to have a few pockets on the sides, top, and front for snacks, spare maps, documents, sunglasses, and so on. Most cyclists keep their cameras in the front bag since it is easy to reach.

Front bags are made from a waterproof material, usually nylon, not a water-resistant one. Many people pick bright colors that can be seen by oncoming traffic. I once had a fluorescent yellow one. It was ugly, but no one missed seeing me. The colors of most bags today are more sedate.

Handlebar bags and panniers are made by Astra, Back Country, Bikeology, Bellwether, Brooks, Cannondale, CyclePro, Eclipse, Ensolite, Kangaroo, Kirtland, Karrimor, Nashbar, Needle Works, Overland, Performance, Sojourn Designs, Velo, Versatile, and several other companies. For a ride lasting over a week, a bag should have a stated capacity of 600 cubic inches or more and weigh less than 1.5 pounds. A good front bag costs $35 to $60. The bag's compartments close with zippers or Velcro, and most bags have a strap that allows you to use it as a shoulder bag, making it convenient to carry around when walking.

Rear Panniers

Most riders store the bulk of their equipment in the rear panniers. If this is going to be true for you as well, then get the largest pair. They clip on or slide through the top of the rear luggage rack and attach at the bottom near the hubs. It is good to have several separate

This handlebar bag from Cannondale has an easy-to-use attachment to the handlebars, so it can easily be taken off the bike when needed.

compartments in the pannier, otherwise the equipment gets mixed together and you have to take everything out in order to get to something small at the bottom.

A 2,200-cubic-inch pair weighs less than four pounds and costs $80 to $150. They should have a solid backing of metal or plastic to keep them straight and should be easy to put on and take off the rear rack. Since the bicycle gets plenty of bounce, the clips that hold the panniers should be strong and well attached so they do not give you a jerky ride.

Because of its size, the rear pannier is not usually made from nylon but from a thick water-resistant material. Look for quality material, good stitching, and a guarantee. You need to make sure that your feet clear the pannier during pedaling and that neither it nor the rear rack obstructs the chain on the smallest gear of the freewheel. Waterproof covers that fit over the panniers are also available, but they are never 100 percent effective. Cyclists often use plastic bags inside the panniers during bad weather.

Front Panniers

To balance the load and allow more packing space, some people find it advantageous to fasten a rack on the front fork over the wheel and attach a pair of front panniers. Unlike a relatively small handlebar bag that keeps the weight high, front panniers give you more room at a lower center of gravity. They are smaller than rear panniers since the front rack is shorter and can only take on smaller bags. They weigh under four pounds, cost between $50 and $120, and have about 1600 cubic inches.

I recommend front panniers for people who use smaller rear panniers to balance the load. Personally, I use a front luggage rack and attach my tent, bicycle tools, and spare tires without panniers. I believe that large-capacity rear panniers packed with light items, a good-size handlebar bag with heavy items, and a loaded front rack can carry all the necessary equipment. If you need more room, you're probably taking too much.

Important: Nothing should be loose near the front wheel that has the potential of getting caught in the front spokes and locking the wheel. If the rear wheel locks, you'll have a spill; if the front wheel locks, you will be thrown you over the handlebar, which is worse.

CHAPTER 8

Camping Equipment

The science of taking the right camping equipment can only be perfected by experience. If you plan to spend some or all of your nights camping, a large portion of your outfit will be items required for camping. Let us go through the equipment.

Tent

Tents are mandatory for camping. In a large group the night may be the only time you have to yourself, and you may prefer to sleep separately. Naturally, it is best for the overall weight and size to get the smallest required tent. Remember, each additional pound means an extra pound to pedal up hills.

It is impractical to take any tent that weighs over eight pounds and is fatter than six inches when rolled up. You can get a decent two-person tent that weighs four pounds and costs under $150. Do not take a tent without either mosquito netting or a rain fly or you will regret it. Tents made out of plastic-coated materials that do not breathe are uncomfortable and unhealthy.

Backpackers often use one-person bivvy sacks, usually made from Gore-tex. These small and light—1.5 pounds—tent sacks are popular with rock climbers. Since you cannot sit up in them, they are only for sleep, and they tend to give a claustrophobic feeling.

Dome tent suitable for bike camping

Although they are said to be waterproof, they, like the best tent, will take in a little water during a heavy rain. They are not popular with cyclists who demand a good rest.

Tent Types and Materials

Most campers prefer free-standing tents since they do not need to be staked in the ground. Everyone comes to places where the earth is too hard to stake, and it is annoying not to be able to sink stakes well. You find yourself trying to hold the tent with ropes tied to trees and weigh down the edges with the bicycle. A tent has been introduced in Europe that sits above the ground. Since the cold ground robs the body of heat, such a tent would be good in cold weather, but it is heavier and feels like sleeping in a hammock.

Over twenty manufacturers market tents, including Adventure, American Camper, Camp Ways, Caribou, Chownard, Coleman, Cannondale, Diamond, Eureka, Famous Trails, Jansport, Kelty, Moss, North Face, Pacific Trails, Patagonia, REI, Sierra Designs, Sierra West, Slumber Jack, Trailwise, Walrus, Wenzel, and Wilderness Experience. Several mail order houses make their own in an array of shapes: triangles, domes, ovals, A-frames, and flashlights. Unless you know tents, stick to the reputable brands. Examine a tent's size and structure, and get inside it to see if you feel comfortable. You will want room for your panniers inside the tent. See if you will be able to set up and take down the tent quickly—in less than five minutes. Compare the weights and packed sizes.

Most manufacturers make tents from ripstop nylon (it stops rips because it is a weave), a thin, breathable material that seeps water as soon as you touch it. They use a protective rain fly to keep the inner material dry. Look for good construction: floor material doubled together and stitched in two rows and other seams taped so the end of the material does not un-ravel. Tight, double stitching is crucial, and the poles and eyelets should stand up to pressure. It is one thing to have a tent problem in Kansas, but the matter can be distressing if you are in the middle of Africa and a pole breaks, as has happened to me. Go to several camping stores and inspect many tents. Since tent manufacturers introduce a new line of tents peri-odically, stores often offer the old line at a consider-able discount, usually in the fall. Remember, you have to treat the seams with two generous coats of sealer every year so water does not go through the needle holes.

Store the tent dry. On a trip you often need to spread out the tent for five minutes in the middle of the day to dry the morning dew, but keep it out of direct sunlight.

Sleeping Bag

As with tents, one of the biggest problems in buying a sleeping bag is the indecision that comes from having too much choice. Before deliberating which to buy, consider how cold the night will be where you are going. Sleeping bags are rated by how much cold they can tolerate, a highly exaggerated figure. A sleeping bag rated for –10°C (14°F) will be cold if the temperature drops below freezing. You need a bag rated 10°C less than the rating given on the label. The lower the rating, the heavier and more expensive the sleeping bag.

Couples can use a double bag or a pair of sleeping bags that can be zipped together. Sleeping bags come in different lengths for shorter or taller people. Cyclists use sleeping sacks that are tapered at the feet, called mummy bags or backpacking bags because they weigh less and keep body warmth better. Cyclists also make sure that the stuff sack that comes with the bag is durable and waterproof. Most bags come with a choice of zipper on right or left side—a quality zipper is important.

People are moving away from goose down (down does not necessarily mean goose down, but a combination of down and waterfowl feathers) since it is expensive and will lose 90 percent of its warmth if soaked. If you go somewhere where it might rain hard, your sleeping bag has a chance of getting wet. Quallofil, PolarGuard, Hollofil, and polyester are common fills. Look for a sleeping bag that can be easily washed.

So that the filling does not lump up, a good sleeping bag is sewn in small segments or baffles. Plenty of fill at the bottom of the bag is most important: feet get cold first. For a medium-length sleeping bag, you do not need to buy heavier than four pounds at a cost of $100 to $150. Before you buy a bag, remember that it is better to get one that is too warm rather than too cold since you can always unzip the bag. Daytime temperatures, especially in high altitudes, have little relationship to what your toes are going to feel like at night. It is also not out of the question to bring along a hot-water bottle.

Youth hostels often require a sewn sheet of their guests, and this can also be used as a sleeping bag liner, a cleaner way to sleep. You can get a light sleeping bag for summer and use a liner with it in slightly cooler weather. Camping stores sell liners that can reduce a sleeping bag's rating by ten or more degrees, or you can make one by sewing a flannel sheet into a sack.

Mattress

A camping mattress or sleeping pad, another essential piece of equipment, not only makes sleeping more comfortable, it insulates you from the cold earth. An inflatable foam mattress called Therm-a-rest, which costs about $45, is most practical for cyclists. Although cheaper, the semi-hard foam sleeping pads used by most budget travelers are bulkier and do not protect as well. An air mattress and the Therm-a-Rest are vulnerable to punctures. You can repair punctures with inner tube patches, but before setting up camp, make sure the place you decide on is free of sharp objects. Air pillows are also available, or you can use clothes in a stuff sack.

I know people who have taken a hammock on cycling trips to Mexico. They are small and light (although the really comfortable ones are heavier and bulkier since they use wood spreader bars), and they

Camping out in Illinois. Don't get this close to the tracks in parts of the world where trains run frequently if you want a quiet night's sleep.

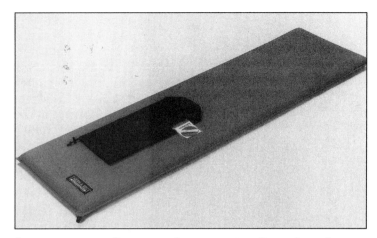

Therm A Rest inflatable pad with foam filling: compact and light to carry on the bike, yet comfortable to sleep on.

keep you away from crawling insects. Consider a hammock made from rope, not canvas, for trips to tropical areas.

Cooking and Accessories

If you want to prepare your own food you will need a small stove and camping pots and pans. Camping stores have a large selection of small backpacking stoves using different types of gas. If you are going to other countries, you should pick a stove that uses a fuel that you know you can get. It is hard to get Coleman gas or special propane cartridges overseas, whereas kerosene is sold everywhere and International Gaz (butane) is available in the U.S. and Europe. Coleman, MSR, Optimus, Primus, and Svea make efficient small stoves. A few campers use Sterno fuel

Small backpacking stoves are most suitable for bike camping.

cans. When I am on my own I cannot take the trouble to cook and clean dishes, but with another person the evening meal is something to look forward to. Those who want to avoid aluminum can use coated pans that are not much heavier. Cookware is an individual decision. Its bulk requires judicious limits.

Other camping necessities include a flashlight and/or reading light, either battery-operated or a candle—you will have no problems getting batteries and candles anywhere. A lighter is as good as waterproof matches. Camping stores have pocket knives and other useful gadgets such as soap and toothbrush holders. I find a pen that has a light in it good for writing my journal at night.

PART III.

PLANNING AND
PREPARATION

CHAPTER 9

Transporting Your Bicycle

Bicycles are checked in as luggage at all airports. Planes have plenty of empty space in the cargo section, so do not feel guilty about taking too much room. Within the United States and to some European destinations, you must pack your bicycle in a box and have it specially handled for an extra fee that varies from carrier to carrier. You can get a box from a local bike store.

On international flights weight, not size, counts. You are usually allowed 44 pounds—more on transatlantic flights—and your bicycle gets counted in the total. Your panniers and sleeping bag can be secured and also handed in as luggage. You should take most of the air out of the tires in case the pressure in the baggage compartment drops. Since a touring bike with all the gear weighs 60 to 75 pounds, you may face an excess weight charge. By the way, if you are carrying much more than 75 pounds you are taking too much stuff.

Taking Your Bicycle Apart

The pedals come off first. They require a heavy flat wrench and muscle power to take off, and it is easier to do that while the handlebar is still on. They come

If a box is not available, most airlines will accept a bicycle taken apart and tied together.

You may have to tap the handlebar stem's expander bolt to loosen the stem.

off where the pedals meet the crank arms. The left and right pedals are threaded in opposite directions, so the pedaling motion tightens the threads, and after many miles of hard cycling, it can be an athletic feat to force them off. Turn each wrench toward the rear wheel. Struggling with hard-to-remove pedals makes you realize the advantage of greasing all threads.

The seat comes off next, and it is easy to do. First, mark the seat post at the point where it touches the frame so you know how far to put it back in, then loosen the bolt on the top of the seat tube. After it is loose, the seat pulls out with a twisting motion.

The handlebar and stem come off together. The stem is attached with one long bolt through the top of it. Again, mark where the stem meets the headset so you know how far to replace it. Loosen the bolt, hit it to release the lower catch, and pull out the stem. The handlebar is draped over the top tube for packing. Most manufacturers use Allen head bolts. These wrenches are light, so take the ones you need for the trip.

After you take off the front wheel, you are set to put your bicycle in the box and seal the box. The front wheel fits on the side of the frame, and the entire bicycle slides in. If you do not have a box, tie all the loose parts to the frame carefully.

Note: When you replace the seat and handlebar, make sure the stems are held at least two inches in their tubes, and apply grease to the sections of tube that fit in the frame. You must tighten the bolts well: it's dangerous to ride with a loose handlebar or seat.

Trains, Buses, and Ferries

Trains do not require taking the bicycle apart. The bicycle goes in the baggage car. Take off panniers, handlebar bag, and pump, and turn the bicycle over to the clerks. In most countries the fee for shipping a bicycle with you is minimal. However, crossing a border with a bicycle can sometimes involve a customs declaration routine. Procedures vary, so ask before you buy a ticket. In Europe the bicycle may not travel on the same train as you and may take a couple of days to arrive, so take your bicycle to the station 2–3 days before you leave.

Ferries are equally easy. You bring the bicycle up the auto ramp and lean it on a wall in the parking area. Tie it to the wall in anticipation of rough seas.

Some companies accept bicycles for no extra charge; others add a small fee.

Bicycles fit in the luggage compartment of a modern bus or on top of almost any vehicle including three-wheel motor rickshaws that are popular in Asia. Make sure the bicycle is securely attached, and nothing, such as water bottles or pump, is able to fly off. Use your common sense, but do not expect a bicycle to be free from scratches after having it thrown on or under a bunch of boxes and crates. If I have to go by bus in a poor country I always try to carry the bicycle to the roof myself and make sure it's safely tied with the rope they give me. Buses in the United States require the bicycle to be boxed.

For car transportation you have the choice of several styles of carrying racks that either attach to the front or rear bumper and carry bicycles on hooks, or that fit on the roof with up to four bicycles either right side up or upside down. These racks often can be used for skis. A few companies make racks that allow you to lock the bike to the rack, but the locks should not be considered safe enough to leave your bike in the middle of a large city. If you do not have a rack,

Many suitable racks are available to transport one or more bikes on the top or the back of a car. (Photo courtesy Grabber Products)

you can take off the front and rear wheels and probably fit the bicycle somewhere in the car. I used to take one inside a VW. Many cyclists who live in cities drive out of town and begin riding on the weekend or for a training ride.

Knowing that a bicycle can be easily transported means that you do not have to worry about being stranded, unable to take your bicycle with you. If you hitch a ride, be prepared to take off all your bags and perhaps your wheels when someone stops for you. There is a lot to be said for panniers that snap on and off easily, for quick release hubs, and for handlebar bags that double as shoulder bags.

CHAPTER 10

Timing Your Trip

The importance of planning your trip to hit good weather—dry, mild, and windless—cannot be over-emphasized. It is impossible to ride through Asia during the rainy season, Wisconsin in April, or Somalia during their hot season. Most parts of the world have clearly predictable seasons. It rains during certain months, gets hot and cold in other months, and experiences a dry spell.

The rainy season for one part of a continent can be entirely different from that of another part. The monsoon in southern India starts weeks before it does in the north; the hot season in East Africa is the cool season in West Africa; it does not rain in California during summer, the time for Midwest thunderstorms. When making plans, be sure to check the specific places to which you want to go. The weather on the east side of a mountain range may not be the same as the west, and that nice dirt road may have turned to mud.

Prevailing Winds

Cyclists should also investigate prevalent winds. If you plan to cycle south along South America's Pacific coast during their summer, you will encounter a terrible headwind all the way. Winds in many sections of the

On the bus: bikes transported by bus in Argentina to traverse a particularly muddy stretch of road.

world can be predicted accurately; unfortunately, winds in other regions are not as reliable, but they can be fierce.

You can use the information in Appendix 2 to check the monthly average temperatures and rainfall for most large cities around the world. Appendix 3 describes the prevalent winds during winter and summer. These charts are designed to help you plan the time and direction of your travel. For multi-month excursions, arranging the tour to hit good weather can be quite complicated.

Planning to Save

Travel arrangements to your starting point should also be considered when planning the timing of a bicycle tour. This often means airline bookings. If you need to take more than one flight, especially if you need to make a series of one-way trips, a poorly planned schedule can be costly, forcing you to pay the unnaturally high standard fare, like buying a car at the suggested retail price. For example, the one-way fare from England to India is over $1,000; but if you shop around you can get a round trip for under $800. My advice is to shop around. Naturally, it is preferable to avoid the high tourist season when hostels, camping areas, and hotels are crowded, but since most of your time will be spent away from the major tourist centers, this should not be the major concern.

Information and tickets for ferries in the Mediterranean and the Far East are usually available from travel agents. Reservations are often required during peak season, but other travelers and I have found that if you do not need a reservation it is better to buy your ticket at the point of departure.

CHAPTER 11

Health and Medical Considerations

You should always take a first aid kit, even on a weekend trip, containing supplies for treating minor cuts and sprains. You need an antiseptic (if you take iodine you can also use it to purify drinking water), small and large adhesive bandages, sterile gauze or cotton, medical tape, and an Ace or similar bandage. You may also want to include medicine for diarrhea such as Kaopectate, aspirin for headaches, a small pair of scissors (many pen knives include one), insect repellent, sunscreen lotion, vitamins, a snake bite kit, malaria pills, and prescription medicine. Keep the medicine kit handy and dry—a plastic bag will do. If you break the skin even slightly, clean the wound, apply antiseptic, and bandage it.

Apart from minor lesions, most health problems for distance cyclists involve stiff shoulders, saddle soreness, and minor sickness from eating food or drinking water that is not necessarily bad, but contains bacteria different from that to which the body is accustomed. These minor sicknesses usually last a day or

Relieve neck and shoulder strain by doing this exercise: Tighten your shoulders for a few seconds and roll your neck in both directions.

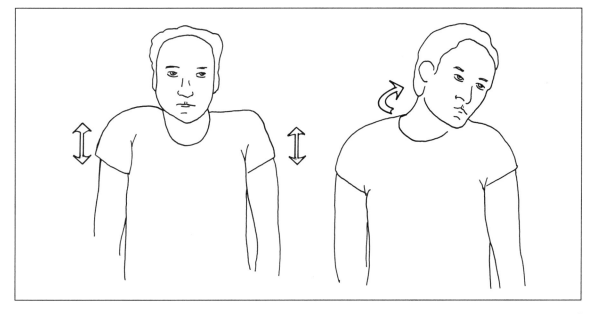

two, and more often than not they do not limit normal cycling activity. Stretching exercises and massages help combat sore muscles; lotion in the crotch area reduces chafing.

Experienced athletes learn to monitor their bodies and not overextend themselves. If you have not trained before, get a physical. On a taxing bicycle tour be good to yourself: eat foods that help keep your bowels in good shape—fruit, fibrous vegetables, and grains; get a full night's rest; drink clean or purified water; never allow your body to dehydrate; exercise your muscles before riding; and massage yourself or have someone give you a massage during breaks. Some cyclists bring medicine for digestion irregularity (if you get diarrhea drink more liquid than normal). Others take vitamin supplements on the road. Staying healthy on a trip also means keeping clean, washing produce, and being sensible.

Sunshine

Sunburn can be a real problem, especially for the light-skinned, but it is relatively easy to prevent by wearing light clothing over the sensitive areas, usually the arms, back of the neck, and thighs, or applying a sun block. Those uncomfortable sunburns occur when the skin has not seen the sun and suddenly gets eight hours of it at the beginning of a trip. Break your skin in gently, exposing it to the sun a little more each day until it gets used to it. Oily sunblocks attract dirt and mingle with sweat, forming a greasy, grimy mixture. Use lotion that the skin absorbs.

Sunglasses are a must to keep your face muscles from straining. A lightweight pair that keep out ultraviolet light and fit high over the eyes is a good choice. People who need prescription glasses have found photosensitive lenses a good choice. They lighten at dark, requiring the cyclist to carry only one pair of glasses.

Heat, Cold, and Altitude

All campers should be aware of hypothermia and altitude sickness, disorders that affect the nervous system so that victims do not know their own condition until it is too late. Hypothermia usually occurs in high altitudes when it is cold and wet. The victim is usually tired and has not eaten, and the body does not have the energy to keep its warmth. For cyclists, this can happen after a hard climb into cold, windy mountains while the body is wet from rain or sweat. Usually, the rider has not eaten (it is not good to climb mountains on a full stomach). Candidates for hypothermia should cover themselves and eat high-energy foods immediately, such as dried fruit and nuts.

Altitude sickness affects people who are not used to the thin air, and they often do not sense anything wrong until they keel over. Although light-headedness usually does not hit below 13,000 feet, cyclists accustomed to sea level find that they have to breathe deeper and stop more often when they reach 5,000 feet. You cannot fight it; you have to go slowly and allow your body to gradually accept the altitude. If you start feeling sick, you must relax. Since it takes about three months to truly adjust to the altitude, if you feel yourself becoming sick, it's probably better to drop down to a lower altitude and cycle elsewhere.

I know of few cyclists who have suffered from hypothermia and altitude sickness, but several have been afflicted by heat exhaustion when it is humid and oppressive. I was stricken to a point where my skin broke out in a painful rash. It is tremendously uncomfortable, and once it starts you cannot do anything about it except go to a cooler climate. It makes you not want to cycle any more, ever. When cycling one feels deceptively cooler since the wind runs across the face. Heat exhaustion, which can occur when cycling in over 104°F, will affect you before the local people not only because you are not used to the heat, but because you are physically active under the hot sun.

Children flock around touring cyclist in an Indian village.

Heat exhaustion attacks people riding in humid regions, not deserts. Avoid riding in the heat of the day, drink a lot more than you usually do, force yourself to eat regularly, keep your head shaded, and expect to go more slowly. If you feel sick to your stomach, consider a way to transport yourself and your bicycle to a cooler area, such as the mountains; otherwise, it will take weeks to recover.

Insects and Animals

Campers can protect themselves from biting insects by going into the safety of their tents or by using a repellent. Desert cyclists need to check for scorpions both before they set up camp and when they venture out of their tents in the morning. Flies are a sanitary menace; keep your food covered and wash before eating.

Despite their bad PR, snakes are docile, usually harmless creatures that shy away from human presence. However, wilderness campers often carry a small snake bite kit that cuts open a wound from a poisonous snake bite and extracts the venom by a suction cup. If you are worried about snakes, before coming into a high weed area to camp, shout, stamp your feet, and make a lot of noise.

You do not need to worry about wild animals except in African game parks. However, domestic dogs can be a serious and dangerous menace, and many will bark at you viciously. Few will actually bite, but you can never tell which ones will. You can usually out-cycle

Elephant crossing in Zimbabwe

them—they do not have the stamina of a cyclist and can run fast for only a short distance. Almost always it is best to leave them alone and ride out of their territory quickly. Occasionally you need to take off your pump and start swinging it at them, making sure they don't bite into it. Some cyclists, like mail carriers, bring a can of Halt for dogs that persist in their attack. A 50/50 mixture of ammonia and water in a squeeze bottle is equally effective. Spray only when under attack, but spray the attacking animal directly in the eyes (its blinding action is temporary).

It is a bad idea to stop when being pursued by a dog, but if you are off your bicycle you may have to put the bicycle between you and the dog until you get help. If help does not come you will curse yourself for not buying dog repellent. I remember once in Peru when I was camped by the side of a river a vicious-sounding dog came in the middle of the night and started barking right outside my tent. I did not know what he was going to do, but he did not give up barking until dawn. Then there was the time in Kenya when I heard the terrifying roar of a lion while lying in my tent. I wished I had been back in Peru with the dog.

Inoculations for Foreign Travel

Thanks to the United Nations, smallpox no longer poses a health danger, and doctors have stopped inoculating against it. But yellow fever, cholera, tetanus, malaria, typhoid, and hepatitis remain prevalent all over the world, not just in poor countries. These diseases can be prevented by vaccinations or pills. Other diseases require precautions. World health conditions change. Up-to-date information on recommended inoculations is available either from the embassies of the countries you are going to visit, from the State Department of Foreign Ministry, or from local travel inoculation clinics located at international airports or large urban hospitals.

Your method of travel exposes you to every disease. You are probably not frequenting luxury hotels in the main cities, but pushing out to rural parts of the country. I strongly urge you to go out of your way to protect yourself against every disease you might contract. If a country recommends but does not require inoculation, go ahead and get it. Two French cyclists touring West Africa without taking malaria pills both got the disease and spent six weeks recuperating.

Immunizations

SHOT	DURATION	POSSIBLE SIDE EFFECTS
Tetanus	10 yrs.	Fever, aching, tiredness, and pain at point of injection and arm for one or two days.
Typhoid	3 yrs.	Same as tetanus.
Cholera	6 months	Same as tetanus.
Yellow Fever	10 yrs.	Muscle aches and tiredness 3-10 days after injection.
Globulins	n.a.	Pain at injection site.
Meningitis	3 yrs.	Pain at point of injection, possibly fever and tiredness.

Immunization table

They were on the road again, but it was a lot of uncomfortable wasted time.

The standard recognized certificate for vaccinations, the yellow *International Certificate of Vaccination* booklet, is issued by the World Health Organization. Whenever you get inoculated, take the booklet with you and ask the doctor to sign and stamp it. This booklet, available from the United Nations and travel inoculation centers, is for your records as well as for showing border guards of countries where proof of inoculation is required.

Typhoid usually results from drinking bad water, and it requires an effective inoculation that lasts three years. Tetanus is caused by an infection through the blood, usually from a puncture of the skin. Since cyclists have a good chance of falling on the road and scraping the skin, often the same place where animals walk, they need to protect themselves with a tetanus shot wherever in the world they go. The inoculation is good for two years and is effective. If you cut yourself put antiseptic on the wound. Yellow Fever vaccinations are good for ten years, should you be going to a country where such an inoculation is required. Cholera towers its ugly head over many Third World communities, but the inoculation against it is not effective, and some centers have stopped immunizing against it.

Malaria and Mosquitoes

Malaria, the most common of the dangerous diseases, comes in three strains, two of which you can protect against moderately well while the third strain is rare. For most parts of the world you can shield yourself by taking a 500 mg. Cloriquin tablet once a week, beginning two weeks before arriving in an infected area and ending six weeks after leaving. The other strain of malaria in parts of Africa and Asia can be avoided by a 500 mg. tablet of Fansadar taken the same way. For a reason far beyond my comprehension these pills are given in the United States by prescription only, and they are expensive. Both pills are only 80 percent effective; missionaries who spend years in malaria-infected areas usually get the debilitating disease even if they take the tablets religiously. The pills are not unpleasant, but it is easy to forget to take one each week.

Avoid mosquitoes, or at least minimize the number of bites you get. Mosquitoes are responsible for spreading a disproportionately large number of diseases, and they can turn a camping or cycling trip into an painful experience. You will have no problem with mosquitoes while riding, for the wind will not allow them to land on you. Once you stop they will find you, especially in the late afternoon. If you are not in the safety of your tent or using a repellent in a heavy mosquito area, you are in trouble. Some campers swear that if you take vitamin B-12 along. With a B-Complex, your skin will emit an odor that turns mosquitoes away. It does not work for everyone, but B-12 is soluble and will not harm you if you want to try it. If you use repellent, get the lighter cream type rather than a spray can.

Other diseases such as hepatitis can be controlled with good sanitation. Some doctors recommend a shot of gamma globulin to increase the amount of gamma globulin manufactured by the body. These shots are effective for only a short time, and they are a relatively small dose—2.25 mg, only a fraction of the gamma globulin produced by the body—and they are blood-based. The best remedy for hepatitis is washing fresh fruit and vegetables and washing your hands before eating and after going to the bathroom.

Bilharzia, which you can get on the shore of some lakes and rivers in Africa and western Asia, results from a microscopic crab boring its way through the skin. Avoid those bodies of water.

Insurance

Travel insurance is not cheap for decent coverage, but since our way of travel is vulnerable, travel insurance appears to be a sound investment. Used mostly by people who travel by air and see the sights in capital cities, travel insurance can cover accidents, illness, and loss of baggage. Remember that in order to be paid you must get full documentation for the problem—including police reports and doctors' bills.

CHAPTER 12

Food, Water, and Nutrition

Eating is as sacred to distance cyclists as chanting is to Buddhist monks. No one has to tell a cyclist to eat—after a strong ride there is no restraining the appetite. A 150-lb. person can burn up to 700 calories an hour while riding on flat ground at 15 mph. As the speed increases, the caloric output increases geometrically. Cyclists on a 100-mile ride can use up to 5,000 calories a day.

Food Types

Carbohydrates are the necessary food for cyclists to replenish the energy lost to exertion. The body craves that heavy food, and you must satisfy its need if you want to have the energy to continue riding with the same strength. On the road, cyclists may eat twice as much as they do normally, but they usually finish the trip weighing less. The heart beats faster, the lungs work harder, and energy is expended at an alarming rate. You need carbohydrates, but you also need a good diet.

The fixation on getting adequate protein is exaggerated and often misdirected. The protein controversy boils down to eight amino acids (proteins) that your body cannot manufacture and that you must eat. Except for meat, fish, and dairy products, individual

Two German cyclists in Tunisia, North Africa.

foods contain only a few of those amino acids. If you do not eat meat, eat foods containing a combination of those amino acids. Thus, wise eaters make sure that they not only eat carbohydrates, but that in lieu of animal products they eat a balanced combination of foods such as rice and beans for at least one meal. Eating beans for one meal and rice for the next will not enable your body to have a complete protein complex. Examples of protein-rich foods include nuts and fruit, beans on a tortilla, Chinese stir-fried vegetables and rice, or Arabic hummos.

Exotic Food

One of the exciting aspects of traveling is trying new foods, so try everything. Exotic fruits are wonderful, especially the first time. In restaurants where you will have a language problem do a lot of smiling and, if you can, go and see what the owner is trying to serve you. You often have to leave yourself to his or her mercy. Be a good sport. Almost everyone will want to serve you well.

On a trip you may be invited into people's homes for dinner. It is an opportunity to meet and talk to people. At someone's home a household might spend more on you for the meal they put before you than they would spend on themselves for a week. I give up my vegetarian diet and eat whatever my host puts in front of me. Once in a poor black community in South Africa a family took me in and fed me beef and Cadbury chocolate, and I know they do not eat like that. Do not be surprised if someone else wants to pay for your dinner in a restaurant, or if the owner will not accept your money. Perhaps you can leave something as a gift. I buy sweets and other treats in a city and give them away as I go, but I confess that I also eat a lot of them while riding.

In poor countries a restaurant often means a hut or a movable stand where you sit on a bench and get served by an eight-year-old boy who sticks his finger in the water glass as he serves it to you. Your ideas of sanitation will fly out the window. You can do little to be careful in such a situation, but the meals are usually healthy, and since the food is boiled or cooked at a high temperature, you will seldom get sick from contamination.

Major cities in the poorest country have plenty of food, and you will see supplies of food in the countryside. You will rarely see starving people unless you ride into a massive famine area, but you may see people eating a poor diet, especially in the belts of poverty that surround large cities. In parts of the world people eat only one food, rice or corn, sometimes little else, filling themselves but failing to satisfy the body's nutritional needs.

Water

On a hot day and a hard cycle your body can perspire, burn up, and breathe out two gallons of water. If you do not replace that fluid your body will rebel and begin to break down. It is next to impossible to over-drink on a hot day, but it is a serious problem to let your body burn off water without replacing it. This cannot be stressed enough: you must drink often and a lot. If you wait until you feel thirsty then it is already too late, and although you can drink and quench your thirst, it will take hours to regain the strength you lost to the dehydration. It is quite natural to drink half or a full liter of water during a rest break, but keep drinking a little at a time while riding. That is why water bottles are kept handy on the frame.

The test of how much water you are replacing is how much you are urinating. Many days you'll drink plenty and hardly go to the bathroom. This means that you are not drinking enough. It is good to urinate and flush salts and minerals. While we are on the subject, you should follow nature's call and go to the bathroom as soon as you feel the urge. You will get rid of excess weight and allow your body to function better. A full bladder can rupture in an accident, such as taking a spill on the road—an unnecessary risk.

Water is available wherever there are people, and only a handful of roads pass long uninhabited stretches. But the quality of water varies from place to place and from rainy to dry season. Water may become more salty or polluted at the end of the dry season. Some drinking water comes from reservoirs where the water is purified. Other water is diverted from lakes, rivers and small streams, collected from rain or taken from wells. A lot of water looks or tastes bad, and it is obvious that it needs purification, but most of the time it is not possible to tell: those little germs that cause sickness are invisible, odorless, and tasteless. The local people may have no problem drinking their water, but they are used to the germs. They may have as many problems with your water, especially if it's not chlorinated.

Health and Water

Bad water kills millions of people every year in poor countries. Although this is an important subject for the world community of concerned citizens, only in a few places is it a problem for cyclists who can carry up to three water bottles on the bicycle frame between the crank and gear shifters—two facing the rider and one facing the front wheel—in addition to reserve containers packed on the luggage racks. Large-capacity water bottles are popular with tourists.

At times a touring cyclist has no choice but to drink local tap water—it is not possible to always bring along enough bottled water. Sometimes tap water will make you sick for a day or two, and your body will build up tolerances as a result. You can purify water by adding chlorine, adding iodine, boiling it, purifying it through charcoal, or a combination of the above. Boiling a huge amount of water during the day is often impractical, but you can feel safe drinking coffee or tea at the local cafe. If you add chlorine or iodine, tablet or liquid, add a minute amount, wait 15 minutes, then drink. Water purification tablets sold in camping stores are easy to use.

Camping stores also carry charcoal filters, including a purification straw and a flip cup that slowly filters water. Filtering will not kill as many of the harmful germs as will chlorine and iodine, but chlorine and iodine are poisons and should be used sparingly. Iodine can cause throat problems after continued use (a bottle of iodine antiseptic warns that it is for external use only). Use those poisons only when you do not trust the water, especially if the water looks brown or yellow.

Bottled soda and fruit juice are available everywhere. Many people add a powder mix such as Kool-aid or Gatorade to make lousy water taste good. After water has been sitting under the sun in your water bottles, it needs spicing up. Powder is heavy: you can only bring a small amount of it along, enough to last for a few quarts of water, though mixes that use artificial sweeteners are lighter.

CHAPTER 13

Maps and Orientation

A cyclist's map has to be very detailed, showing the small roads and describing the nuances of the terrain. In most cases a 1:500,000 scale is not detailed enough for cycling. Standard automobile maps for large areas such as Germany or Nevada are 1:1,000,000 or more. On such a scale one inch equals 15.8 miles. That is usually too small, although it depends on the number of roads in the region. In Germany, with its vast network of roads, a 1:100,000 map is advantageous, while in Nevada, where there are only a few roads and fewer towns, a 1:500,000 map may do. Generally, cyclists need 1:250,000 or less.

Where to Get Maps

A few countries or states have good maps readily available from their tourist offices. Other places do not believe in detailed maps. You can buy good maps to Western countries at a map store—Michelin and other tire and oil companies produce good maps—but the selection of detailed maps good for cycling in other countries is often limited. I have found that a large university library has a wide selection of maps in its map and atlas room. By looking through road maps, aviation maps, State Department maps, political maps, and geological survey maps, you can find what

Typical Nepalese road

you feel is the best map for the area, then order it at a store or photocopy it. Write on the map in bold ink the best route, places to see, and other information such as rate of the local currency.

If you look closely at several maps of the same area you can see whether the road will be mountainous. It only takes a little time to learn to read relief indications. Contour lines show elevation, while the contour interval—the amount of space between lines—tells the amount of rise. A curvy line or a scenic road usually means mountains. From the altitude difference you can determine grade. Roads that follow rivers or railroads are usually not steep.

A 1:500,000 scale map is not detailed enough for populated areas.

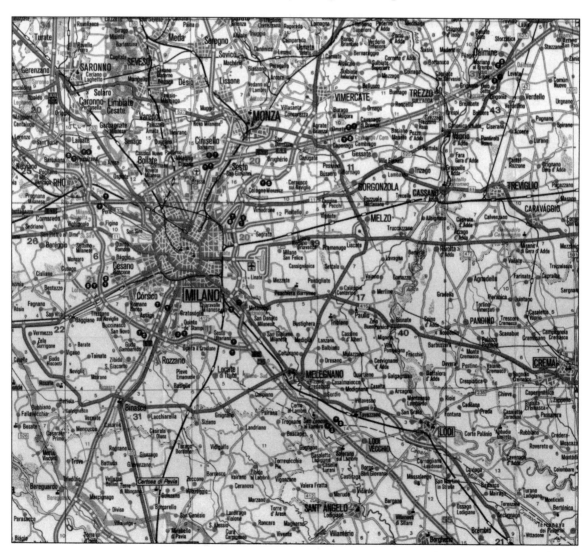

Which way now? Road signs in Arkansas, USA.

A good map informs you about the condition of the roads—whether they are gravel, all-weather, or multi-lane. It should include small roads to remote areas as well as physical landmarks such as railroad tracks, telephone lines, and points where ferries operate. The date of the map is important, as roads change. Although you usually won't have a chance to select a more recent map of the same series, this should guide your choice between different maps, certainly in regions that go through a lot of development.

Select maps carefully to provide the kind of detail that is important to cyclists. Some maps show a fat line for a road but do not say what type of road it is, and when you arrive it may turn out to be small, narrow, and nothing but dirt. Parts of the Pan-American Highway in South and Central America are not only dirt, they are rocky, tire-destroying dirt that brings curses to the mouths of the most pious. Some countries have no paved roads, literally. Some states in the United States have no alternative to the Interstate. You have to do your homework before leaving on a trip. Bicycling is about roads, and where you go will depend largely on finding a connecting system of roads on which you can travel. If you are traveling a long distance, the packet of maps you bring will take up a lot of space in the panniers. Try to trim the unnecessary parts of the map, keep them in plastic, and consider holding off taking maps you know you can get en route.

Mountain bike riders who actually intend to travel off-road especially need to know more about the terrain. You can be sure that if you see several towns near each other without a road that there will be at least a trail or a footpath. If you read about the area you are traveling to in books from a well-supplied library you will have a good idea of the terrain.

It is also wise to carry a compass, not that you are going to get lost in the woods, but a compass helps in many situations where you have to make a decision on roads. Also, you can often tell exactly where you are on the road with a compass and a good map. I put mine in the map case. A compass helps you find your way out of a big city. Find the direction of the road you want and follow main roads in that compass direction. The trick is to keep on the main roads and keep going in the direction intended.

As soon as you get out of the congested area you will either see a sign or have to ask someone, and you will see that if you are not on the right road you are not far off. Believe me, this technique works. It is often hard to get out of a big city otherwise. Since the compass bounces with the bicycle, use a good fluid-filled one. Note that the magnetic north is near Bathwest Island on the northern Canadian coast, while zero is a curved line that passes through Chicago and Miami. In Seattle, you need to adjust over 20 degrees for a true reading.

CHAPTER 14

Borders, Legalities, Bureaucracies, and Money

Dealing with border formalities, conforming to seemingly senseless bureaucratic rules, and overcoming authoritarian barricades can be exasperating and draining. At some borders you present your passport and begin cycling in the new country within two minutes. At other borders you can spend four hours or an entire day. It is frustrating. I am convinced that some countries make a deliberate effort to employ their rudest and most dull-witted civil servants to supervise immigration and travel.

But for most people in the Third World, travel to Western countries, especially the United States, is a far worse experience then it is for a Westerner traveling to the Third World. Immigration and border formalities of Western countries suffer a tremendous cultural/racial prejudice, as a look at the American-Mexican border can attest. I try to think about that when I am impatiently waiting for border guards to finish their three-hour lunch break.

It is impossible to generalize the various policies that affect passport and immigration. To almost all

Which bike was mine? Japanese bicycle parking facility.

places you will travel, borders present absolutely no problem. The authorities are courteous and helpful. They are a good source of information and amusement. Let us discuss the others.

Finding a Country's Requirements

Some countries require no visa (a rubber stamp in your passport); some stamp a visa in your passport when you enter; some require a visa before arriving; a few countries require sponsorship from a citizen of that country; and fewer countries will not allow you to cycle in their country. You need to find out exactly what the country you want to visit requires and when the border you plan to cross is open. Countries change visa policies for political reasons or, more often, for no logical reason. If a visa is required before arriving, apply to the country's consular office before traveling. Visas are free or cost about $10 and take anywhere from two minutes to four weeks to obtain. If you cannot go to the country's consulate office in person, you can mail your passport via certified mail, including a pre-stamped self-addressed certified envelope, which is available at the post office.

The country's consulate or government tourist information office is the best place to find out about their legal requirements. Write or telephone them and ask them to send you information and an application. Many countries have tourist offices located in major cities. You can also get information from travel books and a few reference library books. The United States Department of State publishes periodic pamphlets called *State Department Notes* on all countries. These are informative, and they are available from libraries containing a government documents section. This research is part of planning a trip.

Visas often expire in three or six months, so if you are expecting that it will take you longer to get to the country, you have to stop at another capital city en route and visit the country's consulate. You usually need to give them passport-size pictures of yourself. It is a good idea to pack with your documents a few passport-size pictures of yourself in case you need to make a visa application on the road. In the words of Earl Wilson, if you look like your passport photo, you need the journey.

Make sure you know all the country's requirements. Some need special permits to certain areas of the country. Other countries will not let you in if you have a valid visa for Israel, South Africa, North Korea, or a country hostile to the one you are entering. The onus is on you to show that you are a decent person who has no political agenda.

Not only does each country have its own border procedures, but border procedures at different entry points of the same country can also vary. It is fair to say that countries treat visitors who arrive by air better than those who cross borders, but almost always, people both in and out of uniform enjoy seeing cyclists and treat them cordially. However, if some little thing is out of place, you may be thrown into a tidal wave of bureaucracy and can only hold your breath until it passes you and allows you to swim again.

Frontier Crossing

When you do arrive at a frontier or an airport look neat, bright, and self-sufficient. Every bureaucrat, the lowest flunky to the boss, may ask for your papers, and you must show them your passport. Be genial; indicate that you have an adequate amount of money and that you will stay in hotels and campgrounds, but do not flash around your money unless they demand to see it. Give your employment as teacher, cultural research specialist, merchant, or student. How you are treated usually depends on how you look and what you say.

At some borders you will be asked to show proof of inoculations, at which time you will bring out your

Egyptian desert road

World Health Organization booklet of vaccinations and point to the inoculations you have had. Many countries require proof of inoculation only if your passport says that you have recently been in a disease-infected area. Regulations change. I can remember being asked for proof that I was taking malaria tablets only once, on the Costa Rican border.

Keep your camera out of sight at border crossings. Borders are sensitive areas, usually military zones, and it is illegal to photograph military zones. If the authorities see you taking pictures, or even suspect that you are, they may expose or confiscate your film, a terrible thing to have happen if you have just taken the best pictures of your trip. Some countries prohibit photographing trains, harbors, bridges, or military installations.

You and your equipment may be searched by the border authorities, mainly to see if you are bringing anything that requires duty, usually a cursory check of part of your pannier. Some borders employ drug-sniffing dogs; others search you thoroughly, but most will take your word that you have nothing to declare. I do not need to point out the consequences of being caught trying to smuggle firearms, antiquities, or illegal drugs. You can never yell, threaten, or otherwise override the power of the authorities. If you get mad, keep that anger inside you. In rare instances bribes are called for: use your ethical and practical judgment.

Once you are in the country you have to show your papers to anyone in a uniform who asks you for them. They often do not know how to read your passport, but give it to them anyway, and let them thumb through it. Generally, I have found the less you say in that situation the better; just show your passport, let them look, answer their questions, and continue on your way.

Handling Money

A handful of countries want you to change money on the spot at the official exchange rate. This is unfortunate. Change as little as possible, as it is probably a bad rate for you. A few countries demand that you spend a certain minimum each day, and you change money according to the number of days you will stay in the country.

There is an active black market for hard currency in countries with a high external debt. In a few countries, changing on the black market can lead to trouble with the authorities. Near many borders unofficial money changers roam looking for business. Changing money with them might be illegal, often immoral. Money changers supply the rich of a country with hard currency to enable them to buy what they otherwise cannot, robbing the country as a whole of badly needed foreign cash. Be careful.

Sometimes money changers are the only way to change money, and it is most advantageous for you if you have dollars, the world standard. Ask a few people for the current exchange rate so you do not get cheated. If you feel unsure about a money changer who approaches you—and they will approach you—trust your instincts.

How much money to take and in what form depends on where and how long you are going. Travelers checks are all right for Europe and where there are tourists, but are a nuisance anywhere else. Not only do you pay when you buy the checks, but you usually have to pay an extra commission when exchanging them. Figure your budget and allow 20 percent extra. Take a combination of cash and a few travelers checks, and keep the money in different places. Some cyclists carry their money on them in a nylon money belt that fits comfortably around their waist under their jersey. I put a small amount of money in the handlebar bag or panniers and store emergency money rolled up inside the handlebar behind the end plug. The passport should remain safe in a dry plastic bag together with airline tickets and other documents.

Credit cards are useful, especially American Express, which in major cities has offices that allow you to withdraw money. VISA and MasterCard allow you to withdraw from an associate bank. If you are an American Express customer (credit card or checks) you can have mail sent to their offices abroad. It is morale boosting to get a letter on the road.

Language and Social Customs

Over 2,000 languages are spoken around the world. If you plan to travel to other countries you cannot possibly know many words in even a hundredth of the world's languages, but over 80 percent of the world's population speak eight languages, and you can learn a few words of those. The more you know a language the

Sometimes, the realities of our industrial age cach up with the touring cyclist. But on the positive side, there is unspoilt scenery that you quickly reach by bike not too far from these cooling towers.

better you will know the people, but you only need to know a few words to be able to get around and communicate.

Due to several hundred years of colonization, the official language of many countries is a European language, the Americas being the largest example. That does not mean that the people you are going to be visiting in the rural areas speak the official language. For example, English is one of the main official languages in India, but studies show that only a small percentage of the people speak decent English. Nevertheless, those few people will come out of the woodwork in the most remote areas to talk to you and will enable you to get around.

Knowing a few words of English, Spanish, French, and Arabic will do you amazingly well almost everywhere. Other important languages include Russian for the Soviet Union, Mandarin for the Orient, German for Eastern Europe and Turkey, and Swahili for East Africa. English has become the Lingua Franca for business, travel, aviation, and technology—some people in every city speak English.

I get a short phrase sheet of often-used phrases and expressions and keep it in the map case. While I am riding I try pronouncing and remembering the words I know I am going to need, such as 'thank you,' 'water,' 'where is the way to....' I had a devil of a time trying to pronounce East European languages, so I had to show the sheet to people in order to be understood. People go out of their way to help you. Two words of greeting make all the difference.

Of course, sign language also gets you a long way. I have traveled through places where I understood not one word of the local language and no one understood me, yet I sat with people for tea and felt we somehow not only understood each other but became close friends. A large portion of human communication is non-verbal, and sometimes not being able to communicate is an even more profound experience. People invite the whole town over to try to talk to you. Do not worry about being able to communicate, but do try to learn a few essential words and phrases or carry sheets of those words with you.

Ethnocentrism

It is hard to dump your prejudices before beginning a trip. We usually do not know what prejudices we have.

Rather, bicycle trips make you gradually more open to new cultural values. The more you travel with an attitude of discovery, the more sensitive you will be to others. Part of the planning of a trip is learning the social customs of the place you are visiting. If you read about the place and have a sensitive attitude, your trip will be much more rewarding. The essential element is open-mindedness, not to think you know more than they.

Prudent bicycle tourists, whether they are riding in Louisiana or Syria, try to act within their host's social framework. If an Algerian offers you something to eat, and you refuse, you will offend him and reject the Algerian culture, greatly limiting your experience. Generosity, an Algerian social value, is prized as much as financial standing is on New York's Upper East Side. Men who go to Malaysia with long hair will violate Malaysian sensibilities. Women wearing skimpy tops or men wearing no tops while cycling in rural Greece will remain outside Greek life, even though most foreign women seem to go topless on the beaches in Greece.

Sign in the Jewish section of Jerusalem.

Keeping Track

Almost all cyclists keep a journal of their travels. This rewarding discipline helps you to look back and see not only where you have been, but your attitude toward different places. Write down what roads you took, what cities you passed, how many miles you traveled, and interesting highlights during the day. If you take photographs, keep accurate notes about just where and when you took each particular picture and if applicable the names of people involved. This will make it much easier to reconstruct your trip afterwards.

CHAPTER 15

Where to Stay at Night

The nights spent while on a bicycle tour will encompass the richest and most remembered experiences of the trip. Cyclists have many accommodation alternatives: camping in a public campground, staying at youth hostels, finding a spot not far from the road and setting up your own camp, staying at cheap, moderate, or expensive hotels in towns, or accepting hospitality and staying with local people in their homes.

Camping, the cheapest way to travel, allows you the opportunity to be in and with nature. Youth hostels are usually jolly places where one can meet other international travelers. Hotels provide an opportunity to rest, while accepting local hospitality gives you a chance to experience a regional culture. A well-rounded trip will include all five alternatives.

Campgrounds and Youth Hostels

Youth hostels and official campsites are available in Westernized countries, but I have found campsites and youth hostels in Zimbabwe and Peru; 'camping' has become an international word. Campgrounds are usually just outside town off a main road. You will find hostels in virtually all European cities and many American cities. Both hostels and camps are usually

Bicycle campers at a French campground.

cheap, reasonably clean, and offer you the opportunity to meet others or, if you want, to relax without the need to talk to anyone. You can do your laundry, write your journal, read about the next place you are going to travel, do preventative maintenance on your bicycle, and take a bath.

Campsites get most of their business from motorized campers. A few camps, especially in American state parks, are government run; most are independent, but their locations are noted on tourist maps. Facilities vary so much from camp to camp that it is difficult to make generalizations. Some campgrounds have tennis courts and swimming pools, while others are rustic. Tourist books list the facilities at different campgrounds, but most cyclists stay at the first one they pass when they are ready to turn in. It is normal to pay $3 to $6 a person for a night's stay (you often have to pay extra for a hot shower). Even during the height of summer, campgrounds have room for an extra one or two cyclists, but large groups may need to make reservations.

Do not be put off by the name; youth hostel are not for the young only: they are open to anyone who becomes a member, except in a few countrys with age limits (see directory). Guests usually share a dormitory which costs from $5–15 a night. In large hostels you must be careful not to leave your equipment unguarded, including sleeping bag, tent, and bicycle, but smaller hostels are usually safe. A few hostels in larger towns with train stations need reservations during the high season, which in Europe usually means during the summer school and university vacations. When you join, you will be given a directory for locating hostels around the world; many European cities have small road signs directing you to the local hostel.

Finding a Campsite

Finding your own campsite is simple. When it starts getting late in the day, or when you are ready to stop, begin looking for a place to camp. In heavily populated areas it is hard to find empty space. Ask a local resident if you can pitch your tent on his farm or yard. In open areas look for a secluded place, preferably surrounded by trees. Forests and state-run parks are excellent places to camp. If you are on a busy road, take a side street that leads you away from the noise of the road.

Look for level, smooth ground and sweep the area with your feet. You can often find a nice place to camp on the side of a stream or river. You need to use your judgment and follow your discretion: if you feel at all uneasy about camping unprotected, if you feel that someone is watching you, do not camp. Get the permission of local residents, enlisting their protection. Do not be afraid to ask if you can camp on their farm, near their house, or behind a fence. Do not camp next to military areas or any highly trafficked area without getting permission.

Bathing and doing laundry can be a drawback to camping alone. Camping near a stream, or stopping at one along the way the next day, usually solves that problem. If you are going through a dry area, this type of camping can only be occasional. A few times the you-make-it camping accommodations have turned out poorly for me. If I want to camp off by myself, I often leave the matter until too late, getting ready to camp when it is becoming dark, then throwing down my tent and dropping off to sleep. Late afternoon and early evening are good times to ride. As the sun sinks in the horizon, the wind calms and the air cools, and I feel renewed energy and often want to put on a few extra miles, but I am unable to see that I have chosen

The rules of considerate and conscientious camping.

Resposible Camping

☐ Never leave litter.

☐ Wash body, clothes, and dishes away from natural water resources with a biodegradable soap.

☐ When there isn't a bathroom, dig a small hole for your waste and toilet paper, then cover with dirt.

☐ Unless you know stream water is pure, assume it is contaminated and either boil or purify with filter or chemical.

a place that becomes a ditch after a rain, or that there is a hornets nest a few trees away, or that it is actually someone's front yard. If you want to avoid this situation, start looking for a spot to camp while there's plenty of light.

Hotels

Staying at hotels, another alternative even for roughing-it campers, has the advantage of a hot bath and a comfortable bed, a well-earned reward after an invigorating cycle or during bad weather. In small towns and villages, whether in upstate New York or Muritania, the choice of hotels is often limited to run-down buildings that do not appear in the region's tourist literature. If you want a hotel for the night, ask the local people where one is and plan to cycle to that town.

Hotels in poor countries cost as little as a dollar a night. Often there is nothing else in the room but a bed and small table. Ask the owner if your bike will be safe before abandoning it for dinner. The owner may say that it is not necessary to lock the door, and you can trust his or her judgment as well as your own. If you suspect the bed is unclean, use your sleeping bag or sewn sheet on top of the bed.

Cheap hotel rooms usually do not have mosquito netting on the windows. A 6 x 3 foot piece of mosquito netting weighs almost nothing and can easily be taken with you. Prop it up in the window and try to get rid of all the mosquitoes in the room. On occasion in heavy

Transporting a bicycle in Peru

mosquito areas I have set up my tent on top of the bed, tying it down with rope. At times it is the only guarantee of getting a decent night's sleep.

Local Hospitality

By far the most rewarding experience is to accept the hospitality of the local people, for hospitality will come your way, especially in South America, The Middle East, Asia, and Africa. Arabic hospitality is beyond words. By eating, talking, and sleeping in people's houses you will become part of their country, not an outsider taking a trip through a foreign country. The country will be yours, the people will become your brothers and sisters, and you will be sharing your common humanity.

You do not have to be a bold person to invite yourself into someone's home. I do not consider myself an extrovert, but I have slept in the homes of many. Here is what I do. When it is late and I want to quit for the day, I will see someone near the road and stop and introduce myself—in a language I know, from poorly pronounced words on a phrase sheet, or in sign language—saying where I am from and that I am traveling through their country. I then ask if I can please pitch my tent on their property, saying that I have all the necessary equipment and will leave early in the morning. Who could refuse such a request? I ask for nothing more, except perhaps to fill my water bottle. I smile and show politeness. A few times that is all that hap-

Staying with a family in Tanzania

pens: I pitch my tent in their front yard, and we hardly exchange any more words.

Most of the time, however, I am invited into their home and treated to food and a lively discussion. The simpler the people are, the more elaborate the hospitality. I make it a point to have food with me that I share—such as bread or fruit or sweets—and we have a fine meal together. I tell them about the places I have visited, and they tell me about their country. Hospitality works both ways. I have never had any problems staying with people, but I do not use this method of securing accommodations in the city. Generally it would be impolite of me, a man, to approach a woman and make such a request. Generally, men should ask men, and women should ask women.

CHAPTER 16

Safe Riding Techniques

Traffic conventions differ from region to region, and you need to adjust your riding habits accordingly. In certain places you will have a wide lane reserved for bicycles, whereas in other areas cars and trucks have the absolute right of way; if there is not enough room for the both of you, they will honk at you, and you must get off the road quickly or they will run you over. Do not argue or try to change their driving habits, just get out of their way.

I strongly recommend a rear-view mirror. Although these weigh little, they do perceptibly increase wind drag. Yet, their advantage outweighs other considerations. After you have had one, you will not know what you did without it. Three types are on the market: those that fit on the end of the handlebar drops; small mirrors that attach to glasses or helmets; and others that attach to the brake lever. The last choice, made by Cateye, Rhode Gear, and Mirrycle, is becoming the most popular.

Wearing a Helmet

Statistically, country riding is safer than city riding: there are fewer accidents per mile traveled on country roads than in the city. On the other hand, the accidents that do occur on rural roads tend to cause more

On your way to safe tea: road safety sign in India.

serious injuries. A car hitting an adult cyclist from behind is, the figures say, a rare event, although the fear factor of that happening is much greater. Cars and trucks make a lot of noise coming from behind, and they often count their clearance in millimeters. For both cars and cyclists most accidents occur at intersections, usually close to home. The statistics also say that four out of five of all fatalities from bicycle accidents are due to head injuries. In the United States almost 1,000 people a year die and 20,000 suffer injuries on bicycles, almost all in urban areas.

It would be nice if all distance cyclists could ride on quiet country roads, but too often you have no choice but busy, crowded roads through hectic cities. The first safety question distance cyclists need to consider is whether to wear a helmet. Everyone with any sense agrees that a helmet is a must in the city, but cyclists disagree on country riding. Although cycling organizations and magazines exhort people to always wear a helmet, many long-distance cyclists find the extra weight hard on the neck after spending hours in the saddle. They also say helmets are hot, and that carrying a bulky helmet is not worth the low risk of injury. Frankly, few long-distance cyclists in foreign countries wear helmets.

This does not mean that you should agree with the majority. If you have a bad fall and break a bone in your leg, it will heal in two months. If you break your head, it will not heal. One woman cycling through Scotland told me about the time she was going rapidly downhill when something caught in her front wheel and threw her over the handlebar. She landed on her helmet, and although her front fork cracked, she walked away unhurt. Had she not had a helmet, she would not have been alive to tell the story.

Avoiding Danger

Whether you wear a helmet or not, remember to be careful at intersections where so many different traffic maneuvers are taking place. Never trust what cars and trucks may do at intersections. Never pass a car on the right near an intersection; always slow down, make yourself visible, look carefully, and listen attentively when approaching an intersection. Intersections are especially difficult if you are riding on the opposite side of the road than you are used to. Stay especially alert.

You cannot use a Walkman in traffic. On a narrow winding road it is safer for cyclists to stay 3 to 4 car lengths apart so cars can overtake one cyclist at a time. If you see or hear a car coming from behind and you think it is dangerous to be passed, move toward the center of the road to stop it.

Riding at Night or in the Rain

Safe riding excludes night riding where there are no street lights, even if you are equipped with your own lights. At night you cannot see the road surface, and you never know what you may be running into, especially if you do not know the road. Although there have been improvments in recent years, most bicycle lights hardly illuminate, and most American cyclists don't carry them. They weigh a lot, and unless you go slowly, you may not see enough. Approaching car lights are blinding, and cars put on their high beams when they see something in the road—you are the last thing they expect to find. All you can do is stop and freeze until the cars pass, a dangerous position. Plan your afternoon so you are not in the middle of nowhere at sundown.

Riding in the rain or fog also presents extra hazards because cars may not be able to see you. I am sure you have been in a car where the passenger-side windshield wiper hardly worked, and the driver could not see anything on that side of the road. I hope I am not describing your car. When cycling in poor visibility wear something bright and flashy and be on guard. I

Reflective devices aid in making the cclist more visible to motorists, but they are no substitute for proper lighting.

glue a large strip of reflector tape on the back of my panniers before I start a trip, the type of tape used on road signs available only from companies that make road signs. Some people use flags or bright-colored vests used by road crews. Flags create wind resistance and often get in the way when mounting and dismounting. In rain and cold weather you will need to make sure that your clothing does not obstruct your vision.

Drafting and Holding on to Vehicles

Riding in a bunch, following each other closely to minimize the effect of wind resistance is referred to as drafting in the U.S. This technique, usually following another cyclist, but sometimes another vehicle—one of the favorite and most efficient riding techniques—calls for special safety considerations. Drafting cyclists should know each other's cycling habits. The person in the back must remain attentive, and since the rear cyclist does not get a good view of the road surface, the front rider should maintain a straight line and point out potential road hazards to the person behind. For example, if the person in front sees glass on the road, he or she should point to the ground and yell out "glass!" Both the hand signal and the sound are necessary since wind often disperses the sound.

Drafting a slow-moving truck or a farm vehicle makes cycling many times easier, but it can be dangerous. Trucks turn, stop, and hide dangers such as potholes. Anytime you are near a motor vehicle you take on more risk and have to be that much more careful. If you draft a vehicle keep your hands on the brakes and maintain a safe distance. Try to stay close to one edge of the vehicle so that you always have a ready escape.

Another trick is holding on to a slow-moving vehicle up a steep hill. In reality you can rarely do this since you and a slow-moving vehicle seldom come together at just the right moment up a hill, unless you are prepared to wait for one to come along. Often you are able to grab a ride on a truck but find that its exhaust is too awful, or that it strains your arm and would be easier to pedal up the hill. Before deciding whether to take hold of the vehicle, you have to make sure that the road is wide enough for both of you so that if at anytime you feel uncomfortable you can just let go and be safe. You should only hang on to the end of the truck, not to the side. Also, you have to let the driver be aware of your presence so he can ensure your safety.

If, while you are struggling up a hill, you hear a slow truck coming up behind you—slow trucks are usually more noisy and spew out blacker smoke—signal the driver with your hand that you are going to hang on. Almost all truck drivers do not mind; in fact many will slow down and make sure that you are able to grab the back. While the truck is approaching, start pedaling faster to match the truck's speed. Find a good place for your hand, and do not stop pedaling until you have a firm hold. You can usually see the driver in the mirror. Signal again with your face to make sure the driver alerts you to any hazards. To prevent your arm from getting tired keep pedaling in a higher gear.

You must always keep your eyes open, and if you get too close to the side of the road, let go and continue struggling up the hill. However, many truck drivers will see that you have let go and will slow down for you, allowing you to grab on again. Almost all hills have to be taken by yourself, but the occasional 'free ride' makes you feel as if you have just gotten away with something.

Cornering

A packed bicycle takes corners differently than one without the extra weight. Physics tells us that the relationship is as shown on the next page:

Dutch touring cyclists in Malta

CENTRIFUGAL FORCE = MASS x RADIUS x SPEED

This means that putting on extra weight—35 pounds of gear—will directly increase the force. When going down a winding hill you cannot take the turn as fast as you can on an unloaded bicycle. The only compensation you can make, the formula says, is to reduce your speed or increase the radius of the turn.

Experienced cyclists take a turn by lowering their center of gravity and leaning into the turn. They tuck their heads into their arms and stick out the turning knee to shift the lower part of the weight to the center of the turning circle. If the road surface is wet, cyclists take turns and grades slowly, holding the handlebar securely and slowing down using the front and rear brakes alternately so the rims do not overheat.

CHAPTER 17

Efficient Riding Style

Cycling is the most efficient and practical use of human power for motion. By using time-tested and laboratory-proven cycling techniques you can ride to the same place in the same amount of time by expending less energy. Riding should not only involve leg muscles, but the whole body should be employed when you need power to climb a hill or fight a wind. As well as using the muscles properly, cyclists should sit in a comfortable position. Strain in any part of the body will reduce your efficiency.

The Riding Posture

When non-cyclists look at a cyclist leaning over the handlebar they often think that it must be painful for the back. It looks as if the back is bent over and stretched. Actually, doctors often recommend cycling for their patients who suffer from back problems. The cycling position should never feel uncomfortable.

To avoid stress while riding, your back should be slightly curved, but the majority of bend comes from the hips. Vary the position of your arms when you are in the saddle. With a dropped handlebar you can periodically move your arms, gripping the handlebar at different points and taking pressure off your shoulders. When riding, especially when your hands are on the drops, your head naturally points down at the road. However, when you are in heavy traffic requiring constant attention, or when you are on a bad road and need to keep looking up to avoid holes and rocks, your neck gets locked in an awkward position. Exercise it while you are in the saddle.

As with any athletic activity, you must breathe deeply and use as much of your lung capacity as you can. The main force for breathing comes from the diaphragm, just under the rib cage. Many people breathe backward, forcing all the air into the small top part of the lungs. Practice taking deep breaths using the diaphragm until that type of breathing becomes natural. Inhale by letting go of the 'stomach,' and exhale by pushing it in. Singers learn this type of breathing. As your cycling ability increases, you will probably find that your respiration rate decreases.

Cycling is less tiring and more efficient when you use this action of the feet, called ankling.

Ankling

Pedal efficiently by using a circular motion, not an up-and-down motion. People call this 'ankling' since it means that not only does each leg go up and down, but the ankles, legs, and feet also participate. Cleats make the motion more forceful since they directly transfer the forward and backward force to the pedals, but the action is also effective without cleats if you keep the toestraps snug. Toe straps are also safer since they prevent the feet from slipping.

At first this ankle movement feels unnatural. It is easy to press down on the toe when the foot is going down, but the trick of high performance riding is to pull up on the strap as the toe rounds the bottom. This movement has to be conscientiously practiced until it becomes part of the normal cycling motion. Since pulling up on the pedal uses a different set of muscles in the lower leg, ankling can dramatically increase efficiency. Also, make sure you are not riding bow-legged, a sign that your seat is too low. The hips, feet, and knees should remain vertical.

Hill Climbing

Hill climbing not only requires strong ankling, but you must stand and use the entire body to lift yourself and your load over the top. Experienced cyclists often rock the bike back and forth, using the shoulder muscles to help. Grab both brake stems and tilt the bicycle left and right without weaving around the road. Cyclists call this 'honking,' and they use it while sprinting as well. Also when you are sitting and you want to add power, use your back and shoulders to help kick the pedals by moving the entire body up and down. This motion comes naturally when you exert energy and hammer on the pedals. These movements, however, take their toll on the body since they demand that you put out all the energy you have, and you cannot ride at peak performance for a long time before getting tired. Alternate standing and sitting while going up a long hill to give yourself a chance to relax.

When you are going into a valley prepare for the coming hill by keeping your body low (riding aerodynamically) and picking up as much speed as possible. Get into your large front gear and small rear gear and begin pedaling as soon as the grade starts to level off. Then try to keep a steady cadence up the hill, changing gears one at a time as you climb the other side of the valley.

A great deal of the tiredness of hill climbing comes from the heart beating wildly, but no small part of tiredness is psychological. You feel you are supposed to be tired after a hill. You can slowly expand your scope. Once you have done a 3,000-foot hill, climbing 1,000 feet feels like a vacation. Learn to love and respect hills. They make cycling a beautiful experience. Tackle them forcefully, not reluctantly, treating them as a true challenge of your cycling ability.

Wind

Adverse wind is a problem I have never learned to cope with. For a short distance a headwind is a nuisance that you just have to plow through. But after long distances against bad winds, after hours and hours of pushing hard on the pedals, you want to throw down your bicycle, kick the road, hurl stones at the wind, and act irrationally. More than once on the side of the road in Wyoming, bewildered local people saw a wild-looking man standing with a bicycle at his feet yelling four-letter words into the wilderness. That crazed cyclist can still feel what it was like to ride against 400 miles of harsh Wyoming winds, and is writing to you about it now. At that time I did not know that you should cross the United States from west to east.

What wears a rider down is the constant noise that the wind makes over the ears. In a strong wind nothing can drown out its noise, and after miles in a low gear without getting half as far as expected and it becomes the greatest morale deflator if you have to listen to a constant drone.

The formula for determining drag is as shown on the next page:

WIND RESISTANCE = [FRONTAL AREA] X
[AERODYNAMIC COEFFICIENT] X ½[DENSITY OF
AIR] X [VELOCITY]^2

The frontal area depends on the height and width of
the cyclist and his gear, so wind drag is directly related to size—the amount of surface or frontal area of
wind you need to break. By lessening the size of that
area—tucking in your head and arms—you reduce the
wind resistance.

The aerodynamic coefficient depends on complicated aerodynamic design factors. A cruising airplane
has a low coefficient while a bicycle and rider,
designed without aerodynamic consideration, suffer a
high coefficient. It would be better to ride backward,
as a bent-over cyclist traps air like a parade banner.

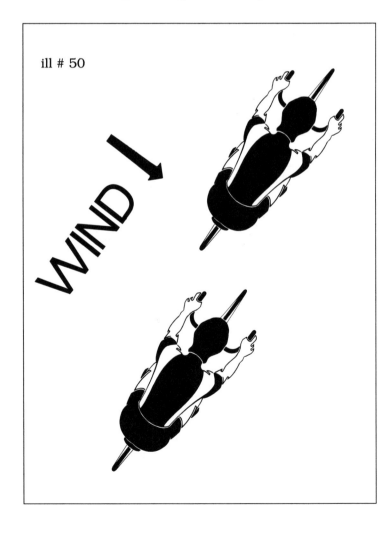

ill # 50

WIND

Drafting formation as dictated by
the direction of the wind.

Air density is affected not only by altitude, but also by the temperature and humidity. A cold humid day has more air resistance than a warm dry one. But the major resistance factor is the velocity squared. That means that going into a 15-mph wind (when you see branches on trees moving) is nine times as hard as a 5-mph wind (when leaves are rustling).

You'll have no control over air density, very little chance to change the aerodynamic coefficient, and a limited ability to reduce the frontal area. Our remaining alternative, reducing velocity, seems intolerable.

While traveling at a brisk 20 mph on flats with no wind, 90 percent of the pedaling energy goes to break the wind created by the cyclist's velocity. All you can do is tighten your pack, get in a lower gear, and make sure you have nothing flapping in the air, not even a piece of string dangling from the panniers. Wear tight clothing, do not let your hair fly in the wind, bring your arms in, and bend your shoulders down as far as you can to take as little wind as possible. Winds are most intense during the early afternoon and are most calm around sunrise.

If you have the opportunity to draft, do it. This is one of the best practical reasons for touring in a group. In a crosswind move slightly downwind. Exchange the lead position every few minutes to renew each other's energy.

Wind resistance far outweighs tire resistance which is controlled by the weight of the rider plus machine and the area of tire that contacts the ground. To keep tire resistance to a minimum, pump the tires up firmly. This also gives the tires longer wear. A well-tuned bicycle has too little friction in the drivetrain worth considering.

Steady Pace Riding

The efficient cyclist keeps a steady pedaling rate, measured in strokes per minute. Studies have shown that a cadence less than 60 strokes per minute is inefficient. Get into a lower gear and stroke 70 to 90 per minute. Racers keep a higher cadence, averaging about 105 rpm. However, it is difficult to keep such a high rate hour after hour, day after day, on a packed bike. Most good cycle tourists keep a 75–90-rpm cadence. You know what pace you feel comfortable at: maintain it. Do not pedal for half a minute, freewheel for a few seconds, and start pedaling again. Slowing down and speeding up saps energy.

Using Gadgets

To help keep a steady pace, many people use a cycle computer, a small electronic gadget that fits on the handlebar and tells you the speed and distance traveled. Those that can read cadence need a special magnetic harness attached to the crank arms. Some cycle computers also monitor heart rate and altitude. A cycle computer also keeps you honest. It tells you how much you actually traveled, not how much you want to believe you traveled.

Devices like this are more useful when training and preparing for your big ride than when you are actually out there. While touring far from home, you'll be better off with as few gadgets as possible. These things are fragile and sensitive, and you will probably not be able to fix or replace them when they break down many miles from home.

CHAPTER 18

Training for Your Tour

People have simply picked up a bicycle and begun cycling around the world. Unless they made the first days of their trip a training ride, cycling only a few miles the first day and slowly increasing the distance, a lot of those people ended up with knee problems, and unless the wild excitement of spontaneously getting up and going overtakes you—and there is something to be said for that feeling of freedom—break your body into the idea of long-distance touring gradually with a training program.

How to Train

If you have not been physically active, you can start. You have to begin improving your heart and lung capacity. Physical training, especially cycling, will actually expand the size of your heart and open blood vessels throughout your body. If your goal is to tour by bicycle 30 or 40 miles a day at a gradual pace, you need relatively little training. But the demanding activity of serious distance cycling—over 100 miles a day—requires stamina. Although it can be done by people of all ages, distance cycling necessitates expending a great deal of energy for a prolonged period. I would like to offer the following training and exercising tips.

A group of French and German cyclists touring in Egypt.

First, I do not know any serious cyclist, whether racer or tourist, who smokes, and I am given to believe that smoking either eliminates or greatly reduces the chance of participating in a long-distance trek at a brisk pace. I am also given to believe that the desire to cycle and develop the body acts as an incentive to stop smoking and helps reduce the desire to smoke. Those who have just stopped smoking may take a little longer to build up strength and endurance.

If you have hardly ridden a bike, start by taking 8–12 mile rides every other day, then slowly build it up to 15–20 miles. That is not far. If you are able to take a ride away from stop signs and traffic signals you should be able to pedal a continuous 12 miles on a flat surface in an hour or less. Once a week, take a long trip. Here, too, build up the mileage as you feel comfortable. Your final goal should depend on how long you plan to travel each day, but the long ride should

Training schedule for casual bicycle touring.

Sample Training Schedule for Casual Touring

Week	Tuesday	Wednesday	Thursday	Friday	Saturday	Sunday
1	12 mi. easy		12 mi. easy		12 mi. easy	15 mi. easy
2	15 mi. easy		15 mi. easy		15 mi. easy	20 mi. slight
3	15 mi. easy		15 mi. slight		15 mi. easy	25 mi. medium
4	15 mi. easy		15 mi. slight		15 mi. easy	30 mi. hard
5	15 mi. easy		20 mi. medium		15 mi. easy	30 mi. hard
6	15 mi. easy		25 mi. hard		20 mi. easy	35 mi. hills
7	20 mi. easy		25 mi. hard		20 mi. medium	40 mi. hills
8	20 mi. easy		20 mi. medium	15 mi. easy	20 mi. hard	40 mi. hills
9	20 mi. easy		30 mi. medium	15 mi. slight	20 mi. hard	40 mi. hills
10	25 mi. slight		30 mi. medium	20 mi. slight	20 mi. hard	50 mi. hills
11	25 mi. slight		30 mi. medium	20 mi. slight	20 mi. hard	50 mi. hills
12	25 mi. slight		40 mi. medium	20 mi. slight	20 mi. easy	

Note: "Easy, slight, medium, hard" refers to the amount of effort; "hills" mean at least part of the ride should include hills; "cadence" means spin the cranks at a higher than usual cadence part of the trip be built up to at least 50 miles. Most people in reasonable health are able to ride 80 miles once a week without much strain, but unless you are experienced you should spend a few weeks building up to that distance.

You do not have to do serious speed or endurance training to tour. The activity is designed for those who love cycling and want to increase their performance. Use the two training schedule charts to custom design your own program. Keeping a calendar of your daily mileage, time, and type of ride lets you see your progress and gives you the discipline to make training a priority.

Once you can do 50 miles without feeling overly tired, you are set to tour. If you have the time, make the every-other-day cycle a daily event, and if you want to build up your speed and endurance, do so by

Training schedule for serious long-distance touring.

Sample Training Schedule for Serious Touring

Week	Tuesday	Wednesday	Thursday	Friday	Saturday	Sunday
1		15 mi. easy		15 mi. easy		20 mi. easy
2		20 mi. slight		20 mi easy		25 mi. medium
3		20 mi. slight		20 mi. slight		35 mi. medium
4	20 mi. medium	15 mi. easy	30 mi. medium	15 mi. easy	20 mi. easy	40 mi. hard
5	20 mi. medium	15 mi. easy	30 mi. cadence	15 mi. easy	25 mi. easy	40 mi. hills
6	30 mi. medium	15 mi. easy	30 mi. cadence	15 mi. easy	25 mi. medium	50 mi. hills
7	30 mi. medium	20 mi. easy	35 mi. hills	15 mi. easy	30 mi. medium	50 mi. hills
8	30 mi. medium	20 mi. easy	35 mi. hills	15 mi. easy	30 mi. cadence	50 mi. hills
9	30 mi. hard	20 mi. slight	35 mi. hills	15 mi. slight	30 mi. cadence	50 mi. hills
10	30 mi. hard	25 mi. slight	35 mi. hills	20 mi. slight	30 mi. cadence	50 mi. hard
11	30 mi. hard	25 mi. medium	35 mi. hills	20 mi. medium	30 mi. hard	70 mi. hard
12	30 mi. hard	25 mi. easy	35 mi. medium	15 mi. easy	20 mi. easy	

Note: "Easy, slight, medium, hard" refers to the amount of effort; "hills" mean at least part of the ride should include hills; "cadence" means spin the cranks at a higher than usual cadence part of the trip going on training rides twice a week, either with a friend, a club, or alone.

Building Stamina

Training rides, designed for seriously building cycling ability, both speed and endurance, usually last two to four hours. They are often, but not necessarily, done in pairs or groups such as a bicycle club, and they go on lightly trafficked roads, usually sticking to one or two familiar routes that include, if possible, hills and flat areas. Keeping a steady pace, the rider or riders gradually strengthen all aspects of their cycling performance.

Riders on training rides maintain 50 to 70 percent of peak effort while cycling. Effort is directly related to heartbeat, which controls the activity of all other organs including lungs. Your resting pulse rate is zero effort while your maximum pulse is peak effort. These rates differ from person to person. Take your pulse when you awaken in the morning; that is your resting pulse. Find your maximum pulse after the most energetic activity, such as a vigorous hill climb, when you are puffing hard. If it is easy for you to take your pulse at that time, you are not at your maximum. As you train, your pulse range increases: your resting pulse drops while your peak pulse rises. Professional bicycle racers have a resting pulse as low as 30 beats per minute.

Let us take an example. Mary has a resting pulse of 60 and a peak of 160, giving her a 100-beat range. Sixty percent of that is added to her resting pulse. Thus, on a training ride Mary keeps her heart running about 120 beats, and this pace she keeps for a two-hour ride with, say, one ten-minute rest break to refill her water bottle. Mary checks her pulse periodically while she is riding, counting the number of beats during a 15-second period and multiplying it by four. Her relatively low resting pulse indicates that she is in good physical health.

To expand your capacity, sprinkle your training ride with bursts of cycling at peak performance: rapid hill climbs, high-cadence training, and short sprints. Put yourself out completely, standing on the pedals and pushing them as hard as you can until you are tired. Practice taking a low grade hill at the same pedaling cadence as you crank on flats. Sweat should be getting in your eyes, and you should be panting before you stop. That is a good time to take your peak pulse. If you use the same hill each time, you can measure your progress. Hills are a cyclist's proving ground. Advanced cyclists practice one- or two-hour hill climbs each week to build cycling performance.

Speed training or sprinting is usually shorter. Get into a higher gear, stand up over the handlebar, and go with all your might for 30 seconds, keeping a 120–150 strokes per minute cadence. In a group this event turns into a fun competition.

Part of the training of a good cyclist is to spin the cranks at a higher rate in a lower gear. High-cadence training is done by getting in a low gear while riding on flats and spinning the cranks fast—over 110 strokes per minute—for two to ten minutes, aiming not for speed but for smooth pedaling. On the road if you feel in a cranking rut of 60–70 strokes per minute, try shifting to a lower gear and stroking 85.

Muscular Development

The major force of cycling comes from the quad muscles in the front outside part of the thigh. The secondary force comes from the rear muscles in the calf, primarily from pushing the toes on the pedals. As you develop your cycling ability you will feel the quads getting bigger and firmer. If you look at advanced cyclists you will see those muscles above the knee bulging, and if you touch that area it feels solid. If cyclists do not also build up the rear muscles in the lower thigh, they can put too much strain on the knee joint. The quad muscles alone are not able to cushion the strain on the knee's soft tissue.

To combat this, cyclists need a well-rounded athletic program. Running, walking, playing tennis, cross-country skiing, and other sports help build up the rear part of the knee, taking the pressure off the relatively tender knee joint. Incidentally, runners who have knee problems should consider cycling in order to develop muscles that their sport neglects. Developing all your leg muscles helps avoid injuries. ATB riding on trails helps develop not only leg muscles but also the top half of the body that road riding neglects.

Few cyclists develop their muscles with weights since weights tend to stiffen and tighten the body. It is best to practice on the bicycle itself, logging miles on a variety of terrains. Triathalon training gives the body a well-rounded program.

Exercising Before Starting

Everybody wants to be in the picture in Southern India.

Nothing feels better than a hot bath and a massage of the legs and shoulders after a strong bicycle ride. Tension around the neck causes strain, which in turn tires the muscles. Rubbing the sore areas calms the muscles and reduces tension. If you do not have someone to give you a massage, rub your neck, shoulders, and legs yourself.

Stretching before a ride and after a long rest break is essential for avoiding injuries. Over the last three decades professional athletes and their trainers have developed exercises designed to loosen the body. These exercises are similar to poses or *asanas* used in Hatha Yoga as well as the exercises of professional dancers. It takes 5 to 10 minutes to go through a complete stretching workout for the legs, neck, and back. The modern exercise idea is not to jerk, bounce, and pull the muscles, but to hold a stretching pose without straining for 20 to 30 seconds. When you are beginning in the morning, spend the first 15 minutes riding slowly, tuning your muscles for the day's ride.

CHAPTER 19

Maintaining and Repairing Your Bicycle

The more you know about your bike and how it works the happier and more confident you will be riding it. Bicycle repairs are not difficult, but they require practice. After you have taken something apart once or twice—and you will make mistakes and take ten times as long as you should that first time—you will have no problem doing the procedure again. It is necessary to know a few essential repairs, but if you are not interested in knowing what the inside of your headset looks like, you can find a mechanic to maintain it, even when you are on a trip.

The tools you need to bring depend on how long you plan to be on the road and how far away you will be from bike stores. If you are going 300 miles in France, there is no point in bringing tools to regrease the bottom bracket. Cyclists should make sure that all bolts and nuts on their bicycles are always tight. No one else will check that for you. Use lock nuts on the luggage rack bolts, and check them often since the shaking of the bicycle may loosen them. The good mechanic also greases all threads—spoke threads,

Maintenance schedule for high-mileage cycling.

Location	Action and Frequency
Chain	Lubricate at least every other day
Derailleur pivot bolts	Lubricate every 4-5 days
Brake pivot bolts	Lubricate every 4-5 days
Brake and gear controls	Grease friction points every week Replace cables every 1-2 yrs
Hub bearings	Grease every 2 months
Pedal bearings	Grease every 2 months
Bottom bracket bearings	Grease every 4-5 months
Head Set bearings	Grease every 5-6 months
Wheels	True whenever necessary
Tires	Check tires frequently
Luggage Racks	Check tightness of bolts every day

crank threads, and brake threads—so they do not freeze.

The following maintenance operations and required tools are accented for bicycle touring. No matter how much you resist, you will probably get your hands dirty from the drive train while on a trip. Take along a little Goop or similar brand hand cleaner.

Repairing a Flat Tire

You need two tire irons and a patch kit even if you are going across town. On a long trip bring plenty of quality patches with butterfly edges, such as Rima brand; dime store or low-grade patch kits do not last, especially in hot weather. Also bring an extra inner tube. Naturally, you must have a hand pump on your frame.

You can reduce the number of flats you get by checking your tire often for glass, pebbles, and cuts, by keeping your tires inflated to their correct pressure, and by using the proper tire for the road. Most flats occur on the rear tire, and they happen more often when your tires are old, not so much because they are worn, but because with age the casing loses its resistance and becomes prone to punctures.

First find the point of the leak. If you know where the leak is (e.g. you see a nail in the tire), you can lay the bike on the ground, take off the tire from the rim 4-5 inches on either side of the leak, pull out the tube, and repair it.

If, however, the leak is hard to find, and the slower the leak the harder it is to find, you need to take off the wheel, take out the entire tube, fill it with air, and go around it and try to see the leak. If you're near water, dunk the tube and check for bubbles. An American couple toured Europe with a wok that they used not only for cooking but for checking tube leaks. If water is not handy, you need to listen closely and try to hear the leak. This is hard if there is wind noise or the noise from a stream of cars on the road. If you cannot hear, run your tongue over the tire a millimeter from the rubber and try to feel the air coming out. If all else fails, slap on your spare tube and repair the leak later.

Rub the area around the hole with sandpaper to clean and roughen the surface. Deplete the tube of air, put a fat drop of glue over the hole, and spread it around with your finger to cover the area of the patch.

Three critical steps in removing and reinstalling a tube.

Top left: Lift the tire off the rim.

Top right: Put all the tube back into the tire.

Bottom right: Push the tire bead over the rim with your thumbs.

Wait until it looks almost dry before putting on the patch. In hot weather have the patch ready to apply since the glue will dry quickly. Squeeze the patch from the middle to the outside, making sure the edges of the patch are tight. Rub the patch with a hard blunt instrument to get rid of the air bubbles.

Before you put the tube back into the tire, sprinkle a little talcum powder or rub chalk over the new patch to prevent it from sticking to the inside of the tire. You can carry a small amount of talc in plastic—it is also good for sore rear ends. When returning the tube to the rim make sure that no dirt gets under the tire. You should not use any tools to put the tire back on the rim; just force the bead of the tire over the rim with your thumbs, being careful that you do not pinch the tube.

Tire Pressure						
lb/sq.in.	60	70	80	90	100	110 (psi)
kg/sq.cm	4	5	6	7	8 (bar)	

Tire pressure conversion table

If you are getting pinching punctures it probably means that you do not have enough pressure in your tire; the squeezing of a soft tire over a bump pinches the tire, causing two little holes on the side or bottom. Keep your tires, especially the rear, pumped hard.

Cleaning and Lubricating the Drive Train

A dirty chain is the major source of premature drive train wear, and a dry chain causes unnecessary friction and lowers cycling efficiency. Clean and lubricate often. On dusty roads your chain needs daily cleaning, while a rain will strip off the lubricant. Bring along a squeeze bottle of lubricant—most people are using a synthetic, teflon base.

At home you can clean a chain with naptha or kerosene, either taking the chain off and soaking it, or brushing the solvent on the chain (use newspaper since it is messy). Also clean the gears on the chainwheel, freewheel, and the two small rear derailleur wheels. On the road you probably will not have solvent, so clean everything dry with an old toothbrush, then put on a bit of lubricant—not too much since it

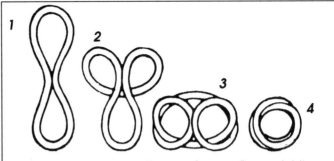

1. Fold tire once in half (tire now forms a figure eight).

2. Fold one half inward, so that it meets the center of the first fold.

3. Draw the other loop in to match the two smaller loops you just made.

4. Draw these three loops together, equalizing them into one tight circle.

How to fold a regular clincher, or wired-on, tire. (Illustration courtesy Bike Nashbar) attracts dirt. Wipe off the excess, and the gears become lubricated as the chain runs over them.

You also need to lubricate the points where both derailleurs pivot, adding a small drop to each pivot bolt. Wipe off the excess so it does not attract dirt. Do not lubricate any other part of the drivetrain—neither the hubs, the pedals, nor the bottom bracket. Those areas are greased; your lubricating oil will only dilute the grease. However, the brake pivot bolts need regular lubrication: two drops (wiping off the excess) every other time you oil the chain. If you run out on the road, then you have to use regular oil, which you can find at a gas station.

Adjusting the Derailleurs

If either derailleur gets out of adjustment, two small screws on each unit will realign them. The adjustment limits the motion of the derailleurs so the rear one does not send the chain into the wheel or over to the frame, and the front one does not move the chain too far in either direction, allowing the chain to fall off the chainrings. The screws move in and out and stop each derailleur.

If the rear derailleur is going too far to one side or the other—you can tell because it sounds like it wants to move over—you have to tighten one of the screws and limit its motion: the top screw limits the inside motion; the bottom screw limits the outside. If you cannot move the chain into either one of the end gears, you need to loosen the appropriate screw until the chain falls over the gear easily. Eye the derailleur from be-

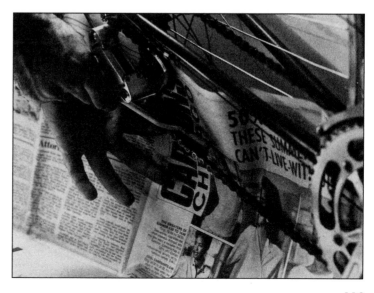

Cleaning can be a messy operation unless you're well organized.

Take care to prevent oil and solvents from entering at the bearings, to prevent washing out the lubricating grease.

hind. At its end points it should line up with its outside gears. You should always check that the derailleur is perpendicular after it has been shipped.

The front derailleur operates on the same principle. If it is shifting the chain too far or not far enough in one direction, tighten or loosen one of the screws. The inner screw controls the motion over the inner chainring; the outer screw controls the motion over the outer one. If you still have problems shifting the chain onto the big gear, you may have to straighten the cage. It should not bulge to the sides and should be about one centimeter wide.

Keep the chain clean and lightly oiled.

The derailleur's range of travel is adjusted with these little screws.

Adjusting the Brakes

Although there are several types of brakes, most have a knurled barrel nut finger adjustment for tightening or loosening the brake shoe opening. Turn the adjusting barrel, and you will see the brake shoes getting closer or farther from the rim. If your wheel gets out of true and begins to periodically hit the brake shoes, you need to true the wheel, not open the brakes. This is important. When you really have to stop, especially after you have picked up downhill momentum, you squeeze hard on the brakes, much harder than you would when testing them in your basement. You need the full movement of the levers.

If you are at the end of the finger adjustment and you need to let out or tighten the brakes, then you have to change the point where the cable is held. If you loosen the cable, the spring on the brakes will let them expand. You have to squeeze them together with your free hand while you adjust and tighten the bolt. The shoes should be close to the rims, separated by a gap of a couple of millimeters. When the brakes close, the entire shoe should touch the rim and not hit the tire. If not, loosen the nut on the brake shoes and change their position so that they close directly on the rim.

Adjust the brake shoes to be close enough to the rim.

Replacing the Cables

Carry a spare brake cable and a spare derailleur cable with you on a long trip. Derailleur cables are thinner than brake cables and cannot be interchanged. To increase their life, apply a little grease to the entire length of the cable, especially the parts that come in contact with metal. It is at these points, especially at the lever ends, that they are prone to snap. The grease helps the cable to move freely in its housing. New brake cables often come crimped with two different cylinders, a button and a barrel at each end; you may have to cut one end off the cable with cutters—saving the cylinder that fits your brakes—to be able to thread it through the housing. Do that before the trip.

To change cables, loosen the small anchor bolt holding the cable at the brake or derailleur end and take the cable out from its housing. Thread the new wire through the hole in the lever, through the housing, and tighten the new cable at the anchor. You need to pull the cable tight before fastening it to the anchor bolt in order to eliminate the subtle twists in the cable. You may have to do this more than once to take out all the play in the lever. Trim the cable one inch past the bolt and crimp a piece of plastic on the cable end.

Wheel Truing

Truing a wheel requires patience. At home you can use a truing stand and get a precisely straight wheel. On the road—and you may need to true your wheels on the road—flip over your bicycle and use the brake shoes as guides to get an almost straight wheel. Out-of-true wheels give you a bad, inefficient ride; the longer you wait to true them, the harder the job will become.

The straightness or trueness of a rim is dependent on the spokes. Rims have little strength by themselves. By adjusting the spoke tension, you move the rim from one side to the other. Spoke tension is adjusted by tightening or loosening the nipples at the rim with a spoke wrench, a small tool that should be taken on a trip. The spokes of the wheel go to opposite ends of the hub in a crisscross pattern. If one section of the rim is too far to the right, then you need to tighten the spokes that go to the left side of the hub and loosen the spokes that go to the right side, thereby centering the rim. You need to both tighten and loosen so you do not lose the roundness of the rim.

Using the spoke tool, go through the entire wheel, tightening and loosening the proper nipples until it turns straight in relation to the brake shoes. You must tighten and loosen gradually, usually not more than a half a turn at a time, to avoid a sharp pull that could damage the wheel. If on the road a wheel becomes damaged, either developing a flat spot or severe bend, you cannot true it. You have to loosen the spokes and rebend the wheel by force: stepping on it, pushing it against a tree, or using any other method at your disposal. This type of guerrilla repair is not mentioned in standard manuals. Only when the rim is almost straight can you true it.

Replacing a Spoke

Front spokes rarely break because they do not take much of the rider's weight. Spokes are most vulnerable on that hard-to-reach freewheel-side of the rear wheel, not only because the rear wheel takes most of the load, but also because the freewheel-side spokes are under greater tension. Bring a couple of extra spokes on a trip, and if you break spokes, use thicker ones the next time or lighten your load.

Replacing a spoke on the front wheel or on the other side of the freewheel in the back is a ten-minute operation. Unscrew the old spoke from its nipple on the rim. Since you have already put grease on it, it will unscrew easily. The new spoke goes through the hub threads to the nipple the same way the old one did.

Left: Tighten or loosen spokes gradually.
Right: The freewheel block remover fits inside the freewheel block and requires force to use.

You have to bend it around other spokes and into the nipple. Now true your wheel, tightening the nipple until the wheel turns straight. You may need to retrue the wheel after riding a day or two.

When a spoke breaks on the freewheel side of the rear wheel, you will have to take off the freewheel in order to replace the spoke. Each brand of freewheel has its own remover, a small tool that fits inside the end of the freewheel and can easily be taken on a trip. Like the pedals, the freewheel tightens as you ride. You need a vise or a wrench with long leverage. I have never found it a problem to ask a mechanic to use his vise.

Take off the rear wheel and unscrew the quick release. Put the freewheel remover inside the grooves of the freewheel and tighten the remover in a vise. Turn it counterclockwise, and it will come off. You replace the broken spoke in the manner described above and put back the freewheel by hand. It will tighten as you ride.

Replacing, Shortening, or Lengthening the Chain

You can tell when the chain gets worn or stretched by measuring. The links are ½ inches each, so if you measure 20 links and it is 10⅛ inches, replace it. However, the gears on the freewheel and the chainwheel also wear down, and putting a new chain on old gears may cause the chain to skip, especially in the smaller freewheel gears where only a few teeth catch the chain at any given moment. If after putting

A chain tool is used to separate or join the links of a chain.

124

on a new chain you notice it skipping when you apply force to the pedals, you need to replace either the freewheel or the worn freewheel cogs, usually your favorite gear. Chainrings need to be replaced less often.

Carry with you a chain tool, a compact and easy-to-use device that removes the pins or rivets uniting the links of the chain. Put the tool on one of the pins and turn the handle of the tool until the pin is pushed slightly out, then do the same to the adjacent pin. With the pins sticking out on one end of the chain, you can take off the chain, clean it, add or remove links, or replace it.

Replace the chain through the front derailleur cage and around the freewheel and rear derailleur. Do not put it on the chainwheel until the chain is united. The rivets are replaced by lining up the holes of both ends of the chain and having the chain tool push the pin through. Sometimes a replaced rivet tightens the links too hard, making it stiff at that joint. If this happens, bend the chain laterally until the link frees up.

Regreasing Bearings

Regreasing is a preventative program. If you feel your wheel is not turning as smoothly as it should, you have not been doing your job; it is already long overdue for regreasing. On a long trip you may need to regrease bearings, the hubs, bottom bracket, and pedals. I have never regreased the headset on the road.

Cone wrenches are used to adjust the hub bearings or to disassemble them, exposing the parts of the bearing.

After you have done it once, regreasing is easy. The hubs require two thin tools called cone wrenches, which can be taken on a trip, but the bottom bracket requires a couple of heavy tools. If you can get away

Overhauling the bottom bracket requires some relatively heavy tools.

without regreasing the bottom bracket, do so, and save yourself the weight of the tools.

You can spin the wheels and feel if they need regreasing. Put your ear to the saddle and spin the cranks while the chain is off the gears. If you hear a grinding noise amplified through the seat tube, it is time to regrease the bottom bracket. Water does not hurt the bearing, unless it is a torrent of water, but dirt gets into the bearings and causes friction and excessive wear. If you are on dirt or mud roads, you should do a lot more cleaning.

PART IV.

TOURING THE WORLD
REGION BY REGION

In the remaining chapters, we'll look at each section of the globe and examine the roads, weather, costs, customs, and terrain. When trying to figure out your route, read each section with a map in front of you. If a region has many good roads for cycling, such as Europe and North America, specific routes are not discussed. Plan your own route by using a detailed map.

A good road is a relative concept. French cyclists complain about rough roads in parts of Spain. However, bad Spanish roads are better than the best roads in Zaire, none of which are paved. A good road in the Andes may mean a packed dirt surface, good for that region, while a good road in Japan means one that does not have heavy traffic.

More information can be obtained by writing to appropriate sources listed in Appendix 4. Note that legalities and road conditions change. New roads are under construction, while a heavy rain or a damaged bridge can negate what was once a good cycling route.

CHAPTER 20

Touring Europe

General Information

Unquestionably, Europe is the finest place to cycle, as hundreds of thousands of cyclists who have toured there will attest. Except in pockets of East Europe, roads are well paved, the best in the world, and cars generally treat cyclists with respect. You will find bike lanes and quiet country roads that pass through incredible scenery. Bicycling through the Alps is a fairy-tale experience.

Not long ago we would have treated East and West in separate sections. Striking differences between East and West will remain for years to come, as have differences between North and South, but Europeans, whether Bulgarian or Irish, share a common history and outlook. In the interest of unity, let us take the entire continent as a whole.

The best part about cycling in Europe is that you can take any small road and go anywhere you want. This will make our description here different from other chapters in which we suggest routes and discuss road conditions: here we only need to make general comments. Several bicycle-touring guides of the region specify scenic routes to follow, but it is more satisfying to make your own agenda by studying small-scale

Many Europeans cycle daily to work—and unlike their American counterparts, most of them don't dress up in cycling gear to do so.

maps and following a network of secondary roads. In the populated industrialized areas—England, France, Germany, Austria, Northern Italy, Holland, and Belgium—the primary roads or national routes are either a noisy hell or dangerous for cyclists. This includes primary roads that parallel Europe's extensive system of motorways.

Use the secondaries that yield cycling connections everywhere. With literally millions of miles of roads in Europe, all one has to do is decide the region in which to travel, pick up a map, and select the roads. Most cyclists prefer 1:200,000 scale Michelin maps. It is cheaper to buy an oversized paperback atlas and tear out and fold up the necessary pages.

English has established itself as the base language—many young people in northern Europe speak English better than native speakers. In lieu of knowing the local language, German will help you in most of Eastern Europe. I think you miss a lot if you do not study basic phrases of the language of the country in which you are traveling.

Rail service throughout Europe is excellent but can be expensive. Trains take bicycles for a variable fee. Many buses will also accept bicycles. If you ship your bike across a non-EEC border you can be asked to pay a customs fee, and some trains can delay your bike. Inquire at the station before transporting by rail.

Since cities are only a short cycling distance apart, cyclists need not be athletes to tour. Some cyclists pedal only 30 miles a day, going from town to town, examining the architecture or the town's historic significance, or people's lifestyles, or just having a good time. Many people have spent six months touring only France or Italy—it is the best way to get to know the country and the language.

Borders

Gone are the days when once you arrived at an East European border you had to make a detailed currency declaration, stay at approved hotels, spend a certain minimum each day, be searched for anti-communist or religious literature, and be treated rudely. However, East European countries still have restrictions and require visas. Border requirements are changing at the time of writing—all of Europe is changing—check before leaving.

Often when West European border guards see cyclists they just wave them through without looking at their papers. Between EEC countries and associate members border formalities are minimal, but in every country theft is on the increase, so be careful of your belongings in urban areas.

Climate

Southern Europe and the Mediterranean get too cold for riding in the winter—although people have done it—and northern Europe remains cold from early October to late May. Many people do not realize that it snows in Madrid. The mountains stay cold longer, and the night chill, even in summer, requires a comfortable sleeping bag. Also, youth hostels and campgrounds close off season, making mid-spring to mid-fall the best time for visiting. I think northern Europe is best for cyclists in September, and southern Europe is ideal in October.

Generally winds come from the north and west, so the best bet is to plan your trip to head east and south. Local winds can be strong almost everywhere, especially if there are mountains nearby. Rainfall is less easy to predict, but most rain comes during

Relative traffic densities in selected European countries.

Country	number Of Cars (in thousands)	paved road (in miles)	dirt roads* (in miles)
Albania	158	.N/A	.N/A
Austria	2,984	65,000	0
Belgium	3,701	75,000	3,200
Bulgaria	.1,000	21,300	1,300
Czechoslovakia	2,790	43,900	.500
Denmark	1,629	43,400	.200
Finland	1,930	28,100	19,200
France	23,105	.491,200	0
Germany	.34,000	.382,900	0
Greece	1,420	53,200	11,100
Ireland	820	52,900	3,378
Italy	24,623	.185,100	0
Holland	5,282	61,900	8,400
Hungary	1,795	30,900	27,300
Norway	1,580	35,600	17,500
Poland	4,560	.134,000	84,800
Portugal	.1,789	7,600	5,100
Romania	855	21,700	22,900
Spain	11,220	.109,400	85,200
Sweden	3,602	56,800	24,100
Switzerland	2,805	41,200	2,200
Turkey	1,202	27,500	.168,200
United Kingdom	22,080	.214,900	0
(former) U.S.S.R.	12,400	.716,200	25,300
Yugoslavia	2,988	42,300	30,600

Notes:

* Includes only primary and secondary roads.

This chart will give you a good idea of the extent of each country's road network and the amount of traffic to expect.

winter and spring. The Mediterranean region is virtually dry during the summer, while Bavaria seems perpetually wet. Heavy three-day rains are not unusual. The United Kingdom and Ireland often have bad years when they see the sun a handful of days a year. Europe has a high latitude—Rome is the same distance from the equator as Chicago—so if you are riding during summer you will have many hours of daylight; northern Scandinavia has the midnight sun.

Bicycles and Money

You do not need to worry about finding bike shops in the Western countries, but a couple I met brought 27-inch wheels and were unable to buy extra tires in Spain, France, or Italy. Many people have flown to the place they wanted to start, bought a bicycle, and began touring. A good idea, but you need to have a notion where to look and spend time shopping. People in East Europe cycle less, rarely using multiple speeds, but you can find tires and parts in the large cities.

Although cycling is the cheapest way to tour Europe, it can be expensive. Most cyclists camp at official camping sites or use youth hostels. Armed with a list of the hostels and campgrounds, you can plan each cycling day to end at a hostel or a camp. In August it is good to arrive at popular hostels early since they fill up. In a relatively cheap country like Greece an economical cyclist would spend perhaps $8–10 a day, while in Germany the same person would probably have to shell out double. Most of East Europe is a bit less expensive than Greece, but that is changing. Hotels and restaurants in the industrial countries can be costly. If you go in late summer you can find fruit trees on the side of the road, but do not tell anyone that I told you to help yourself.

The hostel and camping facilities in Eastern Europe are much simpler than they are in the West, but all the large cities have hostels; many small countries such as Bulgaria and Romania have 100 campgrounds each, as well as an abundance of low-priced hotels. Eastern European food, trains, and bicycle equipment are also inexpensive.

Europe Country by Country

Great Britain and Ireland

The weather often makes Ireland and Great Britain difficult for cyclists who are at the mercy of the elements. If it is not actually raining, it is threatening to rain. Your best chance of hitting good weather is during summer, but even then it can be drizzly all year with generally west to southwest winds that are strong on the west coasts. Scotland's weather seems eternally gloomy, but if you wear the right clothes and take good camping equipment, you will find riding these islands a rewarding experience, especially once you leave the vast London area. Place your rearview mirror on the right.

Scotland, Wales, and southern Ireland are the only places with real hills, but they pose no major difficulty. Scotland is an especially interesting experience, culturally and naturally. Its terrain is more challenging, but its roads less trafficked and its people more inviting. Most of England and Ireland are either flat or rolling hills. When you get away from the urban areas you will find many lightly trafficked small roads. If you land in London, Dublin, or Dover stop off at the first travel bookstore and pick up detailed maps or an atlas. Ferries run between the islands and the mainland, bicycles on trains travel free, and hitchhiking is usually possible.

Down the Alps in Austria

France

France has earned the title as the cycling capital of the world. You can find many small roads, miles of flats, mountains, coastal roads, and beautiful, unspoiled forested areas. It is hard to sing enough praises on French riding. The French people have gained the reputation for being unfriendly, snobbish, and distant, but cyclists have found this to be entirely untrue. The French may not gush with emotion, but they will go out of their way to help you.

Most French roads are rolling hills, except the flats in the Loir Valley, the area south of Bordeaux, and parts of Bretagne. The real mountains are of course the Pyrenees, the Alps near Switzerland, and the central mountains around Lyon. As you go toward the borders of France you will have to get into your low gears and sweat your way up difficult mountain passes. Through the mountains you will be able to take roads that parallel rivers, such as in the Rhone Valley, making the ascent gradual, but if you are approaching Italy, Switzerland, or Spain (except on the coastal road to San Sebastian), expect hard work.

The Alps are spectacular, with several hard climbs over winding roads, a few containing grades of over 10 percent. The motorways with their tunnels and viaducts are reserved for cars; cyclists can look down at the motorway cutting through the mountain they just climbed. Yet the rewards that await you make the climbs more than worth the labor. Every part of France is recommended.

Spain and Portugal

Roads in Spain and Portugal are less well cared for than they are in the rest of Western Europe, but they are still good and less crowded. Southern Spain with its up and down terrain is excellent to ride, as is the lively Basque area, but the entire Iberian peninsula is hilly, some of the roads being difficult for even advanced cyclists. The central parts of Spain and Portugal contain dry mountain regions, the roads continually going up and down, making riding a challenge. Distances between towns can be over 30 miles. The most interesting rides are in the southern and northern parts of the country and along the northeast coast.

Portugal is often missed by tourists because it is out of the way, but it is highly recommended for riding because of its quiet roads and rolling countryside. The

Map of Europe

northern region and coast is flat, while the south is more hilly, though less difficult than Spain's hills. I remember all the secondary roads being wide, the primary roads light with traffic, and the people gregarious.

Italy

When talking about Italy we have to talk Bicycles. Many small towns have their own framebuilder, and on Sunday the streets are full of riders. The entire country is a work of art, but again, once you get away from the coast you will run into mountains. With the exception of certain parts in the north central Alps, there is nothing too hard to ride. In Italy as well as many other European cities the streets are cobble, pretty but terrible for riding. You feel as if your behind and hands are getting a real shaking as you go over the stones, a contrast to the smooth country roads between cities. Northern Italian main roads are heavy with cars and trucks, but the road network becomes less intricate as you ride to the sparser and poorer south.

Some people have ridden all around Italy on the coastal roads and through the flat Po Valley. Many of these roads, such as the popular Via Aurelia that comes around the French coast through Genova, are heavy with traffic. Go inland and see the towns and villages that are the country's backbone. Ferries operate between Sicily and Sardegna (Sardinia), both of which are recommended places to ride, with scenic coastal roads and mountainous interiors. You can go around Sicily's volcanic Mount Etna and visit dozens of historical places.

Germany

Germany offers a different but equally inspiring cycling experience. You see castles—too many castles— drink beer for breakfast, dance to live polka bands, and cycle over clean roads next to manicured lawns. The further north you go the flatter the terrain, while the area near Czechoslovakia is quite hilly. Stay clear of the principal roads that are dense with traffic. If you are on the secondaries the cars will give you the right of way, but if you are on a busy road they will whiz by. The Black Forest, Bavaria, and the Rhine Valley are recommended areas, but cycling anywhere is satisfying. Although you'll probably meet more bicycle tourists from Germany than from any other European country, Germany is no cycling Mecca but a heavily automobile-dominated country.

Austria and Switzerland

These two countries have less traffic but equally high-grade roads. However, here you are into almost nothing but mountain roads. I strongly recommend these countries because their stunning natural beauty that you can best be seen either skiing or cycling; but do not tackle this area unless you have trained on hills. I remember more than one climb where I had to get off and walk, where even small cars could not make it up the hill. The eastern part of Austria is less hilly, but the part that is wedged between Germany and Italy is as tough as Switzerland. You can find easier passes, such as the road north through Bolzano across the Brenner Pass, and if you get tired you can probably ask someone with a camper for a lift.

Holland and Belgium

Many of these countries' roads, especially in and near the cities, have separate lanes for cyclists, and you will see the natives riding alongside you. They are easy countries to ride, flat and small, though Belgium's region near France rises to a plateau. Ferries cross Holland's waterways, helping you to cut across the country. It is pleasant to go down the Netherlands to Belgium then cycle across to the Rhine. These countries have a thick system of farm or secondary roads. Most cyclists to the north integrate riding in the small northern countries with a trip through Germany or France.

Denmark

Denmark is another flat country—its average altitude is under 100 feet—reached through Germany. Ferries and bridges link the island of Fyn to Jutland and Sjaelland to Falster. Bicycling is a popular form of transport for everyone. Because it has a slightly milder temperature than northern Germany, many people make Denmark their last country before returning home in September. It is an easy, pleasant cycling country, though it can rain there anytime.

Italy: rounding the Colliseum in Rome by bike.

Norway, Sweden, and Finland

These huge countries to the north are open cycling areas: the farther north you travel, the less populated the region, and the more you need to depend on main roads, for that is all there is up there. You can hop a ferry from Denmark to Sweden or fly in. Cyclists often take the coastal road around the bottom of Norway and Sweden, and in the summer a few nature-oriented cyclists find touring the less inhabited northern part of the three countries worthwhile—Norway is over 1,000 miles long, and much of it is mountainous. If you like to get in many hours of daylight riding, this is the place to come since the sun hovers over the horizon all night.

Sweden gives you the biggest choice of roads, and travelers going north use that country's roads, even if they are going to northern Norway. Most cyclists stay in the southern part of the countries, which have dense road network. The weather in the north is similar to Alaska. Finland is often neglected by cyclists because it is difficult to get to and does not seem to have anything interesting to offer travelers, but with the opening of Russia and the Baltic states, that may change as travelers can cross over to Helsinki from picturesque St. Petersburg. I know of no one who has traveled to northern Finland, though several people have gone to northern Sweden and Norway. Finland's roads are weaker, and during summer the forests are infested with insects that get in your mouth while riding. But since the terrain is flatter than that of Sweden.

Greece

Greece is one of my favorite cycling countries, although the mountains make central and northern Greece difficult. Athens is east of three East European capitals, but it is clearly not East European. If you only cycle around Athens, you have not really seen Greece. There are a handful of national highways in the country that skirt the mountains and are easier to ride. If the highway has a road next to it, such as the one to Corinth, take it. The small interior roads are in neglected condition; some are dirt. Riders to Greece either come down from Yugoslavia or Turkey (both are good rides), or they fly in or take a ferry from Italy. Greece is not a large country, and it is easy to cycle right across it, east to west, from Igoumenitsa to Istanbul via Thessaloniki and Kavala, or north to south from Yugoslavia, either Bitola or Gevgolij, to Athens. The roads near the sea can be windy, but the friendliness of the rural people makes Greece highly recommended.

At the time of going to press, civil strife in Yugoslavia appears to effectively halt any tourism—whether by bike or not.

Eastern Europe and Russia

I requested to cycle in the Soviet Union in 1981 and again in 1985 and was turned down both times. That has changed, or more accurately it is in the process of changing, and cyclists have been able to ride through the European part of Russia and Ukrania. Until the situation clears up, it is difficult to give advice on entry to Russia, the Baltic countries, Ukrania, and the Southern Republics. Russia is huge, three times as long as the United States. The western part of the country up to the Yenisey River is generally flat, with the exception of the mighty Urals which, as far as I

Map of Norway, Sweden, and Finland.

know, no cyclist has ever crossed. The region in the south near Turkey and Iran is also mountainous and tough to ride. Between the Yenisey and Lena rivers rises the West Siberian Plain, and east of Lake Baykal come several mountain ranges. The country's short summer is the only time to ride.

The cyclists who rode through Russia were surprised to find a strong infrastructure, with a large network of wide roads. Some of the roads carry heavy truck traffic, but many secondaries crisscross European parts of the country. One American cyclist I interviewed spoke Russian and said that it would be difficult for foreigners to cycle because few people can speak anything but their own language. He said that he got maps before leaving and was able to put his bike on an inexpensive train part of the way. At that time it was one country, so there were no border problems between republics. Another cyclist had to take a government guide with him. The Baltic countries are generally flat and should offer easy cycling, while the southern republics would be difficult. The farther east the fewer roads and people—this remains a virgin area for us.

Yugoslavia

With civil war raging at the time of going to press, you will probably not find this a good destination. Even if the country returns to normal, you will find that most of Yugoslavia is difficult cycling—a lot of it is unpleasant as well. Tourists tend to go to the picturesque

Yugoslavia: Parts of Eastern Europe contain Muslim communities.

Adriatic coast, the area of intense fighting during the civil war. Inland, the roads are narrow, and the few bike lanes are not paved. Since there are not many secondary roads you are forced to stick to the main routes. Also, the country is hilly—it is difficult to find a flat road anywhere, even on the Adriatic—with narrow winding mountain roads. Certainly it is a beautiful place, but it has not earned the enthusiasm of many cyclists. The main motorway going through Zagreb, Belgrade, and down to Greece is off-limits to cyclists. It is best to follow the Adriatic road if you are going north and south. There are several border crossings to the east, and it gets less hilly as you move away from the central part of the country. Yugoslavia still has deep social and ethnic problems, making it uncomfortable for visitors.

Albania

Although Albania is changing, too, at the time of this writing it remains off-limits to tourists unless they obtain special permission from the government, something pleasure cyclists have yet to do. The small country has a stern history of allowing no outsiders. Since the 1940s it has probably been the most closed nation in the world, and as soon as we get cycling reactions on it, we will pass them on. It is poor, but clunkers are popular, competing with donkeys for a share of the paved and dirt roads.

That's 3,700 ft up: many parts of Europe, such as Austria, have their share of steep climbs, even on main roads.

Poland

Poland is easy riding because most of it is flat. It is a big country with a developed road system, though you see a marked difference in road quality if you come across the border from Germany: the cleanliness and fanatic attention to precision ends. Many secondaries are dirt, but the hectic German traffic gives way to a more relaxing ride. You will find plenty of farm roads through the country, as well as several campgrounds.

The best riding is the southwestern part where towns are close together and the roads become rolling and even hilly. It is possible to cross the country at many points along the German, Czech, and Ukrainian borders. The Bialowieza National Park on the eastern side of the country as well as the roads around Lublin afford good riding. Because it is so long and flat, it is a bit monotonous. Hitchhiking is possible. Most national routes are all right for cycling, but you will find enough small roads to be able to avoid the truck fumes on the main roads.

Czechoslovakia and Hungary

These two countries in central Europe have entirely different landscapes and cultural backgrounds. German gets you around easily, especially in Czechoslovakia, a country full of mountains and rolling hills. Bratislava is a pleasant afternoon ride from Vienna, although Slovakia or the western side of the country is mountainous. The eastern part of the country becomes more rural and less Westernized, and you will encounter steep grades. Southern Bohemia with its net of small towns and old hamlets, offers some of the best riding in Europe, while east of Bohemia, toward the Moravian mountains, is not as interesting. The area west of Prague is hilly. The country has a few motorways where cyclists are prohibited, and in the rural areas you do not encounter the poverty that you see in other East European countries. Overall, the country wins prizes for its beauty and cyclability.

Although Hungary is also interesting, it has fewer mountains and a landscape more similar to Poland. Since it is small, it is an easy country to ride. The area around Budapest is crowded, but most of the other roads are easy to tackle. Travelers tend to cross over from the forested section of Austria and roam the country. Do-it-yourself camping is prohibited. The northern region has small villages and small mountains, while the area from Budapest to Romania is a large plain.

Romania and Bulgaria

The mountains continue in Romania and Bulgaria, although the routes near the Black Sea are flat and pretty. Bulgaria is a fascinating place. While struggling over the central mountains you run into a monastery in the middle of nowhere. You need to find out the status of border crossings into Greece and Turkey, as they used to close, otherwise there is a good road to Istanbul. Small roads suddenly become motorways. From Romania you can cross the Bulgarian border near the Black Sea and take the coastal road down, passing many resorts between Varna and Kavarna.

Map of the Balkan region

South of Varna it becomes more rural and hilly. The ancient town of Nexebur on the coast is as beautiful as Dobrovnik. Between the two countries you can cross the Danube by bridge at Ruse and by boat at Vidin. Also recommended is the road north from Sofia that follows the Isker River to Pleven.

Romania has a central plateau surrounded on the south and east by fairly rugged mountains. It has weaker roads. The Bucharest area is flat, as are the roads going to Constanta on the Black Sea and to Tulcea and Galati and back to Bucharest. However, the road west to Brasov and to Arad is not easy. Also, the main road from Belgrade to Timisora is heavy with traffic and should be avoided. This is a poorer country, ideal for budget travelers. Both countries are cold in winter and suffer from unpredictable winds all year.

CHAPTER 21

Touring North Africa

General Information

North Africa is not a homogeneous region. The culture changes from country to country as well as through sections of each country. Most of the population live within 50 miles of the Mediterranean or Atlantic or within 10 miles of the Nile. However, a surprising number of quiet, sensitive, and hospitable people live in the Sahara, and it is an unforgettable cycling experience for those who like deserts and are able to exert the effort to bike across long, empty scorching stretches.

Riding in North Africa can be conveniently and economically integrated with a tour of Europe, a strategy that might be considered by more European cycle tourists. Ferries connect North Africa with Europe and Mediterranean islands, operating from Tangier, Ceuta, Melilla, Algiers, Tunis, Tripoli, Alexandria, and Port Said. Air service is also plentiful. Locally you will find buses and, along a few routes, trains. It is easy to put a bicycle on a bus or train, or if you stick out your thumb you can probably get a lift on a truck.

Although the road system is not as elaborate as Europe's, road conditions in the northern region are good—well-paved and wide. The principal roads near cities have traffic, but the main inter-city roads are

A French touring cyclist who crossed the Sahara on his bike.

ideal for cycling. The Mediterranean section of North Africa is a developed region, whereas the Sahara has very few roads. Some roads near borders are restricted, and roads in the Sahara require permits. No one will stop you from cycling anywhere else.

The Arabic language dominates the region. Formal or written Arabic is standard, while spoken dialects vary. English is Egypt's second language, and the majority in Morocco, Algeria, and Tunisia (those three countries are called the *Mughreb*) speak fluent French. Two Arabic words of greeting will earn you respect.

Although the North Africans come from different ethnic or racial groups, most practice Islam, which has a tradition of warm hospitality. People will put you up in their homes, feed you, and help you. You do not need to ask: you may be resting in the shade and suddenly someone will bring you something to eat, and he will insist that you eat it. They do not want anything from you; your presence honors them. Do not abuse your status as a visitor. Many cyclists have been overwhelmed by the abundant hospitality of the Egyptians and Algerians. If you go into the Sahara you will find hospitality and friendliness a hundred fold. No doubt, hospitality is a major memory of a cycling trip to North Africa.

North African ruins and archaeological sites are also unforgettable. Of course Egypt is well known for its pyramids, tombs, and temples, but I believe the

Over Morocco's mountains

ruins in the *Mughreb* are the best in the Mediterranean. Carthage (near Tunis) should not be missed. Libya's Leptis Magna ruins 150 miles east of Tripoli are artistically and historically powerful.

If you are a woman, you may find that some local people will turn their heads in shame when they see you. I believe this might only be a problem in rural parts of Algeria and Libya where men's and women's roles are clearly defined, and women are not supposed to be athletes or traveling without a man. These two countries may refuse entry to single women. Most Muslims, however, do not expect foreigners to abide by their rules.

While cycling in the region, everyone, men and women, should dress conservatively when not cycling. Local people like guests but loathe immodest dress and immodest behavior. Riding without a shirt is a bad idea. The people want you to respect their way of life—it will make the difference in how you are treated. This cannot be overstressed. Cover your body and act maturely.

Borders

Algeria and Libya require visas from all foreigners before arriving. They will not give visas to travelers with Israeli or South African stamps in their passports, including stamps from border stations that lead into those countries, such as that of Rafah, Egypt. Visas for Libya are difficult and can take a long time to obtain. You need to tell them why you want to go there, where you want to go, and what you want to do, all in Arabic. For Egypt, Tunisia, and Morocco most Westerners can get a visa at the border.

While riding in Algeria, Tunisia, and Libya you will hardly meet any authorities or run into any bureaucratic snags. However, Morocco and Egypt more than amply make up for the dearth of bureaucracy in the central region. In both those countries the local police and national military can go out of their way to waste your time. Moroccan authorities may search you for drugs. Egypt and Algeria may force you to change money at the terrible bank rate. I have found that fast talking and solicitations of sympathy for being a poor traveler got me out of this at both borders.

There are no major health problems in the region, and no inoculations are required. The quality of water will only be a problem in the desert and parts of Egypt where you may need to use purification. Most travelers purify tap water in cities, including Nile water, which contains an amoeba that can cause stomach cramps.

Climate

North Africa has a dry climate, but many rivers run through the region, and if you bike along the coast you will see acres of healthy crops. It is dry, but it certainly is not barren. The climate is suitable for good cycling during spring and fall. Winds tend to run south from the Mediterranean to the Equator. Reverses often occur, and stagnant air is even more common.

It is cold and rainy in the winter (snow in the Atlas mountains). I recall once in mid-May riding down a mountain in Morocco and having to stop because of the chilly air passing over my hands and face, but when the summer wind blows from the Sahara, it makes everyone swelter from the Canary Islands to Rome. The Sahara also gets frost-cold at night during the winter. Sunglasses are a must in all seasons. Wearing a headdress like the natives is a practical way to ride. Pull it tight around your face so it does not fly in the wind.

Bicycles and Money

The region is relatively cheap for touring, especially if you can get an advantageous exchange rate. A nice hotel in a big city may cost $40 a night, while you can find cheap hotels for as little as $4. You will probably spend $5–12 a day on food, but you will also be given hospitality from the local people in the rural area. Along the Mediterranean resorts in Tunisia and Morocco you can spend a big wad. You can also pick up trinkets and crafts in all these countries, but unless you know exactly what to buy and are willing to shop around, do not buy.

Since cycling is not popular, the region has few bike shops. You can find a limited selection of spare parts in the big cities. They use 700-mm wheels except in Egypt where they use 27-inch wheels. You should not rely on being able to buy any spare parts or camping equipment in North Africa.

One final point: often you ask for directions and discover that someone told you incorrectly. This may sound crazy, but if you ask someone for directions, he feels he cannot tell you that he does not know. That would be inhospitable. Soon you discover that when someone gives you vague directions about continuing down the road, ask someone else, until you get specific details.

Map of North-West Africa

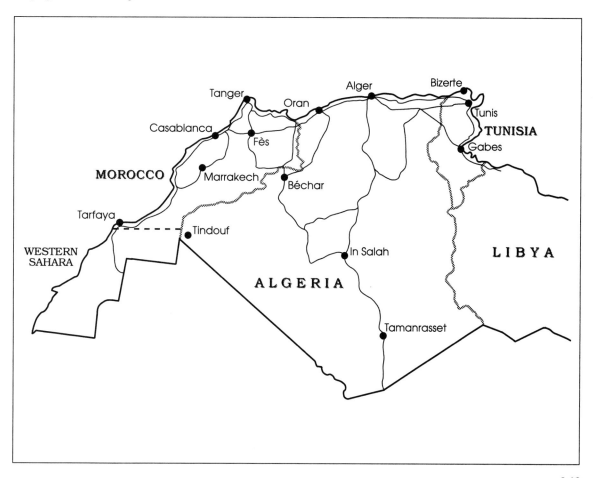

North Africa Country by Country

Morocco

This is a country of contradictions, made up of four distinct regions: the northeast Rif mountains, the central mountains, the Atlantic coast, and the inland desert. This mountainous country houses part of the impressive Atlas range that covers most of the inhabited area and extends to neighboring Algeria. Like much of North Africa, Morocco has Mediterranean resorts along both the northern and western coasts, and its towns are modern and relatively clean. The western coast is good for cycling year around. Many travelers take a ferry to Morocco from Algeciras or Tarifa at the southern part of Spain near Gibraltar. The short sea ride brings you either to Tangier or Ceuta (a city owned by Spain).

Unfortunately, Morocco has developed a reputation for theft, and although most of the population are helpful, hospitable, and honest, this negative element makes riding rough. I suggest that you take care of your belongings all over the country and be careful around young men that approach you. Morocco is a difficult country to understand. Visitors leave with diverse impressions, from pleasure to hate.

The Rif mountain region, famous for its hashish production, presents a tremendous problem for the hapless cyclist who is harassed by a constant barrage of hashish sellers. The police are suspicious of foreigners and can add to a cyclist's dilemma. Drugs breed other crime, and for this reason the northern region of the Rif range, especially the road from Tetouan to Melilla (another city belonging to Spain) and to Oujda is not recommended. For your safety I strongly advise staying clear of drug deals, however tempting. Credible reports have surfaced of corrupt policemen.

The Atlas mountains are beautiful, but they are jagged and tough to ride, with passes well above 6,500 feet, often covered with a layer of fog, reducing visibility. The eastern desert has only a few small roads beginning at Marrakech (a must-see city) and Midelt. The western coastal area, from Tangier to Rabat, Casablanca, and further south, is the main travel area in the country. A good road winds around the coast south of Casablanca to Safi, Essaouira, and Agadir.

You can continue down to Tiznit and Tarfaya on the coastal desert, but further south, including the towns of Tarfaya and Laayoune in the Western Sahara, have been off-limits. The Moroccan army built five concrete walls across the border. Outside of a ferry from Tarfaya to the Canary Islands there are no alternative routes for bicycles. The coastal route used to be a way to get to Muritania and the rest of Africa, generally avoiding the long, empty ride down the middle of Algeria's Sahara.

Those wishing to go to Algeria can take the main road to Oujda from Fes or the desert road from Midelt (recommended). From Oujda you can take a pleasant, quiet road across the border to Tlemcen, Algeria. This used to be the main crossing for foreigners between the two countries since the southern crossing between Figuig and Beni Ounif was closed—check before attempting it. The good road heading south of Oujda to Boudnib is open. You can get an Algerian visa at Oujda, usually while you wait.

A good but mountainous desert road begins at Marrakech and climbs to Ouarzazate, then goes to El-Rachidia and Boudnib to Figuig. At Fes you can take another popular but high-traffic road to Marrakech or the road to Tangier via Sidi Kacem and Kenitra. Morocco has 16,000 miles of tarred roads everywhere except the desert. There are a dozen roads from the main Fes-Marrakech route to the Atlantic. This flat part is probably the best riding area, as is the cooler coastal road from Rabat to Agadir.

Algeria

Algeria is one of my favorite cycling countries. I am not sure how it would be for women since I have not met any women who have cycled there (although women have cycled in Tunisia, Morocco, and Egypt without problems). A woman cycling with her husband (not boyfriend) would probably have no problem. No doubt Algeria is a morally conservative country, but that has its positive aspects: instead of hashish dealers you will find generous, honest, and helpful people who act as noble hosts.

The coastal roads are hilly in parts, but not difficult. The major roads are well-surfaced, wide, and safe, but many secondary roads have been allowed to disintegrate. Expect to find heavy traffic near Algiers and on the main road to Constantine. You can take a coastal secondary between Algiers and Constantine.

Algeria is probably the only place you can experience the Sahara, so let us discuss it. Expandable plastic containers sold in camping stores are useful for extra water, but water is heavy; your spokes need to be strong to support the extra weight. Try out a load before reaching the desert.

Trucks and the few cars traveling the road will stop to give you water. When you hear a car coming, stop and hold out your water bottle to your mouth as a signal to tell the driver that you are running dry. Everyone stops, but trucks only run on the main road. Dates, the staple food of the desert, will give you plenty of energy. Eat them with nuts to give yourself protein.

The sand makes the small desert roads too dangerous for even a mountain bike. One pair of German cyclists said that they want to return with camels and really tour the desert. To ride the entire length of the country you must stick to three main roads; none are easy to ride. This is a serious life-and-death business; you cannot go roaming around. The government requires you to register with the police whenever you come into a desert town.

The first of the three routes down the desert, the Route du Mauritanie, is well paved from Bechar on the western plateau (not very hilly) to Tindouf. A bad sandy road runs into Muritania, skirting the western Sahara and meeting the semi-coastal road from Morocco. Even if the road is open, I do not think you can cycle it, although you can ride to Bechar and to the crossing that leads to the second road—the Route du Tanezrouft—goes into Gao, Mali, straight from al-Golea, and Timimoun to Reggane. After that it is a track. There is a 200-mile unpaved road from Reggane to the third and most popular road, the Route du Hoggar or Trans-Saharan Highway, which leads to Niger via Tamanrasset.

If you take that route all the way from the Mediterranean you will reach In Salah, your last chance to stock up. The road to In Salah is well paved, partly newly paved, but between In Salah and Tamanrasset the asphalt is not as smooth. It also gets hilly as you get to Tamanrasset. You can take a scenic diversion to the mountain hermitage of Brother de Foucauld. In

Tamanrasset check in with the police, meet the fascinating Tuareg tribe (you will begin seeing them along
the road), and if necessary go to the Niger consulate
and get a visa. Thirty miles below Tamanrasset the
road turns to dirt, but there is talk about asphalting
the nearly 400 miles to Niger. Another 125 miles after
the border (nothing there but a few guards), you will
hit asphalt.

Although you will not encounter traffic jams, you
will see people on this road. Sandstorms and erratic
winds hit the desert. You have no choice but to stop
and wait until it is safe to go. The local people take it
in their stride, and you need to as well. The experience
of being with the desert people makes the trip worth
every bit of energy that you are required to muster for
the task.

For those not interested in the long trek through
the Sahara but who would like to experience Arabic
hospitality and desert friendliness, I suggest the road
that runs through Ghardaia, Ouargla, Touggourt, and
into the Tunisian Sahara. This paved road has rough
parts, but it can be cycled.

The rest of Algeria, the northern part of the
country, has enough well-paved roads over its flats
and rolling hills. Bicyclists have several choices of
roads into Tunisia. The most popular road along the
coast through Annaba is beautiful, but it is heavy with
traffic. Other roads from Souk Atras or Tebessa to Beja
are quiet farm roads. Another possibility is the road between the recommended Sahara road and the Souk
Atras road.

Tunisia

This is probably the most European North African
country and hence most visited. Even though small,
Tunisia offers farm roads, desert roads, Mediterranean
resorts, ancient ruins, a big city, and several charming
smaller cities. This diverse country has few roads, but
most are paved; all are lightly traveled except the road
running into Algeria on the Mediterranean. Recommended is the main road from the pleasant coastal
city of Bizerte in the north through Tunis and down to
Sousse, Sfax, Gabes, and into Libya, if you want to go
that far. Except for the heavy traffic around Tunis, this
main road is relatively quiet.

In the Sahara you can go from Gabes to Gafsa to
Tozeur. Farther north a road takes you from Sousse to

Kasserine. From Tozeur you can go to Nefta and into Algeria on the south road. The east coastal road is the only decent road running across the country north and south. In the center of the country there are several roads running between Kef, Kairouan, Makthar, and Sbeitla. Since riding in Tunisia is similar to riding in Europe, many people wanting to experience an Arabic country find it rewarding to take a ferry or plane from Sicily and cycle around the country.

LIBYA

Political complication has made Libya off limits to some Western nationals. The formalities of obtaining a tourist visa can be difficult. Libya, one of the driest countries, has three population areas: the Tripoli area, Sirte, and the Bingazi/Jabal Akhdar (green mountain) district around which run a number of paved roads. Libya has a strip of green on the Mediterranean followed immediately by the desert. The Tibesti mountains, towering over 10,000 feet, sit in the south, but the Sahara requires an impossible-to-obtain permit.

Cyclists can travel along the good 1,000-mile coast road from Tunisia to Egypt. A 750-mile paved road runs to Sabha and Ghat in the interior of the country from near Tripoli. There is a 150-mile paved road from Sirte to Vaddan, and a 380-mile road to Sheba from the Capital. A network of good roads from Tripoli leads several hundred miles into the desert, and other good roads can be found around the Bengazi/Bagda area. The rest of the country is not suitable for cycling. If

Yes, there are pyramids in Egypt, and sometimes you get to cycle right by them.

the Egypt-Libya border is open, cyclists can cross on the coastal road to Alexandria; otherwise, they need to take a ferry or plane to Crete or Cyprus.

Egypt

Riding in Egypt can be a thoroughly enjoyable experience. However, unlike the rest of North Africa, Egypt is a poor country, densely populated in a small area—50 million people are crowded around the Nile. You will see miserable situations. Almost everyone will come over, ask you how you are and where you are from, and offer you cigarettes. Travelers have stories of theft or attempted theft in Cairo and other areas. Egyptians, a spirited, friendly people, will want to buy you coffee and food, find out more about your ways, ask you a lot of questions, invite you to their homes. Unfortunately, some people use the guise of friendliness for other purposes, so watch your belongings. Children roam in gangs looking for foreigners to rob.

Once you step outside the Nile Valley the temperature increases by 10 degrees, the sun becomes a blind-

Map of the Middle East

ing, oppressive white globe, and you will find no decent roads. An exception is the desert road from Alexandria to Cairo (as opposed to the Nile road). In Upper Egypt it begins getting hot at 9:00 a.m.

Coming from the south, there is only a poor coastal road running along the Red Sea from Sudan. That border post has been closed on occasion, but the road is partly paved and little used except to the coastal resorts near Hurghada on the Red Sea. A new road to Sudan from Aswan may be coming. A weekly ferry travels between Aswan and Wadi Halfa, Sudan, the head of another road.

You have two choices of roads from Alexandria to Cairo: one going down the Nile delta and the other, a longer road, running through the desert. Both roads are good, but the Nile road is more interesting. South from Cairo a main road runs down to Luxor and Aswan. Luxor is a must-see for anyone interested in history and art, but several cyclists have reported that children throw stones at foreigners and the mass of children who crowd around steal. Caution along that road is advised. After Aswan you will find ATB trails. You can go from the Nile to the Red Sea beginning at Qena. Otherwise you cannot get out of the Nile Valley: the Nile road ends.

To go to the Sinai from Cairo, take a nice road to Ismiliya along the Suez Canal. The Sinai has several roads through it. Two main paved roads run into Israel. Most people use the coast road through al-Arish and into Gaza. The other road runs straight to Beersheba. Those who would like some desert riding and are afraid of the vast Sahara can easily tackle the Sinai. A unique and interesting culture vastly different from North Africa awaits you. The small road to St. Catherine's monastery is now open. Buses and trucks run that route in case you need a ride along the way. Also a ferry runs between Suez and Aqaba in Jordan. A desert road to Taba allows you to cross the Israeli border to Elat.

Cycling in Cairo is quite an experience: chaos, congestion, confusion, and commotion. You will love it. Keep your eyes open and use your hands to ask for the right of way and occasionally curse drivers. Stoplights have no meaning. Cars go the wrong way. Donkey carts cut off motorcyclists. It will be one of your most amusing stories when you return home.

CHAPTER 22

Touring Africa

General Information

Yes, you can cycle through the heart of Africa, and it is one of life's most rewarding experiences. Africa will leave you with many glorious memories. In fact, it never leaves you. I am not trying to romanticize it; touring Africa by bicycle may turn your life's values upside down. Those who want to ride through the continent from north to south will find that the eastern part is the easier way to go.

Cycling in Africa can be boisterously fun or quietly pleasant; aspects of it, however, are difficult. Road conditions in many countries are terrible. You need to be careful of diseases. Bicycle parts are limited. Borders are restricted. Many areas have no good water. The food, when you find it, is monotonous. Things are just not set up to accommodate travelers.

That is not exactly what makes it difficult. Actually, I cannot put my finger on what makes cycling in Africa so hard. There is a frustration that it cannot be the way we want, a sadness about the poverty, an impatience at having to look after yourself constantly. There is a harsh quality to Africa's raawness.

The Africans, a kind, helpful, and generous people, make the trip through Africa interesting and stimulating. They easily become friends. Moreover, parts of the continent have so much beauty that they make other

Out in the open: getting a haircut in Zambia.

places look bland. Much of Africa remains untamed. Where else do you need to stop until a herd of elephants crosses the road? Where else do you see such an assortment of diverse and colorful cultures?

A main attraction of Africa is wild animals. It is beyond words to see giraffe and zebra roaming in their natural setting. If you take the right roads you will see thousands, perhaps tens of thousands of wild animals. They are only located in certain specifically defined game parks. Wild animals do not roam outside the game parks.

This, of course, can be dangerous; it is a thrill to come upon a herd of elephants playing or see a family of monkeys cross the road, but it is an entirely different story if you run into a lion while cycling. You cannot camp or ride inside a game park after it starts getting dark. All animals, whether in game parks or zoos, are wild. Baboons can be terrible. Some game parks prohibit cyclists and motorcyclists from entering; most have no such control. Use your common sense.

Africa has many, many languages. Malawi, to take one of the smallest countries as an example, has two dozen languages and distinct dialects. In East Africa most languages are related to the Bantu family. Arabic is spoken in some of the northern countries, and there are several language families in the west and southwest. However, most countries use a European language as the official language: French in most of West and Central Africa; English in South and East Africa, and Portuguese in Angola and Mozambique. Government officials and educated persons speak the official language. Swahili is only useful in the east and center. Traffic in South Africa and former British colonies moves on the left; road conditions vary greatly from South Africa's highly developed system to Zaire's nonexistent one.

The tribal system is still strong, meaning that you have to negotiate with an all-powerful chief if you want to stay in a village. If you ask someone on the road, they may direct you to their chief, and you will then put your case before him. If you are polite and cordial, the chiefs will be kind to you.

Borders

You will certainly not have to wait in a queue at borders. Africans themselves are not great travelers. Many

African countries are not welcoming to tourists; several will not allow entry because of unrest. The political picture in Africa will remain in flux for the next generation. Inquire from a country's embassy before you go. You have to register your camera at some borders, but do not attempt to take pictures near borders, military camps, bridges, or trains.

Kenya, South Africa, and Zimbabwe have a range of hotels and shops and tourist facilities including campgrounds. All other countries do not. Most countries require visas that usually cost about $10 and cannot be obtained at the border. I advise obtaining all visas before traveling. Few African countries have tourist information offices overseas, but when you contact their embassies you can ask them pertinent questions. Some West African countries are so small that you can arrive in the morning, cycle through, and exit in the afternoon. French embassies are helpful for visas to their small ex-colonies.

You may be asked for your vaccination document at some borders. You must be inoculated against everything and take anti-malaria pills. Water has to be purified and fruit washed. Your first-aid kit will probably have more medical equipment than many rural clinics.

Climate

Keep your sweater at home. The temperature is directly related to altitude and distance from the equator, but you feel the heat much more in the tropical areas in central and west Africa where it is impossible to ride during the rainy season. Rainfall varies tremendously: you will ride through swamps one day and encounter barren mountains the next. The northern desert is dry, but the farther south you go in West Africa the wetter it becomes, then it gradually gets drier. There is more rain in the west than in the east. It is difficult to time a long trip to hit good weather, but use Appendix 2 to determine when it is best to go.

Winds are not a major problem, though there are areas of strong winds, particularly on the coast or over the open plains. The hot season brings warm winds that can be grueling to ride through. Since much of the region has a pathetic secondary road system, rain means muddy roads. If you are planning to ride on anything but the few paved roads, bring your fat tires and do not expect to set speed records. Wear a hat and sunglasses.

Money and Bicycles

With a few exceptions, these are the most undeveloped countries on earth. India might be poor, but comparatively it is highly developed. When you ride you will see people who own nothing but their own torn clothes and are living in empty mud huts. You walk into a store and see completely empty shelves or perhaps a little corn meal. You will not see people starving, but what you do see is disturbing enough.

In South Africa you can expect food and shelter to cost almost as much as in Europe. The rest of the region varies from very cheap to moderately cheap, partly depending on the exchange rate. All major cities have supermarkets and modern conveniences. Hotels cost $15–25, while a meal in the rural area costs perhaps $2. Many rural areas have no hotels, but you can stay with the local people.

In order to combat the black market, some countries make you fill out a currency declaration. If they find you changing illegally, they may either take your money or put you in jail.

Many Africans cycle, riding clunking single-speeds (South Africa is the exception). You will be able to buy basic parts in the large cities, usually from a general store. They mostly use fat 27-inch tires.

Vehicles per 1000 population in Africa

Country	cars/1000
Algeria	26
Benin	3
Botswana	44
C.A.R.	17
Chad	4
Egypt	18
Ethiopia	2
Gambia	11
Ghana	11
Ivory Coast	24
Kenya	9
Libya	251
Malawi	4
Niger	5

Chart of traffic density in selected African countries.

Africa Country by Country

It is best to divide the continent in two: the south and east area, and the west and central area. We will start in the east and work down.

Sudan

Sudan, the countinent's largest country, suffered a long civil war that exacted a brutal toll. The few roads that the country did have were partially destroyed. You may still have a problem getting a visa or visiting the south.

This Arabic-speaking country gets brutally hot in summer, especially in the north which, except for the main road, is closed during summer. Sudan is a hard country to ride, only made possible by the hospitality of the people. Rivers, notably the White Nile, irrigate the area around them and provide transportation; other areas are dry.

Sudan's main road runs north and south through the country, from Juba through Khartoum to Wadi Halfa. If you take the river boat from Egypt to Wadi Halfa, you will have a choice of two dirt roads; neither is good. The shorter desert route follows a train to Abu Hamed where it is met by the river road that goes through Gashabi. The main road then follows the river to Atbara, becomes paved, and goes into Khartoum. At Atbara you can take a good 750-mile paved road to Port Sudan on the Red Sea via Musmar and Sinkat. A dirt road skirts the coast from Port Sudan to Egypt, but the border has not opened to tourists. That is the extent of the main roads in the north.

There is a long bumpy road to Chad from Khartoum via El Fasher and Kosti. From Kosti to El Obeid the road is good, but after that it crosses mountains and becomes too much of a challenge for most of us. To the east a good road crosses Ethiopia at Kassala and goes through Asmera and Mitsiwa before reaching the Red Sea, but that region may also be closed. The best way to reach Kasala is to follow the good road on the Blue Nile.

If you can go south, take the long main road from Khartoum to Uganda—river boats help break up the trip. Two small roads lead into Zaire at Aba and Yambio, but it is usually better to get to Zaire via Uganda or Burundi. A main road runs directly south from

Juba to Kenya. Sudan's winds can be strong, northwest in the top half of the country and southwest in the bottom. Whereas the northern area is desert, the south contains rain forests.

Ethiopia

The news for riding in Ethiopia is not good: unrest has closed many roads. At the time of this writing, all land borders are closed, and internal movement is restricted. Tourists need to go through a lot of red tape to get a visa that entitles them to stay in pre-approved hotels. Instead, hook up with a relief agency if you want to visit. When the country was open, it was the

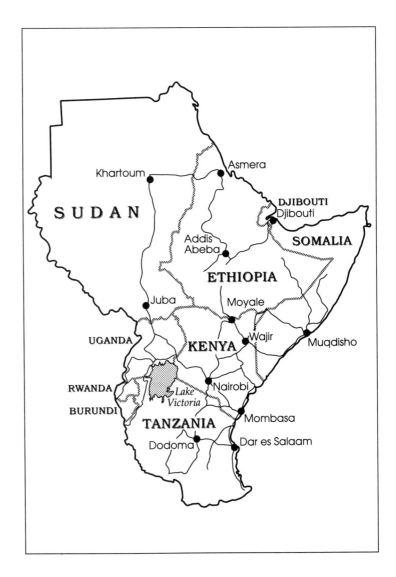

Map of Eastern Africa

hardest to ride because of its mountains. Every part of the country has hilly roads with passes over 9,000 feet.

Also, all roads except the principal highways are poor. A main highway runs from Kenya to Addis Ababa through Negele. Another good road goes from the capital to Djibouti, a separate city-state for which you need a visa from a French embassy. Djibouti is expensive, uninteresting, and unfriendly. A third main road runs north from Addis Ababa to Eritrea via Gondar, the area repeatedly hit by drought. The road to Sudan via Kassala is dirt inside Ethiopia, but another better main road goes to Somalia from Harar and Gorrahei.

Somalia

Also known as the Horn of Africa, Somalia is poor, hot, flat, isolated, and unstable. Yet, if there is peace, it is not unpleasant to ride. The people are less gregarious and more aloof than the rest of Africa. The northern desert is sparsely populated and contains only one decent road. South of Magadishu the country is green and accommodates most inhabitants. The wet season is April to August, and it is hot to roasting hot all year.

The authorities are suspicious of foreigners, and most borders are closed. The main road begins at the Kenyan border town of Libor and takes you on dirt to Kisimayo. From there it is paved to Mogadishu and inland to Belet Uen. Between Belet Uen and Hargeisa and Berbera the road is mostly paved. Except in the north, the road is flat. From Belet Uen another road continues up the river to the mountains of Ethiopia. There is also a paved road from the capital to Baidoa.

Kenya

Kenya is set up for tourism: the roads are well paved; it has hotels; many people speak English; and organized tours are run to all the game areas. It is large, with the most people as well as the best scenery in the south. The north is sparsely populated and quasi-desert. Much of the country is dry and mountainous. If you are traveling from neighboring countries you will find Kenya a place to relax, restock, and get ready for more of Africa. No road has as much traffic, not even in Nairobi.

A paved road is planned to Sudan. A main north-south road runs up to Ethiopia from Nairobi through Nunyaki. Up to Marsabit the road is paved, but slightly after it turns to dirt, runs through Wajir, and reaches the border town of Moyale. The main paved road into Somalia is at Libor. There are also a couple of crossings into Uganda, but the main road goes to Tororo via Nakuru. You can take one of three crossings into Tanzania. The coastal road goes from Tanga to Mombasa (you do not see the coast) and is paved on the Kenyan side, but poor dirt in Tanzania. The roads from Moshi and from Arusha are very good. Travelers can also take a ferry on Lake Victoria to either Uganda or Tanzania.

Throughout the south you will find roads to all game areas, but as you go north, the country and roads become poorer. You will find the colorful Masai in the south and in Tanzania.

Uganda

Uganda's terrain is flatter than its eastern neighbor except in the south, which has the scenic Ruwenzori range with passes over 6,000 feet. It is also wetter and greener than Kenya's dry hills and has a cooler climate. You will ride through forested areas in this small country. You may also see a strong military presence and have to go through several police checkpoints.

Although many roads have deteriorated, Uganda's road system is still good. The main paved road from Tororo goes to Kampala and continues to Masaka and into Tanzania through Bukoba. That is the only road into Tanzania. There are also two roads—they were paved—to Rwanda starting at Kabale: one goes to Gatana and Kigali; the other to Kisoro and Ruhengeri and Kigali. You can also cycle over two roads into Zaire; both get worse the closer to Zaire they come, so many travelers go through Rwanda and Burundi then into Zaire. Apart from the military, Uganda is pleasant to ride, slightly more developed than its neighbors.

Burundi and Rwanda

These two countries are quite different for cyclists: Burundi is scenic and mountaineous—up to 15,000 feet—and has a mild climate, while Rwanda is hotter and flatter. Both countries have good road systems, especially Rwanda. Rwanda's mountain gorillas are located in the Parc des Volcans near Uganda. Apart from the gorilla, these two countries are beautiful. If you wish to visit here, you must make arrangements before arriving. French consulates will often issue visas and advise you on the political and ethnic situation.

The paved road in Rwanda runs as follows: from Ruhengeri to Gisenyi, then a dirt road to Zaire; from Ruhengeri to Kigali around the Kagera Park and into Tanzania; and Ruhengeri to Uganda. Most of Burundi's roads are dirt and hilly, but paved roads run between Bujumbura and Kigoma in Tanzania and between Bujumbura and Kigali in Rwanda. You can also cross into Zaire at Uvira on the top of Lake Tanganyika, but many travelers take a boat on the lake to Kigoma and other ports in Tanzania and Zaire.

Tanzania

I consider Tanzania one of the most beautiful countries in the world. Those interested in wildlife should not bother with Kenya and just visit Tanzania, where five million wild animals roam the Serengeti (sadly, it is too dangerous to cycle there). The mountains are lush with vegetation. Snow-covered Kilimanjaro rises solitary and majestic above the earth.

Two-thirds of the country is mountainous or plateau, giving it a pleasant climate. You should not miss seeing this country, but it is hard to cycle. The paved roads have been neglected for what seems like decades; water is often hard to find; essential supplies—with the pointed exception of beer—routinely become unavailable.

The rotten main roads are the only choice, even though a deteriorated paved road is often more taxing to ride than a dirt one. From Dar es Salaam a main

A family of curious onlookers in Tanzania.

road runs across the country to Ujiji on Lake Tanganyika, passing through Dodoma, the new capital, and Tabora. Another main road goes to Zambia from Dar es Salaam via Iringa and Mbeya. A new road runs from Mbeya to Malawi, and a decent road runs from Dodoma to Arusha. Part of the near-coastal road from Dar es Salaam to Tanga and Kenya used to be paved, but it is now terrible to cycle. Try the road to Kenya via Arusha. There is also a dirt road near the coast into Mozambique, but you need to check on the status of the border. Other roads run between all the major cities, and there is a paved road to Rwanda. There is a trail up Kilimanjaro, where you get the best view in the world. A pair of adventurers used mountain bikes and warm clothing up and down it. The south of the country is less populated and not as interesting as the north.

Zambia

Zambia has its share of hilly roads, but most of the country does not present any difficult climbs. Parts of Zambia are dry, while other sections are lush and tropical. Cooler riding can be found on the plateau. In addition to the standard African diseases, Zambia and the countries around it have the large tsetse fly, whose bite puts people to sleep. Zambian roads are not bad, including 3,300 miles of good paved roads. The Bot-Zam Highway runs from Kazungula to Nata, Botswana. The Great North Road runs from Beit Bridge in Zimbabwe to Tunduma through Chingola and Chililabombwe. Another road from Livingston meets the Great North Road via the Kafice River. There is also a road to northern Malawi. Food and water are not difficult to find, but there are long stretches in the west.

Malawi

Although Malawi has almost no cars or trucks, a number of well-paved roads run through this small, picturesque country. You will find it hilly but enjoyable riding through green areas and game parks. The main paved road comes from Zambia and goes to Karonga in the north, then down to the new capital, Lilongwe, skirting the shore of Lake Malawi. Another paved road goes back to Zambia north of Mozambique from Lilongwe. In the south, which is more developed, a paved road goes from Lilongwe to Blantyre, a large city. From there you can take three roads into Mozambique: one south via Chiroma, another west to Tete, and a third east via Mlanje. You need to check on the status of these crossings.

Zimbabwe

Cycling in Zimbabwe is not much different from cycling in Europe. The roads are well paved, but there is little traffic, and although it has its share of mountains, it is not hard riding. In the south there are long empty stretches, and most of the country is dry, but you will not have problems finding good drinking water. Those interested in seeing Africa without encountering the problems that most of Africa presents and without going to white-dominated South Africa can make an expedition to Zimbabwe.

The main road goes from South Africa through Harare to Lusaka. Near the main road in the south are the impressive ruins of Great Zimbabwe. From Harare you can take another paved road to Mozambique through Umtali as well as a road to Bulawayo. From Bulawayo a paved road takes you south to Botswana at Plumtree. Another paved road leads to the west at Victoria Falls. Not only are the falls impressive, but the area around it is full of wildlife. Boat-safari tours are available on the Zambizi River.

Mozambique

Neighboring Mozambique is probably the poorest East African country. Its flat coast can be hot, and it suffers from strong sea winds from the northeast, especially during the rainy season of November to March. Part of Mozambique is green and tropical, but the majority of the country is prone to drought. Moreover, the country has been ravaged by a brutal civil war. Bicyclists need to be warned that innocent people have often been attacked on the roads. Also, parts of the country remain off-limits.

A partly paved mountainous road runs from Swaziland into Maputo. Another less hilly road from Komatipoort, South Africa, also drops down to Maputo. From there you can follow a paved near-coast road to Beira, then take a good road that parallels a rail line to Zimbabwe, crossing at Umtali. Two mountain roads go into Malawi, one paved leading to Blantyre from Quelimane, the other, harder road from the east leads to Zomba. To Zambia take the long road from Tete through Zumbo. Another relatively easy road cuts across the western part of the country, starting at

Harare, through Tete, and into Zambia. The northern region is not as developed, but a poor dirt road does run into Tanzania, skirting the coastal cities. You need to check on borders.

Angola

Angola, too, has suffered a long civil war with outside forces fueling the fires of destruction. The country does not want tourists, and visas are next to impossible to get. At the time of this writing, borders are closed to foreigners; if you fly into Luanda you probably will not be able to cycle. It has almost no hotels. Peace has come, but it will take years to open.

Angola has a wet, tropical climate over its flat terrain, but its inland plateau makes it pleasant. Almost all roads are unpaved. Exceptions are the roads near Luanda, such as the main road to Malange. Another main road cuts across the country from Benguela on

Map of Southern Africa

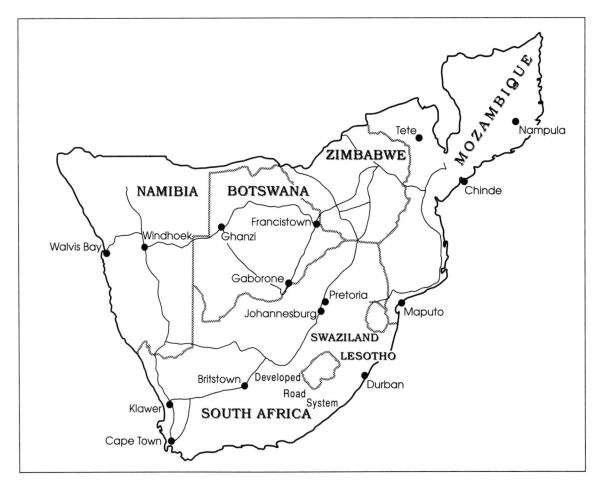

the Atlantic to Malonga in Zaire, via Chinguar. From Namibia a road goes through Mutano, the scene of the fighting.

Namibia

Namibia is an overwhelming desert, sparsely populated, with long hauls between towns. The paved roads that run through the country are mostly in the south. Although the Kalahari is hot, it does not feel as oppressive as the more humid areas in the north. A long main road runs from Angola to South Africa. From Angola to Tsumeb it is dirt. Another paved road runs from Walvis Way to Karibib, and from Windhoek you can go west to Botswana via Gobabis. Unless you are tough, stick to the roads in the south.

Botswana

Botswana is also a mostly unpopulated desert. The country is mineral rich, but the wealth has not trickled down to the people. All main roads are paved and maintained, but the secondary roads are dirt. The non-desert area is northwest of Maun and near the paved road between Gaborone and Francistown. That road stretches into South Africa in the south and Zimbabwe at Plumtree in the north. To get to Maun you can take the road from Zimbabwe, or the road to Ghanzi and Kanye. From Ghanze you can ride into Namibia on tar. The Okavango swamp near Maun is a nature-bird-game sanctuary, but it is also a mosquito paradise. Another paved road goes between Orapa and Serowe and continues to Palapye. Cross by ferry into Zambia over the Zambezi River.

South Africa

In a sense South Africa is not at all Africa, yet it is very African while offering cyclists one of the best riding experiences. At times it looks like riding in Europe, not Africa. It is a big, beautiful country, without heavy traffic but with a solid infrastructure. You will have a hard time getting a visa at the border or in other African countries.

Almost all of the 30,000 miles of paved roads are wide. There are a few motorways on which you cannot ride. Roads run throughout the country. Good maps are available locally at tourist offices and elsewhere. Make your own route, for—excuse the redundancy—all the roads are good. You will not be allowed to cycle through game parks such as Kruger National Park.

Large savannas known as the 'veld' are cooler to ride since they're 3,000–6,000 feet. The country has mountains everywhere, requiring above-normal physical stamina.

Mali and Mauritania

Oasis: Parts of the desert are green and beautiful.

These two countries in the northwest are sparsely populated. Mauritania is an Arab country with almost all its population living near the Atlantic. French gets you by in both areas. The exception is the southern section of Mali, which, like the rest of West Africa, is large and empty. Do not be fooled by a big fat line that appears on the map telling you that there is a road to Algeria from Gao to Tessalit: it is a sandy trail. There is, however, a 650-mile paved road between Nouakchott and Nema, but after that you have to go south on loose dirt. Another road takes you north from Senegal to Nouakchott to Atar. It is paved to Akjoujt and good dirt the rest of the way, but again you cannot go anywhere from there with a bicycle.

The southern section of Mali is about the only place where you will find people. There are dirt roads leading to Bamako from Senegal via Kayes, and another partly paved road from the capital to Guinea, via Kiguiri. Going east, a good paved road runs from Bamako to Bukino Faso, via Sikasso and San (it has many military checkpoints). Half the 340-mile road to Gao is paved, but one American cyclist who wanted to find out what it is like to go to the infamous Tombouctou, a town rightly synonymous with nowhere, discovered swamps and hardships. Mali and Mauritania have about 3,700 miles of paved roads between them; both countries are hard. From June to October strong southwesterly winds bring rain from the coast, but during the rest of the year winds are northeast.

Niger and Chad

Niger and Chad are also sparsely populated, even in the main population area of southern Chad. The countries comprise a hearty section of Africa, but the northern areas are continuations of the desert and have no roads except the Trans-Saharan Highway in Niger, paved from Arlit to Agadez and Tahoua, which goes by the nickname 'the uranium route.' The raincoat you brought for West Africa will sit in the bottom of your panniers except in the south of Chad, which has dense forests and two game parks. Niger also has its share of wild animals in the south.

Visas for Chad are difficult to obtain, and in Niger you have to report to the police every night. You will find a few roads around the Niamey area, but the main road runs east across the country past Zinder to Diffa, where you take a boat across the Komadugu river and continue into Nigeria. There is also a paved road running around Lake Chad to Ndjamena, but if you want to head to the Sudan the road through Abéché is dirt and closes during the rains. Chad has an even weaker road system, with dirt (or mud) roads running to the national parks and Central Africa via Sarh and Doba. If you want to go south it is better to tackle the roads through Nigeria.

Map of West Africa

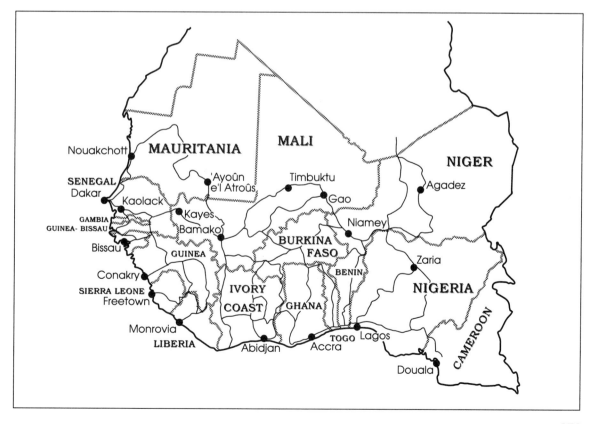

Senegal, Gambia, Guine-Bassau, and Guinea

The countries in the northern area of West Africa are small and basically flat. They have had border closures, so check before leaving. English is spoken in Gambia, Portuguese in Bassau, and French in the others. The coast gets more rain, which is heaviest from July to September. Before that it is hot, humid, and oppressive. Around the coasts there are swamps, but inland you will find open savannas or brush. Bird watchers flock to these countries. Dakar is a modern but wild city—be careful.

Most roads are not paved, but Senegal has the best road system, with paved roads running from Dakar north into the Western Sahara and inland across the country. Another small, mostly paved road runs parallel to the Senegal River, starting at Dagana and working down to Kidira. In lieu of a dirt road you can take a train between Kayes and Tambacounda, and from there, paved roads into Dakar, Gambia, and to the National Park. There are also good paved roads into Gambia from Kaolack; you cross by ferry at Banjul and Mansakonko. Tiny Gambia and Bissau have paved roads from Banjul to Bissau over the swamps (small sections remain unpaved), and inland via Mansakonko to Georgetown and back into Senegal. Another paved road goes from Ziguinchor to Senegal via Kolda. Further south into Guinea the road is not paved. Traveling by river in Gambia is best.

The best way to get through Guinea from the north is an unpaved road from Koundara to Djalon and the paved road to Mamou. There you have a choice of going to Conakry and continuing on the coast or, probably better, taking the paved road to Guékedou. The northern road over the same route to Kankan is not yet paved, but may be soon. Guinea is a slightly mountainous country, probably the most beautiful in the region. The Fouta Djalon area, although not very high, is pretty. Taking the Kindia-Mamou-Pita-Telimele road is the most rewarding experience of cycling through West Africa.

Sierra Leone, Liberia, and the Ivory Coast

These are not developed countries, although the Ivory Coast has one of the strongest road systems in the area—including an 80-mile highway into the modern city of Abidjan—to accommodate the much larger number of cars than you see in the surrounding countries. The coastal area is a wet plain, but inland it becomes drier; as soon as you cross into the Ivory Coast from Liberia you hit a low plateau, and it gets slightly cooler; there's a constant northeast wind. The area offers beaches along the coast, and mountains, forests and jungles inland.

The coastal road (never near the coast) from Freetown to Monrovia is half paved, but the road from Monrovia to Abidjan is good, with only a couple of sections of dirt. There has been a civil war in Liberia—inquire before making plans. From Abidjan you can go north along a paved road straight into Bukino Faso, or take another paved road into Ghana via Abengourou and Kumasi. There are also unpaved coastal roads to Accra and roads leading to the Komoe National Park, but I have no report about them, or about the secondary roads running all over the coastal region. The Ivory Coast has 32,000 miles of roads, many leading to cocoa plantations; all main roads are paved.

Bukino Faso, Ghana, Togo, and Benin

Like their neighbors, these are warm countries, becoming hot and sticky during the summer rainy season. Winds are calmer; there is always a sea breeze along the coast. The official language in Ghana is English, but the other countries use French. There is also several scenic national parks. Benin has periods of friction with its neighbors.

The area has a limited number of roads, but all main roads are paved. Toga has a good road, slightly

Zimbabwe: typical West African small village.

mountainous, running all the way up the narrow country to Dapaong, and good coastal roads to Nigeria and Ghana. If you want to avoid Nigeria, Togo is a better choice than Benin, whose main road between Cotonou and Gaya on the Niger River, though flatter, is partly paved. Ghana has two paved roads to Bukino Faso, both starting at Kumasi. The west road stops at the border and becomes a trail, while the smooth east road through Tamale goes right up to Oaugadougou. There is a ferry crossing at Yeji. Around the Lomé-Accra area you will find several secondary paved and dirt roads. Ghana's poor roads are full of military checkpoints. Bukino Faso is a poor country, and the choice of roads decreases. An uninteresting road runs through the country east to west, through Ouagadougou and into Niger. The coastal road from Accra to Lagos is very good.

Nigeria

The region's most developed country, Nigeria has a reputation for theft. I do not know how factual that is, but I know that there can be a lot of legal problems cycling there. Perhaps I was in the wrong place at the wrong time—I am told that the country's uptightness is changing. It is huge, with a good road network and over 17,000 miles of paved roads, including 200 miles of expressway between Lagos and Benin City, and between Port Harcourt and Enugu. Nigeria pumps oil, and unlike neighboring countries you will find a lot of cars on the roads as soon as you cross any border into Nigeria. Lagos is like Mexico City or Cairo. Since there are paved secondaries, the principal roads are not recommended. With a good map which you can pick up locally (everyone speaks English), you can find the local routes anywhere in the country. Many borders and the northern area are closed—check beforehand.

Nigeria is not only an ethnic mix, it is a climatic mix. There is a plateau in the center of the country around Jos, but once you climb out of the coast the country is either flat or rolling hills. Look for southwest winds during the summer rainy season—along the coast it rains most of the year—but at other times you have winds from the northwest, stronger as you move inland.

Cameroon and Gabon

These are also large countries, and especially parts of Cameroon are much more beautiful than the surrounding area. But Cameroon has been denying permission for people to cycle, so you have to take a bus or Landrover through the area. Inquire. Cameroon becomes very wet from April to September, especially in the mountains; however, rain comes to Gabon in the winter. Gabon is slightly hilly and forested.

There is a footbridge you can take from Ndjamena across the River Chari to get into Cameroon, and there is a main road running down the country to Yaoundé, most of it paved, passing game areas, which is why the authorities will not let us ride (there are also internal tribal conflicts). There are also partly paved roads near the coast leading to Nigeria, but the character of the roads changes greatly once you hit the frontier, from the nice Nigerian to the poor Cameroonian. The country has many dirt roads, mud roads. The main road, Douala to Yaoundé to Ngaoundéré, is partly paved. Further south in Gabon the road network is better. The main paved road runs from Ambam on the Cameroon frontier through Mitzic, Lamparéné, and into the Congo at Ndendé. Another paved road runs from Lamparéné to the capital. I am not sure about the road to Franceville. There are no other paved roads in the country, and few secondary roads. This is not an often-visited country, but during the summer, while it is sweltering in the north, Gabon is dry.

Zaire, Congo, and the Central African Republic

Cycling in Zaire, Congo, and the Central African Republic is not good and not recommended for anyone except the extremely adventurous and hardy. No one has been able to find a paved road in Zaire or the Congo (there are supposed to be some), and the only paved road in C.A.R. is 200 miles long between Bossembele, Bangui, and Sibut. The dirt roads are terrible. These are poor, completely raw areas (C.A.R. is mineral rich). French is the lingua franca here (Zaire has 400 distinct local dialects). Moreover, it is wet and tropically hot, raining at any time. The coastal area in the Congo and the mountains near Rwanda and Burundi offer the only escapes from constantly perspiring, even when standing still. The area is generally flat, but the land rises slowly as you approach Angola.

The Zaire government says that is has over 12,000 miles of roads, but they are awful. This is the place where a mountain bike would pay off. The main dirt road from Gabon goes through the Congo via Loubomo and continues across the border to the surprisingly modern capital of Kinshasa. It then goes to Kikwit and Kananga, and continues to Zambia or to Burundi. In both cases you have to climb hills near the border. In the C.A.R. the main road goes to the Sudan (all the way to Juba) via Bambari and Bangassou. If you cycle in these countries plan on spending a long time, but visas to the Congo only last a few days. I understand that you can still meet pygmies in northeastern Zaire.

CHAPTER 23

Touring the Middle East

General Information

This region includes the Arabian peninsula, Turkey, Iraq, Iran, and Cyprus. It contains diverse peoples, languages, customs, and a radically different physical environment. Much of the area is desert, but the rest is fertile and beautiful. Turkey, Iran, and northern Iraq are very hilly.

The Middle East is a land of hospitality. You are guaranteed to be invited into people's homes, where they will ask you questions—political, social, and personal. Your business is their business. Arabic is the dominant language except in Turkey and Iran, but English gets you around surprisingly well. In Israel, Jordan, Syria, Lebanon, and the Gulf states a high percentage of the people speak fluent English, while in Turkey, Iran and Iraq English is spoken by the educated.

Road conditions are generally good, with wide paved roads being the general rule. Many noisy trucks travel the main roads, which cyclists have found irritating, but they are not a major problem. The region's strong infrastructure breaks down in the sparsely inhabited desert and the mountains of the north, which have predominantly poor dirt roads.

The Negev desert: Parts of the Middle East require desert riding.

To enhance your travels I strongly advise you to read about the area from a political, historical, and cultural perspective before you visit. We could not begin to discuss the splendid cities and the many cultural and political subtleties. The region near the Mediterranean is densely populated, so you will run across many towns. Inland cycling across deserts and mountains, if you can get permission, is recommended only for serious cyclists who carry supplies. All towns have plenty of food—eating well is an integral part of Middle East living—and water is usually purified, though the cities in Iraq, Syria, Iran, and the Turkish interior suffer serious poverty.

Borders

It is a land of political turmoil, and you will see on the roads soldiers and military vehicles. Some countries, especially Israel and Iraq, have unfriendly relations with their neighbors, and borders close either permanently or during times of tension. Since tensions will remain in the Middle East for the foreseeable future, check the political and border situation. It is fair to say that the area's dislike for the West has eroded, but with the exception of Israel, wearing shorts is frowned upon, for both men and women. Modest dress and behavior will win you friends.

In Syria you are required to change $100 at the bank rate and must make currency declarations. Iran and Iraq have tremendous bureaucracies for visa and border formalities, but Westerners have biked there, even during the Iran-Iraq war. Most of Saudi Arabia and the Gulf is closed to tourists who have no valid reason for entry. Except for transit visas, you need sponsorship from a citizen or employer, and I believe that no foreigner has yet bicycle-toured the Arabian peninsula. Lebanon is also currently off-limits, but adventurous people have ridden it.

Many Arab countries refuse entry to anyone with an Israeli stamp in their passport. Get the Israeli officials to stamp a piece of paper, not your passport. Visas to Israel and Turkey can be obtained on arrival, but other countries require visas beforehand. Apart from those two countries, you will rarely find tourist information offices overseas. If you can, visit the country's embassy and ask as many questions as you can.

Climate

The farther north and higher altitude you go, the colder and wetter it gets. The mountain regions in Turkey and Iran are dead cold in winter, and the entire area is harsh in summer. Autumn and spring are the best times to ride, as even on flats you will get temperatures below freezing in winter and over 100°F in summer. Rainfall usually comes in winter, but around the Caspian area, which has a different weather pattern, it can rain any time. Kurdistan and the mountains of Lebanon are the only areas that are pleasant during summer.

Winds can be fierce, especially in the mountains and in Iran where a dusty wind howls from the interior. In the Levant, winds called the Khamsin bring hot and dusty air from Arabia during the beginning and end of summer. The mountain winds can blow from any direction, and wind patterns are not accurate. Traditionally, travelers go east, but that is more out of expediency. Except in summer, the nights turn cold, so bring warm clothes.

Bicycles and Money

These countries are not filled with enthusiastic cyclists, including Israel, which is the only country that has a reasonable, though still limited, number of bike shops. Some people use clunkers in the Gaza and in parts of Turkey, but the terrain does not make cycling a positive alternative for locals. You should aim to be self-sufficient, bringing tools and spares as necessary. I believe you will have a problem buying 700-mm tires but not 27-inch.

It is difficult to generalize about finances. Israel and the Gulf states are almost as expensive as Europe—more expensive for imported commodities—whereas the other countries are much poorer. In Turkey, Syria, Iraq, Iran, and Yeman you can get a meal in a restaurant for about $3 and stay in a hotel for $15. Israel and Turkey have a few camping grounds and youth hostels; the other countries do not.

The Middle East
Country by Country

Turkey

Turkey is a delight to cycle. The people pride themselves on offering visitors an enjoyable stay. Although the country is full of mosques, with new mosques being built, most people do not take their religion sternly. Turkey is huge, 1,000 miles long, and cycling through it is not easy. It has too many mountains—not hills—to count. The Taurus mountains run through the center of the country, and the Pontine mountains stretch to the north into Armenia and down to Kurdistan.

Road conditions are good in the west, but as you travel east the country and roads become poorer. Cheap rail and bus service is plentiful to get you through a rough stretch. The section near Istanbul and the European part of the country is the most populated region; you will find many quiet roads throughout the country. The Göreme area near Neveshir, Kayseri, and Aksaray, where buildings are carved out of the soft rocks, and the Cappadocia

Map of Turkey

region south of Ankara are magical to ride through. I have heard a couple of reports of tourists being hassled in the eastern part of the country where both living conditions and outlook are quite stark.

There are three routes into Iran. The best and easiest is the road straight east from Ankara. The second passes through the Göreme via Kayseri then continues to Elazig, Van, and Agri. That is a hardy travel, but not extremely difficult. The Ankara-Samsun-Trabzon-Erzurum road is harder because part of it is unsurfaced. The easiest way to cross into Syria is through Adana, then to Antakya. There is also a very good and popular road to Greece and another road to Bulgaria via Ediene, where there is an important mosque. Those wishing to ride to the Black Sea can take a partly hilly but good coastal road from Sinop to Hopa. I remember a wonderful ride down the Dardenelles to Canakkale and into the Turquoise Coast, which has incredible Greek ruins, including Troy and Efes (Ephesus).

Syria

Syria looks like a big country, but its large eastern section is desert, and though a pair of British cyclists strongly recommends visiting the desert where, they say, live the true Arabs, such challenges are beyond most of our abilities. The terrain in the eastern section is rougher and more rural. All of Syria's main roads are paved and wide.

Syria and Iraq contain a storehouse of history. Many tourists take the busy road from Damascus to Aleppo, but there are quieter roads throughout the western section of the country, including a road to the coastal towns of Latakia and Tartous. The coastal road is a good way to go between Lebanon and Turkey. Another good road goes along the Euphrates. Those wanting to reach the desert can take a flat road from Homs to Palmyra where a spectacular ruin rises out of the barren sands. From Damascus there is a road over the mountain into Lebanon, as well as a flat road to Jordan. There used to be a road from Damascus to Iraq via Khan Abu Chamat, but soldiers will stop you from going very far on it—the frontier to Iraq has been closed for years.

Lebanon

The situation in Lebanon remains unstable. The country's beauty is renowned throughout the world, but war has made it unsafe for cycling, although much of the northern part of the country has always been safe. The mountains in Lebanon—two ranges—have a few main roads and several secondaries into the small villages. Before the war, the coastal highway used to be one of the most scenic roads. The Lebanese drive insanely, using horns and the bully system, and they are not used to seeing cyclists on their roads. It is a small country; you can travel its length in a day of vigorous riding. I was able to enter only because I was born there, but I hope that others will be able to experience the flamboyance of the people and the beauty of the country in the near future.

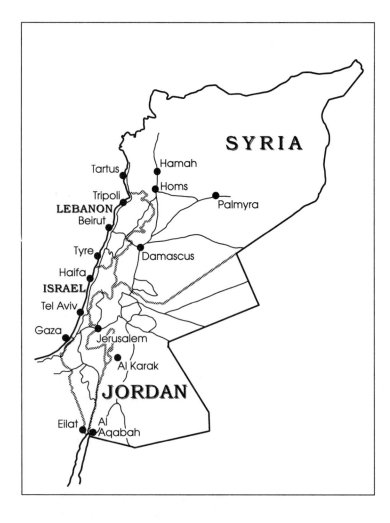

Map of the Levant states

Israel

Israel is open for cycling. Roads are excellent except in the most scenic areas of the occupied West Bank. Tourists must be careful not to upset the local population, who do not enjoy being under military occupation and may throw stones if they think you are invading their small territory. If you show that you are not their enemy they will treat you to an unbelievable amount of hospitality.

This is also a small country. The coast is flat, not interesting, and unfriendly—Israelis have not earned a reputation for welcoming visitors. Once you go inland you climb dry mountains, and if you continue you descend to the lowest points on earth. The climb back from Jerico to Jerusalem is tiring, and the road to Elat is long and dry. The country has many historical and religious sites. The motorways can be ridden, but there are enough secondary roads to make that un-

Map of the Persion Gulf region

necessary. Recommended are the mountains of Galilee and the area around Nablus. Tel Aviv is a city to miss. The Alenby Bridge to Jordan, the only crossing between the two countries, has a ridiculous rule prohibiting bicycles, even if you carry them across. You cannot count on crossing any Israeli border except to and from Egypt.

Jordan

The traffic in Amman, Jordan, shows the degree of westernization that has reached this desert country. Cyclists find it one of the friendliest countries to ride. Most of the population lives in the west; the eastern part is empty desert with one very long desert road running into Iraq. It is not a dangerous ride—trucks and cars will stop for you if you need a lift—but it is one of the world's hottest rides. All other roads are good to ride; most are flat or have small hills. You can ride down the country to Aqaba and take a long ferry to Egypt. While on the way, do not miss the enchanting ruins at Petra in the desert. There is also a strong road system in the east Jordan valley, an area that has to be avoided in summer but is paradise in winter. Trucks use two main routes: one in the north off the Iraq-Jordan road, and the other from Aqaba around the south of the Arabian Peninsula.

Iraq

If the country is not at war with the U.S. at the time, you will encounter a friendliness almost equal to that in Jordan. However, it is a harder country to cycle, not only because it has many hills in the north, but also because it is bigger, has a history of repression, and contains a complicated ethnic mixture. You can plan your trip to avoid hills by keeping your route to the south and cycling along the country's many rivers. The road from Turkey crosses mountains through Kurdistan, but it is not extremely difficult. Iraqi borders are complicated, so make sure you have all your entrance and exit visas and permits to specific areas exactly as required; check on the status of any border you plan to cross. In the United States you can get information from Iraq's United Nations mission.

Mesopotamia, the eastern part of Iraq, is the lush valley that gave rise to our civilization. Most roads are paved, and cycling conditions are not hard even though main roads are crowded. The Baghdad-Basra highway is not recommended, but all other roads are fine. As in the rest of the Middle East, do not take pictures of the military. Every family will come and tell you about their relatives who died during the wars. There is a long desert road from Baghdad to Saudi Arabia used mainly by pilgrims crossing the border at Jumaymah, and a few roads through the interesting marshes in the southeast. Apart from the main road along the Tigris through Mosul, the other roads north are difficult and poor. The entire west is uninhabited desert.

Iran

Iran is a huge country, and unlike flat Iraq, it is not easy cycling. When you push out into the country you will see a lot of poverty. Currently, you can only enter Iran from Turkey or Pakistan. The mountain roads from Turkey to Tehran pass through interesting Kurdish villages. Most of the population lives in the western part of the country; the eastern part is desert, while the interior is a high plateau surrounded by arid mountains. Remember that Iran is not an Arab country, but they observe strict religious rules. Currently, it would be difficult for women to ride there.

Despite the poverty Iran has 40,000 miles of paved roads, including a motorway between Tehran and Qum, and many dirt roads branching out to rural villages. Once it was possible to ride a bicycle from Istanbul to Aleppo, to Baghdad, to Tehran, to Kabul and to Delhi. Political realities have broken that tremendous ride, but if you are strong you can still ride from Bazurgan on the Turkish border right across to Afghanistan. The southern oil-rich part of the country around Ahway and Abadan is much flatter (and hotter), containing many secondaries. If you cross the Elburz mountains north of Tehran you will reach a beautiful coastal road on the Caspian that you can take into Azerbaijan, if the border is open.

The Arabian Peninsula

Most of Arabia is closed to cycling. Saudi Arabia, Kuwait, Oman, And The United Arab Emirates grant, if you are lucky, three-day transit visas. You can only go to Saudi Arabia for pilgrimage (Muslims only), for work, or to see specific friends. It is, of course, a very hot, dry desert, but the country's wealth helped to build 6,000 miles of paved roads. To my knowledge, Oman has one paved road between cities (and the distances are great). The Emirates and Qatar have some roads, but they, too, are long empty rides. Tiny Kuwait has a well-traveled road (especially on weekends) into Saudi Arabia, and a dual carriageway takes you to Basra in Iraq. Kuwait suffers from occasional strong winds from the flat interior, but this is probably your best chance to ride in this part of Arabia, where you will see colorful bedouins once you go outside Kuwait City. Since the 1991 Gulf War, this entire area has been in a state of flux. I think it would be satisfying enough to ride just around Kuwait.

Yemen is the least developed Arab country, and as with most countries in Arabia we do not have reports from cyclists on this land of enchantment. I have been meaning to go for a long time, but it is difficult to get there. For experienced travelers interested in visiting untainted societies, I would suggest they consider a trip. It is a strange country, a narrow coastal plain on the Red Sea followed by mountains that rise 12,000 feet. Even though it is in Arabia, they grow coffee in the mountains where it can rain even in summer.

Yemen has a primitive road system, but paved roads do link the major cities, including the Hodeida to Sana'a, and the Aden to Taiz and Sana'a, going up to Sa'dah. There is also a 40-mile mountain road between Taiz and Muka. All the roads east of Aden are rough tracks except the 650-mile stretch to Mukalla.

Cyprus

Although this book does not cover islands, we should mention Cyprus because of its popularity with cyclists. Much of its center is mountainous, with several hefty climbs. All roads are good, but the tourist areas are crowded in summer. It is a dry island, divided by conflict. The area under Turkish occupation is the most scenic, but there are problems crossing over. I recommend cycling the roads near Paphos and up the Troodos mountains. The area around Larnaca is uninteresting, although it is easy to ride. If you ride to the Turkish side, go to the Kyrenia area. You will find lots of farm roads to take you away from the crowded areas. Traffic here moves on the left.

CHAPTER 24

Touring Central Asia

General Information

These countries—Afghanistan, Pakistan, India, Nepal, Bangladesh, Sri Lanka, and Burma—are extremely interesting and mainly not difficult for cycling. When I first set wheel in the East, my vision of life changed radically. Most countries have decent paved roads and such a variety of terrain that it defies description: some of the world's tallest mountains, lush greenery, rain forests, deserts, and thousands of villages.

Burma is the only exception, whose government does not allow tourists on its limited number of roads. Unless they change their government, the only way to cross the world by bicycle is through Tibet. Even if Burma opened to cycling, its poor system of roads that run north and south would make the going difficult.

Health conditions all over are sub-standard. Many Asians have no idea how germs are spread, and you must do your best to keep clean: wash your hands, wash fruit, and use chemicals in water when you are unsure. Too many people come back from this area with hepatitis, dysentery, and assorted stomach ailments. You have to make a determined effort to keep healthy in the rural areas. Make sure you are inoculated and taking malaria pills.

A rainy day in Bombay, India

Although most of the people are poor, they will treat you well. They will gather around your bike and inspect it, ask you questions about yourself and your trip, and often invite you for tea. Villagers tend to be honest, but you must guard your possessions in big cities and tourist areas. In a village I often left my bike on the street and went in for tea and socializing. Young men came and examined my bike, but no one ever took anything.

The population is generally dense and poor, and except for the desert between India and Pakistan, you will always be near a town when traveling on the roads. In fact, the only problem is being too close to people; you will hardly find time to be alone. Most regions also have rail and bus service, though they tend to be crowded. There are a few youth hostels and many hotels, but outside the main cities the hotels are quite rudimentary.

Language is a source of great controversy in India, but everywhere English gets you around well. Every educated person speaks English.

Borders

Although you cannot legally ride in Burma, you can arrive as a tourist, and since abiding by the law is not a Burmese tradition, people have actually flown into Rangoon, gotten on a bicycle, and ridden out to the villages without anyone stopping them. I have never tried it. Good luck if you do.

War has closed Afghanistan since the late 1970s, and although foreigners can come into the country, the military will stop you from cycling anywhere. Sections of India and Pakistan are also in a state of unrest, and you need a permit to travel to them. These areas include the provinces of Assam, Punjab, and Kashmir as well as the areas near Tibet, Sikkem, and Darjeeling. Foreigners have been killed in Assam and Punjab, so if you do get a permit (you can bribe your way anywhere), carefully consider the situation before going there. Sri Lanka is also in a state of war, and cycling there at the time of this writing is not recommended, although it is a wonderful place.

Most Westerners get visas at the borders of Pakistan, India, Nepal and Bangladesh, but it is a bit easier if you get your visas before leaving.

Climate

Timing the trip is crucial. The monsoon hits the southern part of India six weeks before it arrives in the north. It is too hard to cycle in the rain—impossible in the northern mountains. Perhaps you have read about my experience of riding in 48°C (120°F) in northern India. It was a painful lesson in timing a trip. Furthermore, the wind completely changes direction during the monsoon, and since winds are generally strong, it is important to travel in the proper direction. During the rains, air rushes out of the continent, while during the dry season it comes back in.

Before the rain, the continent experiences a brutal hot season. The best time to cycle is after the rains, though the nights can be nippy. In the northern mountains, the heat is more tolerable, but it is terribly cold in winter, especially in northern Pakistan and Afghanistan. When the snow melts it floods the rivers.

Money and Bicycles

There are millions of bicycles, and each village has a cycle mechanic. They use single-speed clunkers, so they are not going to know anything about your drive train. They can, however, repack your bearings and make adjustments. You can buy only 27-inch tires.

Everything, including bicycle equipment, is cheap. A meal in a rural restaurant usually costs less than 50 cents, and accommodation in a local hotel is perhaps $2. People will invite you into their homes; they are a very curious people. Money is traded on the black market, but not so advantageously.

Taking a dip in Nepal. In the Asian heat, even animals easily overheat, so they bathe when they can.

Central Asia Country by Country

India

India occupies most of Central Asia, but it is made up of different cultures and races. There are 15 official languages in India. The languages of the south belong to an entirely different language family than those of the north. Except for northern Punjab, the southern Ghats, and Kashmir, India is either flat or has only small hills. Kashmir, disputed by India and Pakistan, has been called by many the most beautiful place on earth, but it is hard cycling and not recommended because of the political unrest. You can get a ride on a truck or bus much of the way, but there, as well as in the far eastern section of India, you will need a special pass to enter.

Indian roads are mostly good, although you will have short sections that are unpaved. India's system of national highways links all sections of the country. These are good roads, but they sometimes contain heavy truck traffic. When possible use the secondary roads. The India Motor Club in Bombay and Delhi has good maps of the country, from which you can discover the better roads that run through one small village after another.

More people speak English in the southern part of the country than in the northern part where Hindi is the stronger common language. You can take any road in the country; you do not need to plan a route. Decide how long you want to spend in the country, get a good map, and take one day at a time. I suggest spending two to four weeks riding; you need that long to tackle some of the country, but cyclists experience a burnout after four weeks since cycling there is an intense social experience. It is a unique country—you will love and hate it at the same time.

Pakistan

The feeling in Pakistan is much different, but the people are at least as hospitable. There is a hard road between Hyderabad and Kodhpur, India, but most cyclists cross into India farther north, near Lahore. The central part of the country, the flat Indus Valley, is relatively easy cycling. The unspoiled northern areas, which need a special pass to enter and can only be attempted on an ATB, are beautiful, including Swat, the Chitral Valley, Hunza, and Gilgit.

Avoid March to June, the hot time. Pakistan's roads are not as complex as India's, but you will find 25,000 miles of asphalt, with everything except the border areas pleasant to ride. The Khyber Pass to Afghanistan has been closed, but the long, tough mountain road to Iran via Isfaham, Kerman, and Zahedan enables you to avoid Afghanistan. Most cyclists follow the river highway between Karachi and Islamabad, crossing to Lahore from the flatter south via Sahiwal. The Himalayas rise north of Islamabad—it is not the part of the Himalayas you can ride through, except for the 1,200-mile Karakoram Highway over the Khunjerab Pass from Islamabad to China's Sinking Province.

Map of South Asia

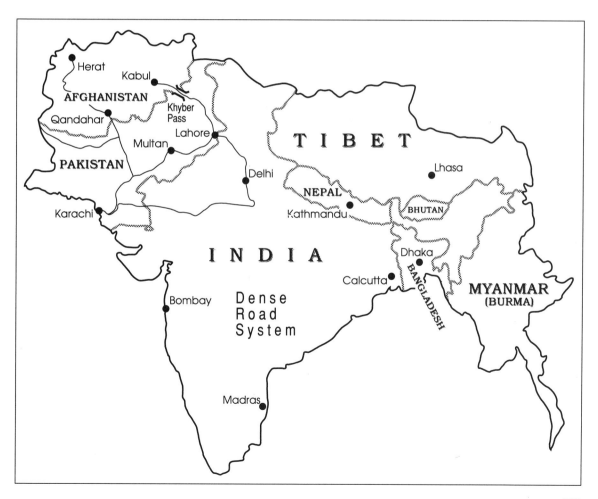

Bangladesh

For all practical purposes Bangladesh is a continuation of India. It is a small country, a densely populated swampy plain, with two main roads leading in and out of India: one to Calcutta and the other to Darjeeling. It is hard to hit the country when there is not a heat wave, flood, or storm. If you go in winter you will find a range of paved roads, not as well kept as those in India, but adequate. This country is recommended for those who do not like being alone, for you are promised to have not a minute to yourself. Many ferries will help you get around. From Dacca you can travel to Akhawra and Sylhat, but the road continues to a sensitive area in India. Another road will take you from the capital to Mymensingh, and a third road goes to Jessore and Benapol and into India. Through the central region try the Jalpaiguri to Syedpur road.

Nepal

Map of Sri Lanka

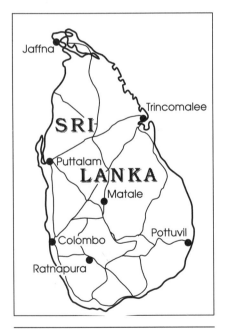

Sri Lanka

Nepal, the cycling goal of many, has four distinct regions. The southern region is an extension of India, dry, and not that interesting. A road runs east and west to Darjeeling province, but you need a special permit to visit that region of India. The western section (west of Pokara) is more remote and poorer, with fewer roads; most areas in the west are only accessible by mountain bike. The third region is the Slwalik mountain range, mostly small mountains that take up most of the country, including Pokara and the Kathmandu area. A few paved and unpaved roads run through this region; all are good for cycling. None of the grades of these lush mountains are steep. Here you begin seeing Tibetan people, but most Tibetans live in the forth section, the tall mountains. You can see these peaks from the lower mountain range, but getting to their bases usually requires an ATB. Many people go off-road into the remote regions. It is a beautiful country, and you do not actually have to be a muscle man or woman to cycle the country. I strongly recommend it. There is a paved road into Tibet north of Kathmandu via Kodari. If the border is open, it is the best way to Tibet. The road between Pokara and Kathmandu is also popular.

Sri Lanka was a wonderful riding country before their civil war. Their roads are as good as India's, with a coastal road running most of the way around the island and good roads over the central mountains. It, too, is a wet country, tropical and wooded, though the northeast is drier. Most people take the crowded ferry between Rameswaram and Talaimannar. The Jaffna area is not recommended until stability returns. From the spread-out city of Colombo you can take a hill road to Kandy where you will find one of Buddha's teeth. If you are not interested in dentures, drop down to the game parks that contain elephants and big cats. Southwest of Haputale you cross a high and windy plateau, then find a sheer drop to the coastal plain. The real hilly area is close to the ancient capitals near Anuredhapura. The beaches on the east coast are better.

Afghanistan

Afghanistan is closed to tourism because of the war. People have reported that it is a beautiful country full of devout, dignified Muslims, but hard to cycle because of the mountains, the Hindu Kush. It is not one hill, but a climb followed by a descent followed by a climb. The main roads are paved and good, though the war has damaged many, but the secondary roads are dirt and hard to cycle.

The country does not experience the monsoon as does the rest of Asia, but it gets rain January through April. Strong winds are possible at any time. The southwest region near Iran is arid and sparsely populated. Summer seems to be prohibitively hot, making autumn the best time to travel its 1,800 miles of paved roads. If you can cross into Uzbek, it is possible to

Pakistan: typical city street scene.

On the outskirts of cities, you see scenes of poverty such as these mud huts on the sidewalk.

take a loop: Herat to Kandahar, to Kabul, to Mazai, to Sharif, and up to Uzbek. The Mugari-Sharif-Herat road is poor, but the Herat-Kabul road via Band, Amir, and Bamiyan is good. Apart from the Khyber Pass, there is another Pakistani crossing between Kandahar and Quetta.

Bhutan and Sikkim

The small mountainous regions of Bhutan and Sikkim have made tourism difficult by imposing many rules. They offer expensive tours to groups, but have been refusing cyclists. Both regions have a limited number of roads, including a 120-mile main road between Phuntgholing and Thimphu.

Burma

Burma rivals Albania as being the world's most closed country. Foreigners have cycled in Burma, but no one has gotten close to any border. If you get stopped on the roads, trains run better than busses, and river travel is possible. A few dollars will get you a long way (there is an active black market). People have traveled all the way from Rangoon to the 'deserted cities' near Mandlay. It's a mountainous, wet country, but since the ranges run north and south, travel in that direction is not difficult.

CHAPTER 25

Touring East Asia

General Information

When China opened to tourism, bicycle-touring groups were among the first to arrive, and now bicycle touring has blossomed all over the Orient. Parts of Southeast Asia remain off-limits, but Thailand, Malaysia, Indonesia, Japan, Korea, and the Philippines offer a variety of cycling opportunities. You will be joined by thousands of others, local men and women, on bicycles, the most sensible mode of travel. Apart from petty theft in Indonesia, this area is one of the safest areas to ride—women freely walk the streets at night.

Not only is the terrain varied, from tropics to deserts to cold mountains, but the people are from several distinct races and ethnic groups. This was the only area where I met a serious communication problem. In all countries some or many people speak English, but in China few do. Because of the complex system of pitch, it is difficult for foreigners to casually pick up a few phrases of Chinese and use them. This makes a package tour seem like a wise alternative.

Cleanliness in East Asia varies from the fastidiousness of Japan to the laxness of inner China. For better or for worse, mostly for worse, the Far East is quickly becoming modernized; that means more cars on the

As a cyclist, you're not alone in East Asia: Street scene in China.

road, more ugly poured concrete buildings crowding out the natural settings, and less room for cyclists. If you want to bicycle tour the East, plan on it soon, before the entire area turns into a hideous sprawling mass of capitalism.

Most of this area is not difficult to ride during the proper season. The exceptions are Tibet and Korea; Korea is probably harder to ride than Tibet because like most of East Asia Tibet is made up of a series of plateaus while Korea is hill after hill. The northern part of China and parts of Japan have hills, but you can usually find easy roads that follow rivers. Most of the islands in the Pacific are hilly or mountainous, usually with a coastal road ringing the island.

Borders

It can be tricky to obtain entry to the war-torn Southeast Asian countries, and travel deep into China, especially Tibet, is restricted. North Korea remains an exclusive regime, and few people are allowed entry, let alone permission to cycle into the countryside. However, other countries have easy borders, with visas obtainable upon entry.

The rules the Chinese have regarding entry and route of travel are not necessarily enforced. Hong Kong is a good place to get a Chinese visa. I found that no one stopped me from going anywhere. But border areas of many countries remain tightly controlled, and you may be stopped near the Thai, Indonesian, and Korean borders. Even some north Japanese islands are off-limits to foreigners. Stability is coming to Southeast Asia, which will probably mean that they will once again be free cycling areas.

Climate

As with Central Asia, the monsoon changes wind direction and brings a torrent of rain. Floods in central China are a yearly occurrence. Avoid not only the rainy season, but also the hot season that precedes it.

In Manchuria and central China the winds blow to the Pacific and Indian oceans from October to April, and in the opposite direction from May to September. Winds are a serious consideration since they tend to be strong. China's east coast has a similar climate to North America's east coast. In winter the temperature drops as you go north. The entire continent has a hot, wet summer, but the north can be bitter cold in winter. The Yangtze Valley has the most pleasant year-round temperature. Along the mountainous borders between China and Southeast Asia the temperature is also much more pleasant, though the summer is terribly wet. Tibet is only cyclable in summer, though the nights are always cold.

China's western interior is a sparsely populated desert that, like Mongolia, no foreigner I know has ridden through. I imagine Mongolia is like riding on the dark side of the moon, only colder and terribly windy. By contrast, Thailand and Malaysia have equatorial or tropical climates that follow the same monsoon pattern. The wet season and the pre-wet season are times to stay away. The northern part of Thailand is hilly, while Malaysia and southern Thailand are jungle.

Japan and Korea get their rain in summer and early autumn, but it can rain there any time. Spring is the best time to cycle Japan; the Bai-u or plum rains begin in mid-June. During winter the air moves southeast; in summer a stronger wind flows northwest. Korea has a short transition between the cold winter and the wet rains. It is hard to hit Korea at a good time. The hilly islands of Indonesia have a variable monsoon, with the rains coming to the northern part November to March and to the south islands from May to September. It is tropical here, with steady temperatures and lots of rain. It is the type of dense weather that causes moss to grow on your sunglasses, and you have to constantly clean out your water bottle.

Civic sewer and water supply: Many Asian cities also have their dark side.

Money and Bicycles

China has 125 million bikes, all black single-speed fat-tire bikes. In the major cities bicycles have designated parking areas. Millions of people in all neighboring countries also cycle, so you will have no problem if something happens to your brake cable and you left your spare at home. I understand that now you can find derailleurs in the major cities. Tires are 27-inch.

Cyclists find this area very cheap to very expensive. Southeast Asia and Indonesia are very cheap, with meals costing $1–2. Thailand and China are a bit more expensive. China has a few hotels that let rooms for $5 a night, but in many cities you cannot find a tourist hotel for under $30 a night. Korea and Malaysia (including Singapore) are moderately expensive, although you can find dormitory-type accommodations for $5–10 a night. Hong Kong costs more, while Japan has the reputation of being the most expensive country on earth, but you can cycle tour Japan without breaking your budget if you avoid staying at the main hotels—it has a few youth hostels but no camping. Most cyclists spend under $8 a day in the budget countries, about $15 a day in China, and $20–30 a day in Japan. It is a bad idea to arrive in an airport at night, when you have to take a taxi to a hotel. Tourists find that airline tickets bought in the Orient are cheaper than they are elsewhere.

East Asia Country by Country

Thailand

Once you get out of Bangkok, Thailand is a good place to cycle. The cities are modern, but the countryside is not. The main roads are well paved and wide, but the secondary roads in the northern part of the country are dirt. Most cyclists take the road from Bangkok down the peninsula to Malaysia. While parts of that road are beautiful (you can stop and swim in the Gulf of Siam), the road is a busy main trunk. Other cyclists recommend going north from Bangkok.

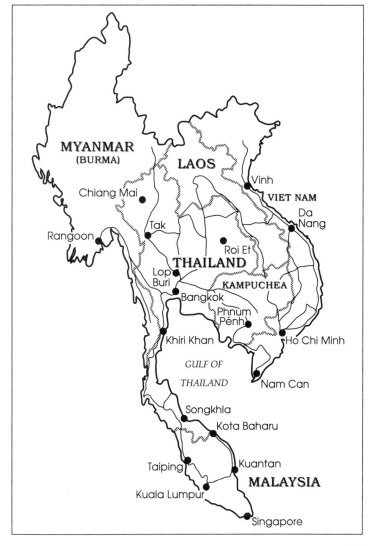

Map of Indo-China

The area near the Laos and Kampuchea borders has been closed, but good main roads run north to Chiang Mai, a much smaller but nicer city than Bangkok. There are no crossings into Burma. Those interested in seeing northern Thailand can make a loop from Bangkok to Khon Kaen, across to Tak, and back to Bangkok. This is an easy and more interesting trek than it would be to ride down to either one of the two coasts, southeast and southwest of the capital. The main road down the peninsula passes near the Burmese border via Hau Hin and Hat Yai, with two border crossings into Malaysia. You have the option of using the trains if you get stuck in a heavy rain, which happens often.

Malaysia

Malaysia is divided into two land masses. Peninsular Malaysia and Singapore are modern countries with excellent roads. The people are friendly, and parts of the country are a tropical paradise. East Malaysia, or Sarawak and Sabah, is not as developed, with only 1,200 miles of paved roads compared to 13,000 miles of paved roads on the Peninsula. Ferries cover the distance, or you can ride over mountain trails from Indonesia to Sarawak (check if the border is open). An important word of caution. Malaysia is a Muslim country that frowns on what they still call hippies. Men with long hair and women in immodest dress have been known to be refused entry. Furthermore, possession of drugs is a very serious crime. If you want to play, do not do it there.

From Thailand you can cross into Malaysia at either Keroh or Changlun and continue on rolling hills down the west coast through Kuala Lumpur, the historic city of Melaka, and across the bridge into Singapore, a city-state. That is the most popular ride, but it is not interesting. Those who like beach scenes will enjoy the road that skirts the east coast, from Kuala Terengganu to Mersing. A few roads cross the mountains, such as the one from Kota Baharu to Kuala Lipis and Kuala Lumpur. They are harder to cycle, but more romantic than the concrete coasts. Trains are available on the Peninsula. Sarawak and Sabah are not popular for cycling since most of their roads are dirt, but a good paved road runs up the coast from Sematan through Brunei, another city-state.

Indonesia

Indonesia is also a Muslim country but much more relaxed. Although not as modernized as Malaysia and Singapore, Indonesian roads near the large, dirty cities have a healthy share of traffic. Java and Madura are as beautiful as they have been pictured in the movies, but most of Indonesia is not easy cycling because it is a surprisingly mountainous series of islands. The hills are not enormous, but there is a good deal of climbing. Also, a group of cyclists advise foreigners to watch their belongings.

A limited number of ferries operate between islands; island flying is also common among tourists. Java is by far the most populated island, but most people live along the humid coast, not the cooler volcanic mountains. The road system on Java is the best, 7,500 miles of asphalt, but many roads suffer from neglect, especially the mountain roads with their truck traffic. The most common route cyclists take, and it is recommended, is Jakarta to Bogor, across to the tourist cities of Yogyakarta and Solo, then to Surabaya and around to Banyuwang and across to Bali, rightly called the island of enchantment.

Besides the mountain roads that cut across the center of Bali, a road covers the touristy part of the island's sea coast, though it is dirt between Seririt and Gilimanuk on the far side of the mountains. Bali is a small island, recommended for riding. Other Indonesian islands south of Bali are also interesting for riders, but once you leave Java and Bali, you leave the most developed islands. The government is busy building more roads to the outlying areas, but if you are interested in reaching remote villages, use your ATB, the

Map of Java

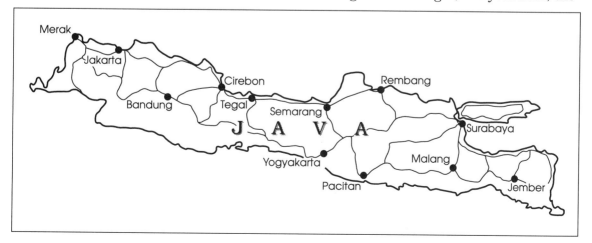

best choice of bicycles unless you are sticking to the main roads on Java and Bali.

It is recommended that you stay away from Timor until peace comes to the island. Kalimantan, the southern part of the island of Borneo, is an undeveloped jungle with a couple of roads on the east side of the island near Samarinda and on the west side near Pontianok, another anthropologist's treasure chest (while on the subject, visit the home of 'Java Man' near Solo). It is better for both stomach and bike to avoid the rainy (muddy) season.

Laos, Kampuchea, and Vietnam

Laos, Kampuchea, and Vietnam are partly open to cyclists, but people rarely go even to the peaceful sections. Cyclists have said that they have been allowed to go everywhere in Vietnam and Laos and have been universally treated to hospitality. Peace is slowly coming to the three countries; currently, cyclists need to find out where they can safely go. Visas to Vietnam and Laos are surprisingly liberal, but Kampuchea has been philosophically opposed to foreigners. Because of the United States war, Vietnam inherited a vast system of mostly empty roads, while Laos and Kampuchea have a weaker road system, only their main roads being paved. With the exception of the flat delta at the southern part of Vietnam, they are hilly countries, but they are not large and can be cycled in a few days. The wet season bring lots of water May through September—avoid that time, as well as January

Chinese bicycle parking lot

through April when it gets hot. Christmas is probably the best time for a cycling there, when winds blow north to northeast.

You can ride from Ho Chi Minh to Hanoi, but you will not be allowed to enter China from Vietnam unless you have a special pass. All border areas are sensitive. If Kampuchea begins to allow foreigners, paved National Highway 1 will bring you from the Vietnamese border to Phnom-Penh. The roads in Laos include the Vientiane and Luang Prabeng road to Ho Chi Minh or to North Vietnam and the Kampuchean border. Another paved road goes between Vientiane to Savannakhet and Phong Saly.

The Philippines

You will see many other cyclists in the Philippines. All the large islands have good roads, although much of the country faces poverty. The islands are under the same monsoon system, which brings rain June to late September, but it does not suffer from excessive heat before the rains. Harsh storms are frequent. Although the country is quite mountainous, it is not difficult to cycle because it is made up of small islands, so distances are never great. Cyclists generally land in Manila, then take the main road north to Solano or south to Nago, then return again to Manila. There is not a good circular route except on Mindanao. With the help of ferries, you can island-hop to Mindanao and climb scenic hills in this more remote part of the world.

Taiwan

Taiwan is one of the most developed countries in the world, similar to Hong Kong. The center of the island is mountainous and pretty, but busy roads, including motorways, run around the coast. The cyclists who have ridden there say that despite the beaches and the developed road system, it is not one of the most appealing countries to cycle in.

Japan

Before visiting Japan or China, you should read about each country, learn a few words, and find out what to see and how to get around. It is impossible to describe the ugly and the beautiful in a few words. As well as Toyota and Sony, the Japanese have cornered the market on bikes and bicycle components. You can buy one there, which is about as expensive as buying one in the United States, or bring your own and cycle on the smooth streets. I never understood why, but traffic moves on the left, and even though there are plenty of cars, all but the motorways are wide enough to accommodate the equally large number of cyclists.

Many cyclists land in Osaka and cycle to Tokyo, but that is only a short distance and covers the most modernized part of the country. Consider going to the eastern part of the country or onto another island. Although the Tokyo-Yokohama area is active, it is probably the least offensive large city to cycle. Kyoto should not be missed, and a bicycle is the best way to get around the historic city. Since the road system—all paved—is extensive and smooth, there is not any need to talk about specific routes. The Japanese have a tradition of honesty. You can leave your bike almost anywhere and no one will take anything.

Korea

We have no reports on cycling in North Korea, which has a restrictive government that grants entrance only on invitation and requires an expensive government guide. It has limited poor-quality roads, except for a Pyongyang to Wonson motorway. There is no international crossing through the Demilitarized Zone.

South Korea is the only alternative, a highly developed country with dense traffic. Most cyclists land in Seoul and ride south to the west coast lowlands, then make a circle to the Sea of Japan, returning to Seoul. All roads are in good condition, but as mentioned earlier, all but the coastal road, which is as heavily touristed as Tokyo and Hong Kong, are tough to ride. Its 13,000 miles of roads are wide and clean, and trains and buses will accommodate bicycles. The country also has a few motorways that prohibit bicycles.

China

While the countries just mentioned have appljied the Western model of development to themselves, China is still developing. Its sense of priorities are different, and although it is developing industry, paving roads and erecting high rises, it will never be a large South Korea or Japan. Now almost anyone can cycle into most parts of China, including the top of the world, Tibet. Most countries bordering China—India, Russia, Nepal, Vietnam, and Burma—have had moments of severe tension; check on the status of any crossings you may consider taking. The best choices of routes into China are from the Trans-Siberian railroad, via Hong Kong, or, most popular, landing in the country by plane or boat. Trains readily accept bicycles; getting a lift on a truck is equally possible. China has no road signs, or, if it does, they are in Chinese.

The Chinese will come over and try to converse with you; hospitality is their natural way. Theoretically, foreigners need permits from the Public Security Bureau to cycle any distance inland.

Hong Kong is an easy entry route. People cycle through the New Territories and take the hovercraft or local train to either Kwangchow (Canton) or the border. A special permit from Hong Kong is necessary to cross by bicycle. This, like most of the east coast, is a developed region of China, and it is flat east of Nanning (Yungning). From Kwangchow you can go south to the Luichow Peninsula, or like 90 percent of other tourists, take the coastal road (it hardly touches the

Map of East Asia

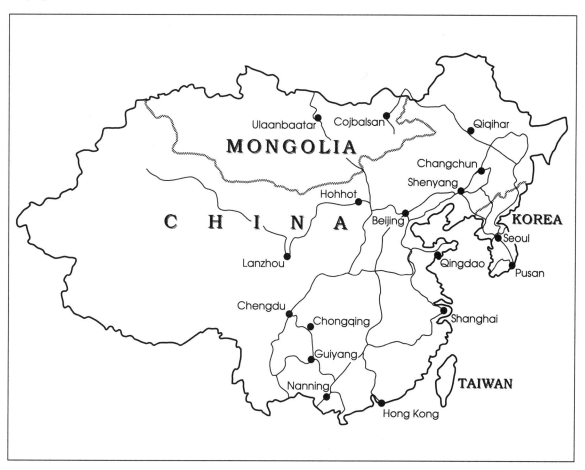

sea) to Shanghai, an enormous place, and continue north.

Also from Kwangchow there is a main road north to Changsha that has some moderately difficult hills. Those interested in Tibet will probably take the road at Pahsien (Chungking), which becomes very difficult west of Chengtu. The mountain area west of the central valley is quite demanding and recommended only for vigorous people who know Chinese language and custom. If you can do it, cross Tibet via the main road from Nepal to Sagyu, to Xigaze, to Lhasa, and across to Chengtu. That is a ride you can brag about for as long as you live. Another road takes you from Lhasa to Sichuan, Xinjiang, Qinghai Hu, and Kathmandu.

The most popular route for bicycle tourists landing in Peking has been south along the flatlands. Many have also ventured to the nearby northern mountains and ridden down the Great Wall, 50 miles north of the capital, but no one takes the hard, barren road into Mongolia via Kalgan (Chang Kiakow) and Ulaanbaatar. Most Mongolian roads are not paved. The road to Russia goes to Choybalsan and Ondorhaan. The southern part of Mongolia is a flat desert, with grasslands to the east and mountains on the west and north. There is an easy road east of Kalgan to Paotow and around the Hwang Ho River all the way to Sian (Siking). If you take that, you will have delved deep into China.

The coast and the Yangtze Valley are flat and easy to ride, and for the majority of us, touring only those populated sections of the country on the good open roads is plenty satisfying. A good map of the country will show the paved and unpaved roads—make sure it is a new map since the road system is constantly expanding.

CHAPTER 26

Touring North America

General Information

Canada is one of the largest countries on earth, and both the United States and Canada offer more diverse cycling experiences than anywhere else in the world—from the populated East Coast to the empty Nevada/Utah deserts, from numerous mountains ranges to the never-ending Midwest plains, from the breathtaking Canadian Rockies to barren Wyoming.

Not only can you find all cycling conditions, but you can discover good roads to almost anywhere. Cyclists have toured northern Alaska and Death Valley. Although there are numerous tall mountains, all but a handful have roads with mild grades, usually well under 6 percent. There are exceptions, but cycling here requires long-term endurance more than short-term power. North America's diverse terrain also provides excellent ATB riding areas.

Canada and the United States operate an extensive park service, encompassing huge areas of natural beauty. You can spend an entire vacation exploring a park by bike. Some parks prohibit ATBs or limit them to specific trails. State and national governments sell detailed maps of parks and wilderness areas; see Appendix 4 for addresses.

You will find many campgrounds, both private and government run, all over North America. The government-run grounds are usually cheaper and more scenic. Most have running water and showers and sell

No pomp and grandeur here: Civic headquarters of Mound City, Illinois, USA.

a limited amount of groceries. The hostel network in-cludes about 100 hostels located throughout the country, many run by cyclists. All states and pro-vinces have tourist or transportation offices that dis-tribute maps and information, and some of these maps, especially of the low-population states, are good enough for cycling. A few states have established bike lanes, recommended bicycle routes, and special bicycle trails.

Much of the area in which you will be riding will be farm lands, and that means that you will be able to fol-low a network of quiet secondary roads. However, in a few sparsely populated areas there will be only one road, and you will have to take it. In states that have no alternate route—Nevada, Wyoming, the Yukon—and the entire northern region, you are allowed by law to ride on the Interstate or main automobile road. A long network of roads for cycling has been established in the United States across the continent called the Bikecentennial Trail. The number of roads included in the Bikecentennial system is constantly growing. Maps and information about these routes can be obtained from Bikecentennial.

Risks in America

North America has drawbacks for cyclists. The United States suffers from having the highest rate of robberies and violent crimes of any country. A disproportionate-ly large percentage of crimes occurs in the metropolitan areas. You should not leave your bicycle out of your sight in any city. You cannot lock it with anything but a heavy U-lock. In rural Canada and rural America, crime is not a major problem; like rural people everywhere, North Americans are honest. How-ever, the United States can be unsafe for traveling women. Many women cycle the United States, but women need street smarts to handle potentially dif-ficult situations.

Rural areas suffer from an attacking-dog problem; urban streets are littered with broken glass near the sidewalk. And of course there is the traffic. It takes miles of pedaling in thick traffic to get out of the big cities and their suburbs and reach the quiet country roads on which we like to tour. To aggravate this problem, many states have narrow roads, so you have to put up not only with gasoline fumes but with horns and aggressive drivers. Avoid traveling through an urban area during morning and evening rush hours.

Finally, distances between towns can be great in the lightly inhabited areas, especially in the central and northern part of the continent. You need to carry a stock of food and water with you because you can ride fifty miles or more between towns. Water is plentiful in the mountain areas but scarce over the long hot stretches of the desert.

Climate

Only the West Coast has a clearly defined rainy season that lasts during the winter. It can rain anytime everywhere else. The important cycling considerations are temperature and wind direction. Winds fluctuate with the moving pressure systems, but generally winds come out of the west and north. In altitudes over 3,000 feet, west winds can be very forceful, so plan to ride east and south.

The farther north you ride the shorter window of travel you have. Spring and autumn weather is unpredictable. Most people ride in summer, when it is hot to very hot all over. The deserts and the south are best ridden in autumn. It is possible to ride in Florida in winter, but not really anywhere else. September is usually the best month to ride in almost all regions. Night temperatures can be cool even in summer.

Bicycles and Money

North America is expensive for food and shelter, but I believe it is slightly cheaper than northern Europe. If you eat in restaurants and stay in nice hotels you can easily spend $50 per person per day. Most cyclists buy food at the grocery store and prepare it themselves, and they camp. However, it is hard to take a trip and spend less than $8 per person a day. Probably $12–15 a day is a good average.

You will have no problem finding bike shops: cities have many, and smaller towns have parts available in hardware stores that also sell lawn mowers. If you want to transport your bicycle, you can stick it on a Greyhound bus. There is no extra charge for this, but you have to have it in a box. Amtrak trains take the bicycle as it is, but trains are more expensive, often more expensive than flying. You can often pull into a gas station and ask for a ride to get you over a hard stretch.

There are many commercial bicycle tour operators in the U.S., who run vacation packages to the most beautiful areas of the United States and Canada, including tours that cross the continent. Prices, distance, and average daily distance vary. Appendix 4 includes a limited selection of such companies.

North America Region by Region

The territory is so vast it is hard to know where to start. The popular places for bicycle touring are often the hardest to cycle. The mountains are beautiful, but so are the painted desert in Arizona and the rolling hills in Wisconsin. Let us take the continent by sections.

Alaska, the Yukon, and the Northwest Territories

Touring Alaska, the Yukon, and the Northwest Territories flowered with the popularity of mountain bikes. Most roads, including the Yukon highway, are unpaved or partly paved, making road bikes the wrong choice. The farther north you go the weaker the road

Map of Alaska and West Canada

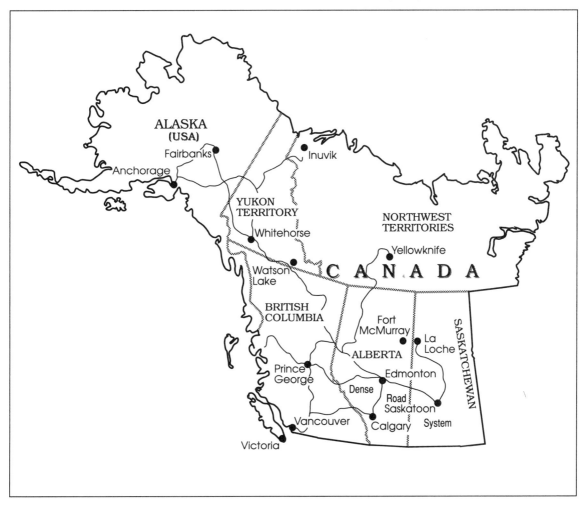

system. Starting at Grande Prairie, a paved road runs to White Horse, and dirt continues to Stewart, Dawson, and all the way up to Inuvik. Inurik is probably the highest mountain bike riders ever climbed, using special studded snow tires and covering themselves in parkas during the summer ride. From Dawson you can enter Alaska and drop down to Tanacross and up to Fairbanks. The Alaska section of the road is paved, as is most of the highway down to Anchorage. The Alaska Highway from White Horse to Tanacross is mostly dirt, as are many of the other roads that lead to the northern communities.

The road system in the southern section of Alaska is good, while from Fairbanks you can ride to Tok, take a rough road to the gates of the Arctic National Park, just inside the Arctic Circle, or follow the Alaska pipeline to Prudhoe Bay. Be sure you know what you are doing: there will be no one to help you. All these roads have been tackled by riders who love solitude and challenge. The only roads in the Northwest Territories that have been ridden are the ones from Hay River to Yellowknife and Wrigley, both dirt.

Western and Central Canada

Most of western and central Canada look equally isolated but in reality have many towns and farming communities usually an hour or two ride from each other. I think that area is better to ride than the northern part of the United States, which is more sparsely populated. Ninety percent of Canada's population lives within 100 miles of the United States border, so the farther you move north, the more open space. British Columbia has a milder climate, but most of it is mountainous. The Vancouver area has a strong road system, but as you move east the choice of roads narrows, and cycling becomes difficult. After you cross those beautiful mountains you suddenly hit flat farmlands that extend across Alberta, Saskatchewan, and Manatoba, all of which have good road systems in the south and central sections of the provinces. This area is recommended riding, with small towns and mainly straight roads.

Eastern Canada

Roads in eastern Canada are more limited to the section near the United States, although a couple of roads shoot up north. Most of Ontario is barren; the only section that has a population is the section around the

Great Lakes that sticks down into the United States and has many choices of roads. When you go west past Sudbury you will be forced to take main roads part of the way. The same holds true for Quebec, as the area south of the St. Lawrence Waterway has a wealth of small flat roads, whereas to the north there are roads that the lone cyclists who hit the Yukon seem to miss. Those interested in scenery should consider New Brunswick, Newfoundland, and Nova Scotia. Roads there are more hilly, and there are fewer choices, but it is an area for nature seekers and sportspersons. Eastern Canadians, when you can find them, are friendly and hospitable. You will have no problem finding a camping place, the most sensible way to spend nights. Most touring cyclists in Canada tour one section at a time, taking roads from Montreal to Quebec, riding around the Great Lakes, or touring

Map of the Western U.S.A.

Newfoundland.

The West Coast

The United States West Coast, from Vancouver to the Mexican border, is the most popular cycling area in the world. Its biggest drawback is the massive amount of California traffic around the big cities, especially the seemingly endless Los Angeles area. California has the highest number of bicycle accidents, and although U.S. 1 along the coast is a spectacular ride (it is a rollercoaster road over Pacific cliffs), the number of cars on it makes me dismiss it. By contrast, I highly recommend northern California (especially around Mount Shasta), Oregon, and the interior of Washington.

The valleys in central California are prohibitively hot during the summer, but you will find a mixture of terrain, from flats to good-size mountains, and when you pick the smaller roads you will be spared from traffic. The Sierra Nevadas are among the most beautiful places on earth to ride a bicycle, and I strongly recommend them. You have to struggle getting up there, climbing 7,000-foot passes, and you have to avoid the principal roads, which have a constant stream of vacationers. Take the unnumbered roads, which you can find on a detailed map. You will also discover several ATB trails. One popular route goes through Death Valley (closed in summer) and up Mount Whitney (partly paved and closed in winter).

The Cascade mountains in Washington and Oregon are popular but difficult cycling havens. There is a particularly beautiful mountain ride from Roseburg to Crater Lake. Cyclists not interested in those difficult roads will find eastern Washington a comfortable and scenic place to ride, especially the region south of I-90. There is a good river road that parallels I-84 on the northern side of the Columbia River. A lot of ATB riders hit the trails in the Olympic mountains west of Seattle.

The Southwest

The Southwest—Nevada, western Utah, Arizona, New Mexico, and Texas—is mostly desert with a sprinkling of mountains and forests. This land will take your breath away, either by seeing the majesty of the scenery or from the heat of the desert. Distances between towns can be hideously long—do not ride this area in summer. Texas is especially large; unlike its neighbors, it is populated and has many farm roads, but it is not scenic, and Texas city drivers have earned the reputation of being rude to cyclists. Nevada and Utah west of I-15 are deadly awful to ride, only meant for those who are prepared to travel 150 miles at a time in emptiness. The sun beats down on your head as you grind out mile after mile, passing a dearth of scenery. Because it has a high elevation, the nights get cold.

Southeast Utah has a tough but scenic road running from Sigurd down to Bluff. You can go through several Indian reservations—they appreciate cyclists— Route 264 through Arizona is one that merits special consideration. There are many good roads around the Grand Canyon, and the mountain forests between Santa Fe and Taos are also wonderful cycling locations, but cyclists rarely travel this area, preferring the more populated and cooler north.

Map of the Southern U.S.A.

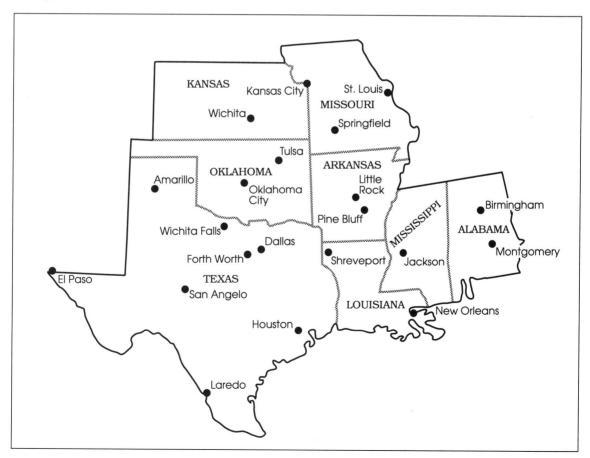

Cross-country cyclists also avoid the far southern route with its flat desert and challenging mountains, preferring to pass through Oregon and Idaho on their way east and through Texas on their way to Mexico. One person toured the southern parts of New Mexico and Arizona after reading Willa Cather's *Death Comes to the Archbishop*. It certainly has its fascination, but do not consider it if you are a 30-mile-a-day cyclist. Northern Arizona and New Mexico are best in autumn.

The Rockies

The Rockies are serious business. Although the mountains climb over 14,000 feet, passes are usually not more than 10,000 feet. Grades are generally manageable on the main roads. Depending on your approach, the mountains either have a gradual rise or a series of hills that lead to the bigger mountains. Many of the secondary roads are dirt and better taken by an all-terrain machine. Rule of thumb: the main road is easier than a smaller road through the same region.

I believe the Canadian Rockies with their white mountains and rich valleys are the most challenging but most rewarding. My second choice is Colorado followed by northern Wyoming. Travel east with the wind direction, and go between mid-June and mid-September. The farther north you go, the more limted your choice of roads. Colorado gives you the most choice; in other states you have to ride on the main road, not unsafe but unpleasant. Montana has a terrific road that crosses Glacier National Park and goes to Shelby, falling gently, then cutting across the northern part of the state at Wolf Point. On other Montana roads you can go over 75 miles without seeing anyone.

Glacier National Park between the U.S. and Canada is a must-see. The two parks in northern Wyoming—Teton and Yellowstone—provide fantastic cycling, and the mountain parks in Colorado are hard to reach but rewarding. Forested mountains and parks continue into northern New Mexico. Roads here vary—the main roads are good, but they are winding and well-traveled. Some mountain roads just end without connecting with any other road. If you have not acclimatized, you cannot comfortably cycle at elevations over 7,000 feet. You have to work yourself up to the Rockies, taking the low passes until your lungs can work normally on the thin air. East of Denver you will experience a gradual descent into rolling flat lands.

The Plains and Midwest

This region—includes the Dakotas, Nebraska, Kansas, Oklahoma, Missouri, Iowa, Minnesota, Wisconsin, and Illinois—iis farm area, full of small roads that are, for the most part, paved. The terrain is flat or mildly rolling, and cycling is almost always good. You will pass miles of crops: potato, corn alfalfa, oats, wheat, and beans. You do not run into national parks, but there are several parks and campgrounds. The Dakotas have mountains, rolling hills, and wide open roads—a bit monotonous. However, it is not an empty land—you do not find big cities, but the low-trafficked roads bring you to small communities every couple of hours. North Dakota is better riding than South Dakota and northern Nebraska. Also, the farther from the Rockies you go, the more rainfall you can expect.

Minnesota and Nebraska have dozens of open roads away from the metropolitan areas. Again, expect to take gentle rolling farm roads and camp a lot. People are happy to have you camp on their land. I enjoy cycling in such areas, but many people find miles of farm land of little interest. Certainly, the roads do not have the wealth of scenery as do other areas. You cycle over hundreds of miles of open roads, seeing a farm

Map of the Midwestern U.S.A.

house every several miles, perhaps a car every half hour. They are good places for a group to develop a closeness and for a hermit to delve into the self. Iowa and Nebraska have annual rides across their states in which a few thousand cyclists pedal on a pre-planned route through dozens of small towns. Cyclists are loyal to Iowa.

Wisconsin is one of the best states to cycle, with a strong system of bike routes and roads marked as particularly appropriate for cyclists. The Kettle Morraine Forest is especially nice, quite different from the Midwest terrain that you will find everywhere else. Again, the north is less populated, but it has roads through Indian communities, and the state has plenty of forested areas. Near the Mississippi River in all states you will meet medium hills. Write the state tourist office for cycling information; the entire state is good to cycle, excellent for those beginning touring.

Illinois is one of the least-favorite states for cycling. Except for the Bikecentennial Trail that passes through the southern part of the state, its roads are narrow and have a high volume of traffic, although the terrain is a continuation of farm land with miles of corn. Oklahoma is also not a popular cycling state, for like Texas it is long, dry, flat, and not that interesting. Be careful of Midwest sewer and cattle grates on entrances to main roads that can trap your tire. You usually have to get off and walk the bicycle across them. Also some smaller bridges use forked expansion joints that can throw you. There is one at the bottom of a hill in Iowa that nearly got me twice.

The South

This region includes Arkansas, Louisiana, Mississippi, Alabama, Florida, South Carolina, and Tennessee. It is unfortunate that cyclists generally tour the north and miss this area. You will certainly meet your share of characters. Parts of this region have tremendous beauty and provide good cycling well into autumn. Although the whole nation is hot in the summer, the south is especially heavy. Florida is a hard state to cycle from top to bottom. Apart from the more interesting northern part, it is flat, and although there are some good roads, it is hard to find a good network of connecting ones that do not make you take high-volume roads at least part of the way; it is the most boring cycling. The northern part of Florida provides cyclists with fine riding, as do Georgia and South Carolina which are especially beautiful in spring and autumn. You have a good choice of secondaries; stay off the main roads, which are narrow and have speeding cars.

The South is car territory. Pick-up drivers think bicycles should not be on the road, and pass with little clearance. A pair of cyclists complained about the people being too conservative and not liking cyclists who have not shaved. Others have said that it is hard to cycle around the New Orleans area because of the lack of quiet roads. Arkansas has the Ozark mountains, which are not hard to cycle over, but Arkansas' road network is weaker than the neighboring states. There is another series of mountains in northern Alabama and eastern Tennessee, but nothing difficult. Tennessee seems to have traffic on all of its roads.

The Mid-Eastern States

This region includes Indiana, Ohio, Kentucky, North Carolina, Virginia, and Pennsylvania. Some of my best road experiences have been in Kentucky and Virginia. Here again cyclists have a good choice of roads and terrain. The mountains in Kentucky are challenging, not

Map of the Northeastern U.S.A.

because they are high, but because there are many of them. They do not compare to the mountains in West Virginia, parts of which are the hardest area to cycle in the United States—harder than the Rockies because there is mountain after challenging mountain to climb. West Virginia is anthropologically highly interesting, but you have to be in good shape to tackle the Appalachians.

You can find good roads throughout this area. Pennsylvania is a large state and contains many green mountains and an array of secondaries. You can pass through several Amish communities and find a variety of terrain. Ohio has many smaller roads over a rolling contour, but few places beat Virginia's beautiful countryside.

The East Coast

This region, though to a lesser degree than the West Coast, is full of bicycle tourists. Vermont, New Hampshire, and upstate New York provide wonderful riding experiences, but so do much of Massachusetts and Maine. Like the West Coast, the main problem with cycling around here is the amount of traffic in New Jersey, around the greater New York City and Boston areas, and at the seaside tourist resorts during summer. I have seen more than one cyclist hit on the road, and I strongly advise you to stay off busy roads, even if many other cyclists use them.

Highway 1 that skirts the coast is generally full of traffic, but the road is wide. In the interior you will find better roads, but they are hilly. There are at least three bicycle touring companies that organize rides through the forests and hills of Vermont. New Hampshire and Vermont have good roads with little traffic, whereas upstate New York, though as beautiful, has fewer such roads. Delaware and Maryland are flat states, easy to ride but not nearly as pretty as Virginia. Connecticut and Massachusetts are a bit more hilly and have more small roads to choose from. The East Coast is nicest to tour in spring and autumn when temperatures are moderate.

CHAPTER 27

Touring Mexico and Central America

General Information

In this part of the world you cycle through a diverse terrain: deserts, mountains—lots of mountains—jungles, forests, and miles of sea coast. The Central Americans, a pleasant and helpful people, are mostly mestizo, but if you venture to remote areas in the central regions you will find many unintegrated Indian communities. More than half of the population of Guatemala, for example, only speak an Indian language. You will not see many near the paved roads. Apart from English-speaking Belize, few people speak any language other than Spanish or an Indian language. You should know some Spanish to be able to get around.

Mexico has a handful of expressways on which you cannot ride and a few tollways where you can ride on the shoulder, although that is not recommended since it is noisy. All other roads are open to cyclists. A vast and sophisticated network of wide and safe roads runs throughout Mexico. South of Mexico the choice of roads becomes limited. Secondary roads in sparsely populated areas of Mexico and the countries below are

Twentyfour-hour service: Mortician's parlor in Guatemala.

weak. Most travelers going south or north through the small countries below Mexico follow the Pan-American Highway, so much so that it goes by the nickname, 'The Gringo Trail.' This well-paved (except in sections of Guatemala), well-traveled ride runs down the Pacific side of the region, usually a bit inland, past the Panama Canal. Along the way you will see smoking volcanoes, have glimpses of the ocean, view lakes and waterfalls, tower over breathtaking scenery, and cycle through dense vegetation.

If you want to travel to more secluded areas I recommend a mountain bike. Central America has almost no roads on the Atlantic side. In Honduras and Guatemala only the main roads are paved. The inland section of the region, from the top of Mexico to the Panama Canal, is mountainous. I found the middle of Mexico one of the hardest places to cycle because of the constant up and down: mountain after mountain after mountain. However, the flat coastal roads are hot and humid. It is best to mix, struggling up the inland mountains and sweating it out on the coast.

The famous ruins, such as Tikal in northern Guatemala, Monte Albán near Oaxaca, the Hanging Gardens, and Tenochtitlan near Mexico City, are impressive but the smaller ruins that you see near the road are also interesting. Two mighty civilizations flourished here: the Mayas whose 1,000-year empire extended from Honduras to the Yucatan, and the Aztecs whose power was in its prime when Hernan Cortes swept across Mexico. The ruins they left reinforce your feeling when you cycle to an open-air market and see the variety of traditional food, crafts, and dress: the area has an old, developed, rich culture.

Drinking water in Mexico and Central America is a matter of great controversy, with bountiful exhortations to travelers not to drink the water. In some places the division between sewage and clean water is not very distinct, and many suffer from internal parasitic problems as a result. However, most water in the big cities is purified, and water is plentiful. Only in parts of central Honduras and Guatemala during the dry season and in the northern Mexican deserts will you have difficulty finding water. Most travelers purify water from rural areas and steer clear of milk products unless they are sure the milk has been pasteurized.

Fruits are plentiful—peel or wash—and sodas are sold everywhere.

Borders

Entry to Central American countries is open to most nationals. Border guards have been known to occasionally give foreigners a hard time. The rule in Central America is that all regulations are subject to exception. If you have a problem at the border, or a guard thinks you have a problem, transform the problem from a legal one to a personal one: negotiate to clear it up, appealing to the guard on the predicament of your personal need as a cyclist. Be patient and polite, and the guards, perhaps after they show you that they are the authority in charge of your fate, will let you in.

Your bicycle is required to be registered as a vehicle—just like a car—and you have to fill in a vehicle form at the border (one of the clerks will type it for you). You will be asked for the name and model of the vehicle, registration number, chassis number, and license number. These categories do not apply to bicycles, but give them names and numbers anyway, so that they can fill in the form. You will also have to pay entry and exist fees at most borders, from $5 to $10 each time.

Your health papers (World Health Organization booklet) may be checked—you cannot travel in Central America without protection against malaria and other prevalent diseases. Since part of Central America is in and out of a state of unrest, your belongings may be searched. Do not carry items that can be used in jungle warfare, including camouflage clothing, combat boots, or a hunting knife.

Climate

The timing of your Central American tour is important. I tried to go through the northern Mexican desert during the summer, the time I was free to take a trip. It was the one time I had to give up cycling and throw my bicycle on a bus. I still remember sitting in air-conditioned bars drinking sodas, unable to contemplate the idea of going outside in the sun. Central America does not have a uniform climate. The northern section of Mexico is hot and dry, similar to the climate of Texas and the southwestern United States, whereas the southern section is tropical. Temperature is also dependent on altitude: while the coast is warm to sticky year around, the mountains are cool to cold.

In the tropical climate of Central America it can rain any time; the most rainfall comes May to September in the Pacific region, and during the winter in the eastern region. Except in the mountains, it is a warm, though often torrential, rain. It seems to perpetually rain or drizzle in the mountains. Before the main rainy season, beginning in April, Central America experiences its hot, humid season, a sultry heat that is difficult to endure, especially along the coast.

It is fair to say that the farther south you go the more rain you can expect. The Atlantic region generally gets more rain. Winds tend to be from the east or northeast on the Atlantic, but it is not possible to gauge the winds in the rest of the region. Generally winds come out of the north during winter. The best riding times are late September to February, but those days are short.

Money and Bicycles

Bicycling in Central America is cheap. It is a challenge to spend more than $6 a day on groceries. Only in the large cities will you find expensive hotels. Most other hotel rooms are under $10 a night. Mexico has a few designated campgrounds, but the other countries do not. Cyclists usually spend about $8–12 a day while touring Central America. Many tourists change money on the black market with convenient money changers who roam the borders looking for hard currency. American dollars are used liberally; leave your travelers checks at home.

With the exception of people in Costa Rica and a handful of Mexican cities, few Central Americans cycle. You will therefore have a hard time finding bicycle shops. However, the main cities have one or two shops where you can buy parts and 27-inch tires. Aim to be self-sufficient and carry spare parts.

Buses can get you through a difficult area. Plan to pay the attendant a dollar or two for your bicycle. Attempts at hitchhiking do not often bear fruit.

Mexico and Central America Country by Country

Mexico

This is a wonderfully exciting but difficult country to cycle. It is bigger than it looks: 2,000 miles from top to bottom. A handful of passes cross over 12,000 feet, but most are lower. Mexico is also home of the word 'macho.' Single foreign women are often harassed—ignoring these men is the best tactic.

Diverse customs, economic states, food, dialects, and mentalities make Mexico a series of regions. You cannot find many secondary roads in the north, especially in the *deserte grande*, where you can go for 60 miles without seeing anything but desert vegetation and vultures flying overhead. Much of the north is sparsely populated, so expect to take food and enough water with you during rides between towns. Often on the road you will find a service station in the middle of nowhere where you can get water, sodas, and junk food.

Baja California, a land of natural beauty, is also sparsely populated and not popular with cyclists. The main road (Route 1) that runs the 900-mile length has stretches of over 50 miles with nothing—no people or water. Such extensive empty expanses of road can make a trip tedious. The scenery is tremendous in places, and there is no shortage of places to camp. Main border crossings into the United States are at Tijuana or Mexicali. Ferries between Baja and the mainland enable you to ride down and not have to turn around and go back.

The mainland Pacific coastal road (Route 15) runs past Navajoa and Guadalajara, passing beautiful scenery and some rather monotonous stretches. The Pacific road becomes Route 200 and continues south to Guatemala, remaining near the coast. Route 45 running from the center of the country through Chihuahua has less traffic than the two main roads running through Monterrey and Tamaulipas. Route 45 forks at Chihuahua, one branch going to El Paso-Cuidad Juárez (Route 16) and the other to south Texas. The east coast road (Route 180) runs through the oil city of Tampico to Veracruz, to Tabasco, then to

Campeche. It is a hot road that gets nicer the farther south you go.

Because central Mexico is more heavily populated it has an abundant choice of roads. The major cities, Guadalajara and the capital, are dense with traffic, but the roads are generally wide. A few expressways radiate out of the capital, but there are also many smaller farm roads. Get a good map and decide where you want to travel. Mexico City is 7,500 feet above the sea, but it sits in a valley. The mountains around it are a challenge. You cannot avoid mountain roads in the central region. The two main roads out of Oaxaca to Veracruz via Tuxtepec and to the west coast are good. With such a large choice of roads in the center and southern part of Mexico, you have the ability to travel freely. If you get tired riding in the hills, put

Map of Mexico

your bicycle on a bus and head for the coast. Also, the people, if asked, are often happy to put travelers up in their homes.

You cycle into a different Mexico when you enter the Yucatan. It is beautiful, but apart from the coastal areas, it does not have many roads. You can ride from Campeche to Merida to Cancun and down again to Chetuma near the border with Belize, or you can cut directly across from Escurcega to Chetuma, a good road on which to travel: flat and wide. The coastal road is breathtaking, and the people away from the main tourist centers are genuinely friendly. You run into a combination of small villages and tourist resorts. I have found that Mexican tourist resorts damage the cycling experience.

Two roads lead to Guatemala: the main road inland from San Cristobal to Huehuetenango and the coastal road from Tapachula to the border, remaining close to the Pacific.

Belize

Belize is pretty well isolated, with few good roads such as the main road from Mexico through Chetuma to the capital, Belmopan, via Belize City. The road continues down to Punta Gorda. Another road goes from Belmopan (an artificial tract-housing city) to Flores in neighboring Guatemala. The few paved roads have deteriorated, but the country has 1,000 miles of all-weather roads. A truck takes six to ten hours to reach Flores. Guatemala and Belize had strained relations and did not have a border open for foreign travel until recently. Belize, a hot and humid country, rains throughout the year, especially in summer. The hills in the southwest are cooler.

Besides speaking a different language, English (though Spanish is also spoken), Belize has a culture that is different from that of the rest of Central America, with a strong African strain. Blacks comprise 65 percent of the population, making it more Caribbean than Central American. Its isolation is further emphasized by a weak road system to neighboring countries, making it a country sparsely traveled by bicycle tourists. Boats operate between Punta Gorda and Livingston and between Puerto Cortes and Belize.

Guatemala

Roads in Guatemala vary from one section of the country to the other. Part of the northern region has neither a paved road nor a decent dirt road. Many Indian villages located in this area remain isolated from modern society and the rest of the country. The military often places areas off-limits. It is difficult to come to any conclusions about this fascinating yet enigmatic country. The people are nice, and the countryside is beautiful, but you can feel an underlying apprehension and submission. The country remains in a partial state of civil war, and this no doubt contributes to that perplexing feeling of discomfort. You will see wide-spread poverty in the rural areas.

You need a mountain bike to reach the Tikal ruins, and expect it to take a long time to get there. A four-wheel drive takes all day from the capital to Puerto Barrios. The rest of Guatemala is good cycling, even though part of the road surface is dirt (mud after the rains). Antigua, the old capital destroyed by earthquake in 1773, can be easily reached by bicycle.

Traveling north and south you have a choice of two main roads, both called the Pan-American Highway. The first road runs from central-western Mexico through the border town of Cuauhtemac, Guatemala City, and into central Honduras, going over many mountains in the process. Part of the road is not paved, and it is a hard ride, but you pass smoking volcanoes and beautiful scenery. The other road goes from the Mexican coast, through the quaint town of Tapachula, along the Guatemalan coast (though I don't remember seeing the ocean), and straight into El Salvador. Although it is easy to cycle, it is a hot ride and less scenic. You can switch roads on either side of the capital; the two roads are not far from each other. About 400 out of the total 500 miles of these roads are paved.

The coastal road can take you through Guatemala in three or four days of cycling, but the inland road through the capital is recommended unless you do not want to spend time in the country. Parts of the coastal road have just received a fresh coat of tar, but as yet small sections of the inland road have not been paved. Since the destination of the inland route is Honduras, you will have to climb up to that road if you want to avoid El Salvador. This sometimes determines the choice of roads. Many other paved roads lead to cities in the central section of the country, including a 27-mile toll road between Escuintla and San José. The mountain roads near the capital are also in good shape.

Map of Central America

El Salvador

El Salvador has suffered a long civil war, and parts of the country remain dangerous for foreigners. The area of fighting as well as the intensity used to change; however, if you are persistent you can ride through the country. It is a thoroughly unpleasant experience, slightly risky, and not recommended until stability comes to the country. Even before the war travelers complained about the unfriendliness of the people who lived under an oppressive class system. Cyclists in the country cannot but notice sad, poverty-stricken towns near elegant seaside villas. A crass middle class in San Salvador deals in throwaways from Woolworth and K-mart. But enough political speeches.

The country is less than 200 miles long, and if you just want to ride quickly, you can make it through in two days of brisk riding: one day from the Guatemalan border to the capital; the next day from the capital to the Honduran border. The Pan-American Highway branches into two sections from Guatemala. The higher road goes through Honduras, then drops into El Salvador and meets the flat coastal road at Santa Ana. That main road goes through San Salvador and down to the town of San Miguel. Past San Miguel there is a junction to La Union and the ferry—sometimes—to Nicaragua. If you cannot take or do not want to take the ferry, the main road curves around to the Honduran border. There is also a coastal road that bypasses the capital. Neither road is terribly mountainous, and I cannot say which is better.

Naturally, you can take small roads to the villages and spend as much time as you like. The small country's good road system has over 1,000 miles of paved roads—twice as much as its larger neighbors—leading to coffee and sugar cane areas.

Those who do not want to go into El Salvador need to take a series of bad mountain roads in Honduras, going through the Honduran capital. Thus, many people go through El Salvador simply to avoid those rigorous mountains. The southern section of the country offers the best riding since it has more roads and is scenic.

Honduras

It is safer but harder to cycle through Honduras and avoid El Salvador. Honduras is a poor, hilly country. The few main roads are well paved and have little traffic, but all secondary roads are dirt. The United States government built roads in Honduras for military purposes. These new roads may take traditional bicycle riders to parts of the country previously only open to mountain bikes.

If you cross from Guatemala on the main road, just after the border station you will have a choice of dropping down to El Salvador or heading to the capital, Tegucigalpa. Currently, the only thoroughfare between Nicaragua and Honduras is over a tall mountain road through San Marco de Colón from Choluteca on the Pan-American Highway. Another easier road—crossing the border closer to the Pacific region of Nicaragua— was closed for political reasons but may now be open. If so, you could ride from the unpaved inland Guatemalan road to Tegucigalpa, then take the short flat road from Choluteca to the southern border.

You can take a trip to the Atlantic side from Tegucigalpa on a newly paved road through San Pedro to Puerto Cortés, passing San Pedro Sula. The eastern side is flat and jungly with a few trails for mountain bikes. The Mayan ruins of Copan can be reached via San Pedro Sula or via La Entrada; neither are good roads. The west coast is becoming popular for its sandy beaches and laid-back Caribbean atmosphere. You can hardly avoid climbing mountains in Honduras.

Nicaragua

Nicaragua is one of the nicest countries for cycling. I found the Nicaraguans most friendly and spirited. As with other countries of the region, over 90 percent of

Roadside restaurant in Costa Rica

the population live on 20 percent of the land on the Pacific side of the country, and apart from a dirt road to Puerto Cobezos, the Atlantic side has only jungle trails and tire-destroying roads. The Atlantic region would be a fine challenge for the hearty on a mountain bike: it is not only entirely different from the western part of the country, consisting of several Indian tribes and African communities that never mixed with the west, many of whom speak English, but it also looks like a land of enchantment. However, most cyclists stick to the Pacific region which, south of Managua on the way to Costa Rica, becomes a thin stretch of flat, unscenic land.

Nicaraguan roads are fine, albeit few. There is a choice of several routes to the capital from the north. After crossing the border the Pan-American Highway will give you a long downhill ride to Somoto and Matagalpa, the country's coffee capital. Before you get to Matagalpa at La Trinidad you could take another road to León and ride up the coast to Chinandega, which used to be a popular place for tourists. Both the León road and the Matagalpa road are mildly hilly and lead to Managua, a large, spread-out and uninteresting city. South of Nicaragua you have only one road, the Pan-American Highway, which continues down the flat western strip to the Costa Rican border town of Penas Blancas. Although that road passes a large lake (be careful, it has sharks) and a smoking volcano, cyclists find the best riding in the country in the northern region.

Costa Rica

Central America's cycling dream, Costa Rica, hosts an annual bicycle stage race for professional cyclists from all over the hemisphere. Everyone turns out to watch the winter event. You will meet several serious cyclists on the road any time of the year. In this most Westernized country in the region you will find a higher standard of living, a network for tourist information offices, and you will be free from bureaucratic headaches common in other parts of Central America. Costa Rica and Colombia are the only two Latin American countries where cycling is popular.

The roads are good, the best in Central America, but the country's small size limits choices. A new paved coastal road on the Pacific runs the entire length of the country, enabling you to avoid the mountain road through the capital, San Jose. Inland, you need to cross 11,500-foot Sierra de la Muerte. The hard climb is worth the breathtaking scenery. There is a restaurant/lodge on top. The mountain roads tend to be foggy or misty throughout the year, whatever the weather is like on the coast. You must wear bright clothing. It is also cold, a mountain cold, especially at night. Once you come down the mountain toward Panama, you will return to tropical weather and soft, rolling roads.

The northern region, a quiet and lightly populated forest with waterfalls and a paradisiac setting, is ideal for cycling and camping. From the Nicaraguan border you ride through the almost uninhabited northern area of the country down to Puertoareas, one of the most gentle rides you will experience. Near Puntarenas you can take the coastal road to the bottom of the country, or you can start climbing mountains to San José, passing coffee plantations along the way. The second road is recommended. Another scenic mountain road runs to Limón on the Atlantic coast, and it is also recommended. You can ride there and take a train back to the capital.

Panama

Panama, by contrast, is not interesting to cycle through. This is not just my opinion but the opinion of almost every cyclist and tourist I have met. The well-paved roads travel over green rolling hills, but they are narrow concrete with many sections having no shoulder. They have a lot of truck traffic, especially around David and Panama City. There are no roads except the main ones. The countryside, a forest or jungle, is sparsely populated. The most interesting part of the country, and about the only thing anyone thinks of when they hear the name Panama, is the canal. You can, of course, cycle along the canal from the capital city to Colón. You will find another main road south of Santiago around the Peninsula de Azuero.

Some 300 miles of riding brings you from Costa Rica to the Panama Canal. If you are traveling south, your trip has to be interrupted at Panama City because there is no road leading to Colombia. The Pan-American Highway continues a few miles south of the capital and gradually becomes a footpath. I have not heard of anyone cycling across to Colombia. Many have backpacked across, but it would take a mountain bike and a lot of walking, and it cannot be done during the rain. There is a semi-dependable weekly ferry to Columbia, and of course plenty of airlines to anywhere in the world. Since Panama City is a center for free enterprise; here you can find bicycle tires and camping equipment to replace anything lost or broken along the way.

CHAPTER 28

Touring South America

General Information

This is such a large area that it really should be discussed in separate sections, but the distinct geographical regions of the continent do not correspond to political boundaries, making it difficult to create sensible divisions. Peru, for example, has three distinct socio-geographic regions: a coastal desert, the Andes, and the Amazon basin. Also, unlike Central American countries that share many similarities, South America is composed of a series of diverse states. The culture, landscape, economic realities, roads, and mentality of Argentina and Bolivia are entirely different. It is hard to find two more different countries. They share no more than a common border and a common language. Similarly, Colombia and Ecuador, Brazil and Paraguay, and Chile and Peru all share common borders but are radically different from each other. You will especially notice the difference in roads: one country will have mostly rocky dirt roads; another country will have European-quality roads.

Along the Pacific coast there is a strip of desert. Inland north run two corridors of the mighty Andes with many of the world's tallest mountains, but farther south the valley between the two corridors becomes a

Ecuador: Cool mountain top above the lush greenery.

plateau, the altiplano. The eastern side of these mountains is lush and rolling, leveling off into the central Amazon basin. The northern part of South America is a mixture of rugged mountains, open plains, and a semi-tropical region on the Caribbean. Around Paraguay lies the Chaco desert and extensive marshlands. You find more mountains near the Atlantic coast east of the Chaco. The lower part of the continent is mostly open plains and rolling roads, the Pampas. Farther south you come to the arid Patagonian plateau which continues down to the cold and windy Tierra del Fuego.

Of the thirteen South American countries, nine speak Spanish. A dialect of Portuguese that sounds similar to Spanish is spoken in Brazil. If you look at a map, you will notice that Brazil takes up a hefty portion of the continent. French, English, and Dutch are spoken in French Guiana, Guyana, and Surinam, the small equatorial countries on the Atlantic. Indian languages are spoken in parts of the Andes (especially Quechua near Lake Titicaca) and in the Amazon, but almost all Indians you will see even in the more remote areas will speak Spanish or Portuguese. English is not spoken by many South Americans.

On the surface it looks as if South America, with its ethnic mixture, has achieved a model of racial balance. To a great extent that is true, much more so than in other parts of the world. If you look deeper you will see prejudices and discrimination. Blacks, for example, are the poor class in Brazil and Colombia, and Indians usually have little say in the government.

Borders

Travel to all countries is open and relatively easy; however, Colombia, Argentina, Brazil, and Venezuela require a visa before entering. Although tourists without visas are often admitted, visas are free and easy to obtain. Paraguay border guards have earned the reputation of looking down on budget travelers. As in Central America, you may have to fill in a form for your bicycle and pay a small fee. Generally, entrance or exit taxes are not required. Border guards seldom search belongings.

Unfortunately, the continent, especially Peru and Colombia, has a bad reputation for theft. Certain cities in Colombia have a high tourist theft rate (one or two barrios of Bogotá should be avoided), but as mentioned, much of the Colombian tourist crime relates to drugs. Stay away from cocaine deals. In Peru and Bolivia the authorities have different drug and cocoa leaf laws for locals and foreigners.

Peru's reputation for theft is well-earned. All over the country, travelers are victims of small but annoying theft. You have to guard your things at all times, especially in areas frequented by tourists. Theft in other areas of South America is similar to any other part of the world, and you have to be sensible.

Climate

Climate variation makes this area difficult to generalize. Meteorologists divide South America into three climates: tierra caliente in the coastal areas and Amazon basin, tierra templada below the Amazon, and tierra fria on the mountains and in the bottom of the country. Generally, temperature can be related to altitude and distance from the equator. The coasts most of the way down the continent have little temperature variance year round.

Most regions have a distinct rainy season. The east coast rains from December to mid-April; every dozen years the northern Peruvian coast is hit with extreme

Brazil: Snake charmer from the Amazon region at work in the marketplace.

storms that go by the name el Niño because they come around Christmas. Precipitation in the Andes occurs September through May, with December to March bringing the strongest rain and snow. The Amazon basin gets its rain December to May, but unlike the cold mountain rain, the Amazon rain makes that tropical area hot and humid.

The Brazilian plateau, a pleasant climate all year, rains January to April, often in short torrents, while south of that area down to the Argentinian Pampas there is no particular rainy season. The Chaco gets its rain from October to March, not a pleasant time to ride through, especially on the dirt roads. The dry western part of Argentina is climatically similar to Chile's coastal desert. Rainfall in Patagonia is low, and the farther south you go, the colder it becomes.

Winds can be strong. Look for constant westerly winds across Argentina. Southern Brazil often experiences easterly winds, but they are not as strong. The western coast has strong and persistent winds from the south, especially during the rainy season. Since it is a long and lonely ride down, it is highly recommended to travel north along that coast. The Caribbean region experiences mild sea breezes most of the year. As a general rule for advantageous winds, travel north and west in the center and northern part of the country, and east in the southern third. Remember also that south of the equator the days are longest when they are shortest in the Northern hemisphere.

Comparative traffic densities in South American countries.

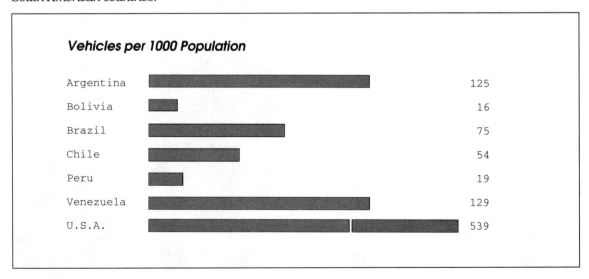

Vehicles per 1000 Population

Argentina	125
Bolivia	16
Brazil	75
Chile	54
Peru	19
Venezuela	129
U.S.A.	539

Money and Bicycles

South American travel is a bargain. Your money will especially go far in the Andean countries of Ecuador, Peru, and Bolivia where you can get a good meal for a couple of dollars and stay in $3 hotel rooms. Brazil, Argentina, and Chile are at least twice as expensive for travelers, while the other countries are somewhere in between. Plan to spend $5 to $15 a day depending on the country and your economy. Venezuela is the most expensive; Bolivia is cheapest. Other cyclists and I have found it easy and satisfying to ask for accommodations from the local people in rural areas. There are many choices of places to eat, from buying food in a store to eating in a restaurant. Many women sell cooked corn or entire meals on the side of the road in villages. The colorful open-air markets are also good places to buy food and other items.

Few people cycle in South America. Exceptions are Colombia—you will meet many cyclists there—and parts of Argentina and Brazil. In other areas some people own and use clunking single-speeds. Aim to buy needed equipment in Colombia or in the major cities such as Lima or Rio. In Colombia you can get 700-mm tires while other areas generally have 27-inch tires. For long rides carry tools and spare parts; the dirt roads exact a heavy toll on the bicycle.

South America has a strong network of public transportation that you can use with your bicycle. In the richer countries of the south, the buses and trains are clean and efficient—the best in the world—while the poorer countries use truck-type transportation called *collectivos,* where people stand in the cargo part of the truck. Since it is a large continent, it may make sense to put your bicycle on a truck, bus, or train.

South America
Country by Country

Colombia

Colombia is wildly exciting to cycle. You will find mountains, flat roads, and a beautiful sea coast, but best of all, you cycle among Colombians. They will make your trip unforgettable, either because you had a wonderful time or because you ended up in jail or without any possessions. Remember what I told you about drugs and theft.

Most people live near the Caribbean or on the plateau between the two corridors of mountains that run down the country. The endless plains on the Brazil side of the mountains are sparsely populated and have almost no roads. The mountains are cool; the Caribbean is warm but not as sticky as the Pacific. Main roads are paved, but the government does not have either the money or the will to keep them in good repair. On the paved roads you have to do a lot of weaving to avoid potholes. The dirt secondary roads are not good either.

The Caribbean coast between the two beautiful cities of Cartagena and Santa Marta is the resort area: romantic, friendly, but expensive. You can take the coastal road from Cartagena to Barranquilla and into Venezuela, passing the border town of Maicao. The two main roads running down the country parallel each other. The west road begins at Cartagena and goes through Medellin (cocaine city), Cali, Popayan (a pretty but high-theft city), and into Ecuador. The second road goes through Bucaramanga and Bogotá from the coast and stops around Huila. These paved roads are mountainous, but they are not extremely challenging.

The Pacific coast does not have a road system. You can take a road from Cali to Buenaventura or a winding bad road from near Pasto to Tumaco (it is terrible going the other way). There are minor roads to seaside communities from Tamaco. Both Buenaventura and Tumaco are uninteresting port cities and should be avoided unless you need to catch a ferry from Buenaventura to Panama.

While you are in Bogotá visit the Gold Museum but watch out for pickpockets and hucksters. From there you can ride to Cúcuta, the main crossing into Venezuela, leading to San Cristóbal. If you are tough and like isolation, there's an 800-mile road from Bogotá down the mountains to the plains and across to Venezuela. The road is dirt, passing untouched Indian communities. That area would be good for roaming by a combination of mountain bike, river boats, and missionary trucks. However, there is another way to the Amazon basin: a thin, partly paved road runs down the mountains from Pasto to Puerto Asís. From there you can find a boat on the Caqueta River, which eventually will take you to the Amazon as far as you want to go, all the way to the Atlantic, changing at Manaus.

Cyclists going south to the Andean countries will encounter the tall mountains that start north of Pasto near Ecuador. The Pan-American Highway going through Popayan to Pasto is a hard but popular ride for cyclists. That winding road requires a lot of up and

Map of the Andes region

down, and it has long empty stretches of barren mountains. The temperature slowly drops as you climb the road to the high mountains in the south.

Venezuela

Venezuela also has a narrow coastal region on the Caribbean that is popular with tourists. However, the country is one of the most often ignored by overland travelers because it seems far out of the way, is not terribly exciting, and has a lot of traffic on the roads. The population is concentrated in the mountainous north, with the plains toward Brazil forming part of the Amazon basin. There are main roads to Colombia and Brazil, but they are painfully long and far from the Andean area that most cyclists enjoy.

Nevertheless, Venezuela is a friendly country, less mountainous, with 15,000 miles of tarred, well-maintained roads. Its heavy traffic is concentrated around the vast Caracas area. A new highway, the Pan Amazon Highway, has been built from Brazil, coming from Manaus and Boa Vista to El Callao and Ciudad Bolivar. You should be able to get a ride part of the way on a truck. Angel Falls, a series of drops that throw water almost 3,000 feet, making it the world's tallest waterfall, is not far from the highway, about 1oo miles from the Brazil-Guyana border, but the area is jungle and hard to reach.

From Caracas—an awful city—you can take three roads to Colombia. The first is the coastal road via Coro, good and mountainous. The second is the northern mountain road via Barquisimento. The third is a flatter road via Guanare that has heavy traffic and is not recommended. Another road leaves Caracas to the Amazon swamps passing Calabozo and San Fernando de Apure and arriving at Apurito. All around the north coast and the mountains you can find a network of good roads—maps are available locally—except the marsh area around Lake Maracaibo. There is no coastal road to Guyana, but there are ferries to Trinidad and other Caribbean islands from Guiria. Expect north winds on that coast.

Ecuador

Ecuador has the best roads of any Andean country. Although the mountains make it at times difficult cycling, it is a pleasure to travel through. Those who want to discover more about Andean life can fly to Quito and cycle only around Ecuador and feel well satisfied. Ecuador does not suffer from many of the social problems of Peru or the economic problems of Bolivia. The eastern part of the country goes toward the Amazon and has neither roads nor villages. Remember to stuff warm clothing in your panniers for the night mountain chill.

The Pan-American Highway runs for 850 miles through the small country and has branches to the coast. You cannot ride along the coast the entire length of the country with a conventional bicycle. The main road runs from Pasto, Colombia, to the border town of Ipiales, then goes through Ibarra and Otavalo (an interesting town much studied by anthropologists), then arrives at Quito. Stop at the mountain villages near the road and mingle with the people.

After Quito the main road continues south to Ambato and Riobamba. Then you can either ride down to the coastal city of Guayaquil and continue south on the flat coast, or continue to Cuenca and Machala, then down to the Peruvian coast. There is a dirt mountain road that stays in the mountains as it drops into Peru, but that road is truly difficult, and you will have to go down to the coast since you run into high, glacier-covered mountains. From Quito you can ride down a mountain road to the Pacific coast. After reaching Santo Domingo de los Colorados there are several roads around the flat coast, a tropical mixture of dry and muggy, not what most people go to an Andean country to experience. You can also cross the border from Colombia at Tumaco on the Pacific, ride to Esmeraldas, then go up to Quito, but the Pan-American Highway is recommended.

Peru

Peru's thievery problem makes cycling uncomfortable. Eighty percent of the tourists riding the train between Arequipa and Puno get robbed—do not let anyone carry your things. The country also suffers from an attacking-dog problem. However, it is the king of the Andes and one of the most beautiful countries in the world. Peru is deceptively large. If you want to cycle through the entire country, plan to spend a longer time than you intended. There are mountains and rough roads and roads that have been completely washed away. There are also interesting villages worth spending an extra couple of days to explore. A schedule never works there.

High up in Peru: 14,500 feet high.

The Amazon region has almost no roads. Iquitos, the main Amazon city in Peru, is only reached by air or by river. I doubt that you can take a mountain bike through that fascinating area. River boats in the Amazon have no route or schedule. You have to negotiate your destination and price.

The coastal area has a branch of the Pan-American Highway running from the top of the country at Tumbes to Chile. You only touch the sea a few times during the ride. It is a terribly long desert trip, a couple of small hills, and little to see in between save a handful of fishing villages. From the coast you can take many roads into the mountains, but the only good, newly paved road is the one from Lima to La Oroya, which goes over a 16,000-foot mountain pass 100 miles out of Lima (take a train or truck if you cannot bear the altitude). There are other popular but bad roads from Arequipa and Nazca. The Nazca area is famous for its miles of ancient lines on the ground. The desert road through the picturesque white city of Arequipa is paved, but a German traveler who took the road through Nazca described it as the 'baddest' road he ever took.

Roads in the Andes are not good, especially in the rainy season. Almost all the road from Huancayo to Puno is not paved. Another 300-mile partly paved road runs from La Oroya over the mountains down to Cerro de Pasco and Pucalipa at the headwaters of the Amazon, and the road continues across Brazil, but I am not sure about it. That is probably as close as you can come to the Amazon in Peru on a bicycle. There are only bad, the 'baddest' roads, in the northern mountain area. It is a place for mountain climbers and adventurers.

From Cuzco you can either take a train or go down a 60-mile mostly paved road to Aguas Calientes, very close to Machu Pichu. The road leading into Bolivia is well paved. The only other way into Bolivia is by ferry from Puno to Guaqui on Lake Titicaca. Motor launches on the lake will take you to the floating reed islands.

The area around Ayacucho gave birth to a revolutionary movement, and there have been many bloody clashes, mostly instigated by the military. You may have to go through checkposts in that area. Peru is beautiful, but it is a heavy, tense country: you will feel a lightening when you cross the border into Ecuador, Bolivia, or Chile.

Bolivia

Bolivia has been called the Tibet of the West. There is more to that statement than the land. If you look at the people, you will see that they appear, dress, act, and work like the Tibetans. Their country is high (La Paz is the highest capital in the world, and you have to climb mountains when you leave the city), and it is also the poorest country on the continent with the worst road system in the hemisphere: almost no roads are paved.

Yet I concur with others who describe Bolivia as one of the most popular cycling countries. The people are poor, but genuine. As you pass on the over 10,000-

Peru: The roads are rough in the Andes region.

foot Altiplano you will notice a barren hard land. Its people were exploited as miners and laborers. Potosí at 13,500 feet was one of the richest cities in the New World, its abundant silver paying for Spain's colonial excess. You can forgive Bolivia's foul roads.

There are paved roads from Lake Titicaca to La Paz to Oruro. Another 340-mile paved road runs between Santa Cruz and Cochobamba. That is it. Most travelers take another dirt road around Lake Titicaca to the border city of Guaqui. There are two dirt roads running to Argentina: the western one running near a train is relatively easy riding but not as interesting as the hard road through Potosí. You cross many mountains before you reach Potosí—terrible in the rain—but from there you can go to the border town of Tarija and into Argentina, or change to the western border town of Villazon. Also from Potosí is a terrible dirt road to Chile via Uyuni and the border town of Ollague. But the more usual way to Chile is a weak road from La Paz through Corocoro and Charaña. There is also a train next to that road, but that route dumps you in the isolated desert of northern Chile.

While we are on the subject of bad roads, let us not forget the one from Sucre to Cochabamba. A better way there is through Oruro, but from the Sucre-Cochabamba road another poor road goes down the mountains to Santa Cruz and toward the Chaco. There is a bumpy road parallel to a railway to Corumbra, Brazil. The northern part of western Bolivia is part of

Roadside stop n Peru

the Amazon basin, but the southern part is the inhospitable Chaco.

Probably the worst road of all is over the 14,500-foot mountain from northeast of La Paz to Coroico into the tropical valley of Santa Ana. That area is lush and beautiful, but, alas, there is a worse road going to Paraguay through the Chaco. Take the 100-mile road from Boyuibe to the border. This is the worst part. Then cycle to Eugenio Garay and Mariscal and the Mennonite community of Filadelfia. Needless to say, none of these roads can be tackled after a rain.

Chile

The desert road north of Coquimbo is only recommended for the hearty. Not only is it dry, but you may have to pedal 100-mile stretches without seeing anything but flat sand. Carry plenty of water. This thin country is not easy to cycle because of the rugged mountains. It is quite Westernized (more European than North American), with a higher cost of living than the Andean countries.

Chile has a good road system,;one or two contain heavy traffic. There is nothing in the southern region except dense forests: Chile's Pan-American Highway stops just south of Puerto Montt. Tierra del Fuego is reached through Argentina. I met someone who was cycling there, but I never discovered if he was able to make it; he was going to take the road to Punta Arenas, cross the Straight of Magellan, and cycle to Ushuaia, Argentina, the lowest city in the world. If you

Wide open space in Bolivia: There are mainly dirt roads in the underdeveloped areas.

meet him, ask him to get in touch.

Since the country has a good infrastructure, a map can get you over the country's 5,000 miles of asphalt. However, you may like to tackle a few border crossings. From Antofagasta you can take a paved road through the copper mining town of Calama and then into Bolivia. Slowly the road disintegrates, but you can also take a train. To reach Argentina from Santiago, go to San Felipe then to Mendoza over the mountains. This crossing is impossible during the wet season, June to November, because of the snow. Those who want a less hilly Argentinian crossing can go south from Temuco to Villarrica and to the border. Then a road takes you to Junín de los Andes.

The Santiago area is large and busy. Many tourists like to go to the most popular beaches at Viña del Mar, which you can reach via Valparaíso. A coastal road takes you up and down much of the country.

Map of Southern South America

Argentina

Roads run all over Argentina, with the exception of the far north and the southern quarter. This big country has a great deal of traffic on its main roads, especially near the enormous but attractive Buenos Aires complex. The roads are generally wide, but the truck traffic on the roads radiating from the capital can be a bit much. You can avoid heavy traffic by taking smaller farming roads. The Argentinians are outgoing and fun and will help make your trip stimulating.

Most of the country is fairly level. The area near Bolivia houses the magnificent mountains that climb to the Andes, and there are modest mountains on the western side of the country. Patagonia is bare and cold and harder to cycle, especially from April to September. There is no need to talk about specific routes: get a good map and make your own route. Argentina has over 35,000 miles of paved roads.

In the north there is a good but endless flat dirt road through the Chaco from Embaración to Formosa. It is paved to the Paraguay border near Asunción. The roads into Bolivia are dirt close to Bolivia, but as you go farther south all main roads are paved. The Pan-American Highway comes from Bolivia through Salto to San Miguel de Tucumán and all the way to Santa Fe, getting more traffic the farther south you go. Through Patagonia you will find two routes running north and south: the main route is the eastern one, which goes from Bahía Blanca to San Oeste, to Comodoro Rivadavia to Rio Gallegos and Trelew. Nearby on the Valdes peninsula you will find a nature reserve teeming with bird, animal, and sea life. The main road goes inland to Paso de Indios and joins the other road to Rio Gallegos, where my Tierre del Fuego friend was heading. The western route goes from Zapala to Bariloche to Rio Mayo. Neither road has any traffic.

There is an unusual way to cross from Chile into Argentina. From Puerto Montt, Chile, ride to Petrohue and catch a boat across Lake Todos los Santos. Bicycle across the border and ride to Puerto Frias (its name is accurate). Then take another boat on Lake Nahuel Huapi to Puerto Alegre near the tourist town of Bariloche. You will be on a main Argentinian road in western Patagonia.

Uruguay

Cycling in Uruguay feels like cycling in Florida, with a mixture of beaches and tropical swamps. The country is small, but it is different from its large neighbors. Again, the roads are good, including expressways, and border crossings to Brazil and Argentina are plentiful. Uruguay is flat farmland with a lot of traffic near Montevidea. It is not unpleasant, but neither is it stimulating.

The main crossing between Uruguay and Argentina is the ferry from Colonia across the Rio de la Plata to Buenos Aires. The secondary crossing is between Bantos and Gualeguaychu, as well as crossings at Paysandu, Salto, and Bella Union. To Brazil the main road crosses at Rivera, but there are other crossings at Artigas, Acequa, Juguarão, and the most scenic at Chui near the coast. Take the quieter road to the border via Montevidea, Mandonado and Rocha.

Montevideo dominates the country. A good map points out the smaller farm roads, such as the road from San José to Trinidad to Paysander, or from Achar across the lake to Sarandi, to Fray Marcos and into the capital.

Paraguay

Some economists argue that Paraguay is the poorest country on the continent. It certainly lacks any jolly feelings, and much of it is not interesting to ride through. I am told that the Chaco is actually the most interesting part of the country. You will find religious communities who came from Germany and made the recalcitrant earth yield fruit. The southern part of the country is the only developed region.

You can cross the Paraguay River into Argentina by a small boat near Asunción, the modern capital. You can use the two main paved roads: from Asunción straight across to the bottom of the Brazilian border near Iguacu Falls, and from Villarrica south to Carmen de Parana. Another boat takes you across to near Posadas in Argentina. Although both these roads are well paved, they are narrow and contain a good amount of traffic.

If you want to travel anywhere else in the country you will have to go on dirt. There are a couple of crossings into Brazil at Pedro Juan Caballero and Bella Vista. The roads there are bumpy. Farther north there is nothing. The Trans-Chaco Highway to Bolivia is flat and empty and hard, except for the first 200 miles out of Asuncion, which is paved.

Brazil

Brazil can be well described as two countries in one. The southern part, where most of the people live, is vastly different from the northern Amazon region.

Brazil built a lot of roads, including roads to the Amazon in the 1970s, during what the military government called the 'miracle.' The main paved road that runs to Manaus can be cycled, as can various roads on the coast to Fortaleza and São Louís. It is controversial whether these roads improved the country or hurt its majesty. You can see how zealous builders have transformed part of the rich Amazon into a desert. Roads to smaller Amazonian towns are mostly unpaved. Brazil has over 800,000 miles of roads, and 70,000 are paved. The Amazon has not been popular with foreign cyclists, who generally travel on the other side of the continent.

The southern part of Brazil is as developed as any Western country, with a large road system. Brazil is not as good riding as Argentina. Generally the roads, though well paved, are narrow and contain a lot of traffic. There are a couple of expressways on which you cannot cycle, such as the one from São Paulo to Rio, but there are also four-lane roads that have a wide shoulder on which you can ride. Although they have a lot of traffic, these roads are usually better than the principal two-lane roads that give you little room. It is often difficult to find a good connecting system of secondary roads.

The lively Brazilian people will make travel through the country a delight. There is good riding on the coastal roads north of Rio to Recife through fishing villages and tourist resorts. South of Rio the coast is impossible for cyclists. Inland near Bolivia you will find few roads. The Transamazonica Highway goes from Altamira to Itaituba, to Humaita, to Porto Velho, and Cruzeiro do Sul. The plan was to link it to Peru.

The best riding is farther up the coast from Rio. A coastal road passes through Salvador (called 'Bahia'), the old capital, and goes to Belem, at the mouth of the Tocantins. From there you can take boats up the Amazon to Manaus, the port city with boats to anywhere. Make sure you have your mosquito-proof tent.

Many travelers cross into either Paraguay or Argentina at the Fox do Iguacu, a short distance from both borders. They are as impressive as Niagara Falls, sitting among a semi-tropical area, now highly tourist developed but still pleasant. There are several other land crossings into most other South American countries. Brazil and Argentina have a few campgrounds.

Other Countries

We have no first-hand information on travel in Guyana, Surinam, and French Guiana, the three semi-tropical countries north of Brazil. A road near the coast links Cayenne, French Guiana, to Paramaribo, Surinam, to Georgetown. There are no roads between these tropical countries and Venezuela, but Guyana is building a highway to Brazil.

CHAPTER 29

Touring Australia and New Zealand

I had better come clean right away and admit that I have never cycled in either country. I have collected the information in this chapter from other cyclists (everyone describes it as a wonderful experience), but I will be unable to give the flavor of cycling in these countries. This should not be a problem, because there is plenty of literature on traveling through Australia and New Zealand. Everything seems to be quite straightforward, so the descriptions can be kept brief.

The region has a lot to offer—sea coasts, deserts, mountains, no language problem—a place for loners as well as party goers (drunk drivers are a problem). Although I do not know anyone who has crossed Australia by bicycle—it is almost the size of the United States—people have done it by car and camel. New Zealand and Tasmania seem like ideal places for touring, with wide first-class roads and plenty of natural beauty. Riding through these countries seems pleasurable, friendly. Cyclists say that New Zealand is much better to cycle than Australia.

Climate

The central part of Australia is dry and mostly flat, but other regions, including Tasmania and both New Zealand islands, are hilly and wet. It can rain in New Zealand any time, but the country is warm to hot year round, as is most of Australia. The northern part of Australia is tropical. On the east coast there are mountains with regular southeast trade winds. The country has a strip of coast, followed by mediocre mountains, followed by flat plain desert. On the north coast between November and April a hot, wet wind comes from the northwest. The east and south coast can have rain anytime, but more during their summer.

Tasmania has a more temperate climate. One cyclist described it as cycling in Oregon; another said it was similar to Ireland. Tasmania and New Zealand suffer from summer heat waves and the occasional 'Willy Willy,' a storm on the northwest coast. New

Zealand has stronger winds, mostly from the west. Winds in the region are generally from the west.

Non-commonwealth citizens need visas before arriving. The countries are welcoming to tourists, and there should be no border problems. They have tourist offices and cycling clubs where you can get more information, and several North American outfits offer package cycling tours there. It has no shortage of bicycle shops, for what they call 'push bicycles,' and they use English-size tires. Cyclists find maps with 1:250,000 scales adequate, although parts of New Zealand's North Island, parts of New South Wales, and parts of Victoria demand more detailed maps.

The area is industrial, developed, and thus not cheap. It is definitely cheaper than Europe, but much more expensive than Asia. There are many campgrounds and a few hostels, and camping cyclists spend less than $15 a day. New Zealand is considered

Map of Australia

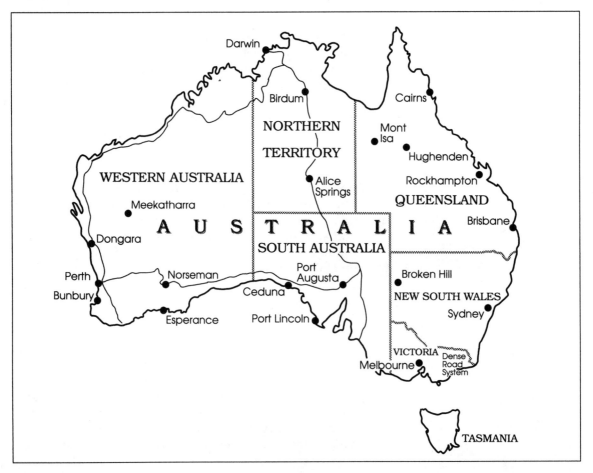

especially good for women cyclists who want to feel safe and comfortable. Trains or buses run to every city.

Australia

Central Australia has no roads running east to west. However, there is a paved road in the Northern Territory that runs from the port of Darwin to the Pacific coast via Camooweal. The Pacific coastal region, especially New South Wales, has an extensive system of roads, but even the coastal roads have their share of hills.

The mountains near Melbourne provide fabulous cycling. Good roads also reach the Outback, and generally the space between towns is not overwhelming. The coastal road running along the southern coast is a different story, with cyclists reporting that the distance between supplies of food and water is large. Such roads are only intended for the highly experienced cyclist.

Apart from the area near Perth, most of western Australia is lightly populated. This means fewer roads and long distances between towns. However, it is possible to take the Great Northern road around the continent back to Darwin—all but 200 miles is paved. Distance is a serious problem, with many points where you will travel over 100 miles without seeing any sign of human life. Before going into the interior you should read about native life in order to gain a better understanding of the indigenous people. All cyclists I interviewed cycled on the west coast, mostly between Brisbane and Melbourne.

The long road in the south linking Perth with Adelaide is entirely paved, and the Stuart Highway from Darwin through the center of the country is 90 percent paved. In addition, ATB riders will find thousands of miles of trails and dirt roads all over the country, especially in Queensland. Many trails are also around Canberra where there is a museum of specialty bicycles.

Tasmania

Tasmania is much more manageable, but it does not have the same network of roads. However, people say that it is a beautiful island and should not be missed by travelers to Australia. Roads run through the farm areas, quiet roads that roll and pass through small towns. I was also surprised to learn that the island has multilane highways. It is a small country with paved and dirt roads running from Hobart to the Launceston and Burnie areas. Sections of the country have no roads, but north of Hobart and between Launceston and Deloraine you will find a strong system of secondaries. It is a mountainous area, and even the main highways are tough. Recommended is the A10 road from Wayatinah to Queenstown and up to Somerset.

New Zealand

New Zealand produces some of the world's best cyclists; I have met many on roads around the world. Both the North Island and the South Island are good for cycling. The South Island has roads going right through the central mountains. You can land in Wellington then tour to Aukland or south to Invercargill. There are plenty of towns and no shortage of beaches and splendid scenery.

The country has 41,000 miles of paved roads, including motorways, and 17,000 miles of sealed roads that cut through mountains and the country's rugged terrain. Although traffic is generally light, it has one of the highest car-to-population ratios in the world, a car for every other person.

The road system around the flat Aukland and Hamilton area is thick, but as you get to the mountains south, you find fewer roads. There is a good coastal road past Whakatane around to Gisborne, isolated in spots. Going south from Hamilton you either have to take the flat roads to New Plymouth or make tough mountain crossings through the center of the island. The road system around Palmerstan becomes more extensive. The eastern part of the North Island is sparser, with many unpaved roads, but a main road runs from Hastings to Wellington.

The South Island is less popular with travelers, but it has a flat road down the west coast for those who like solitude and nature. Other roads run into the Christchurch region and down to the southern part, which is more inhabited. New Zealand is also mountain bike heaven—there are hundreds of trails all over the hills, especially in the North Island.

Map of New Zealand's North Island

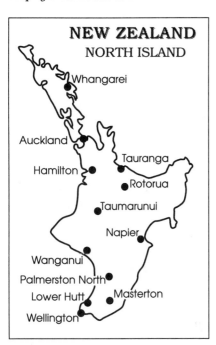

256

BACK MATTER.

_____ APPENDIX

Appendix 1. Equipment Packing List

The following is a list of items you should consider taking, not necessarily items required for every bicycle trip by every cyclist. When reflecting on whether to take an item, ask yourself if you really need it and whether you can get it en route. After a long, hilly trip, you will find yourself rejecting more and more items.

Medical Kit
(Covered in Chapter 11)
Small and large bandages
Aspirin
Antiseptic
Mosquito netting
Sterile gauze or cotton
Small scissor
Stretch bandage
Insect repellent or burning coil
Water purification tablets
Water purification filter
Medical tape
Prescription medicine
Snake bite kit
Sunscreen lotion
Malaria pills
Vitamin supplements
Kaopectate or other diarrhea medicine

Clothing
(Covered in Chapter 6)
Cycling shoes
Gloves
Sandals or spare shoes
Raingear
Thin socks
Cold-weather clothing
Thick socks
Helmet
Shorts
Hat
Tights
Long pants or dress for walking
Underwear
Shirt or blouse
Jerseys
Bathing suit

Camping Equipment
(covered in Chapter 8)
Tent
Eating utensils and plate
Tent stakes
Salt and spices
Light rope
Sweetener
Sleeping bag
Aluminum foil
Sewn sheet
Matches
Camping mattress
Flashlight or reading light
Stove and fuel
Mosquito netting
Pot and/or pan
Plastic food containers
Compass
Can opener

Tools and Spare Parts
(Covered in Chapter 19)
Water bottles
Chain tool
Pump
Chain lubricant
Tire patch kit
Adjustable wrench
Spare tire(s)
Grease and extra bearings
Inner tube
Cleaning brush (e.g. old toothbrush)
Rearview mirror
Extra chain or chain links
Shrader/presta adapter
Brake and derailleur cables
Screwdriver
Spare bolts and nuts
Hex wrenches

Spare spokes
Open-end wrenches
Spoke wrench
Pedal removal tool
Rim strip
Cone wrenches
Lock
Freewheel removal tool
Hand cleaner
Bottom bracket tools

Papers
Maps
Tourist literature
Identification paper for emergency
Passport
World Health Booklet (see chapter 11)
Extra passport photos
Airline, train, or boat tickets

Personal Items
Pocket mirror
Toiletries
Laundry soap
Sunlasses
Diary
Pens
Anti-dog spray
Toothbrush and holder
Towel

Camera Equipment
Camera Extra lens(es)
Film
Haze filter
Tripod
Flash
Lens hood
Shoulder strap

June, July, August

June, July, August

December, January, February

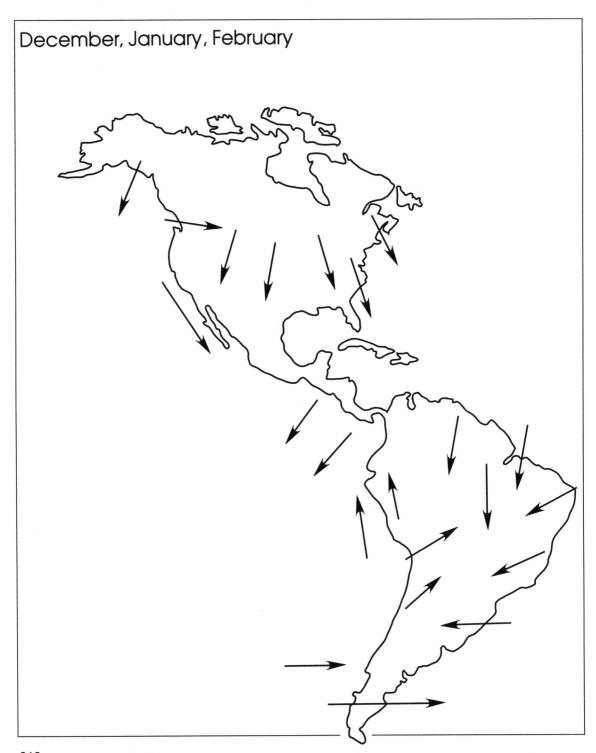

December, January, February

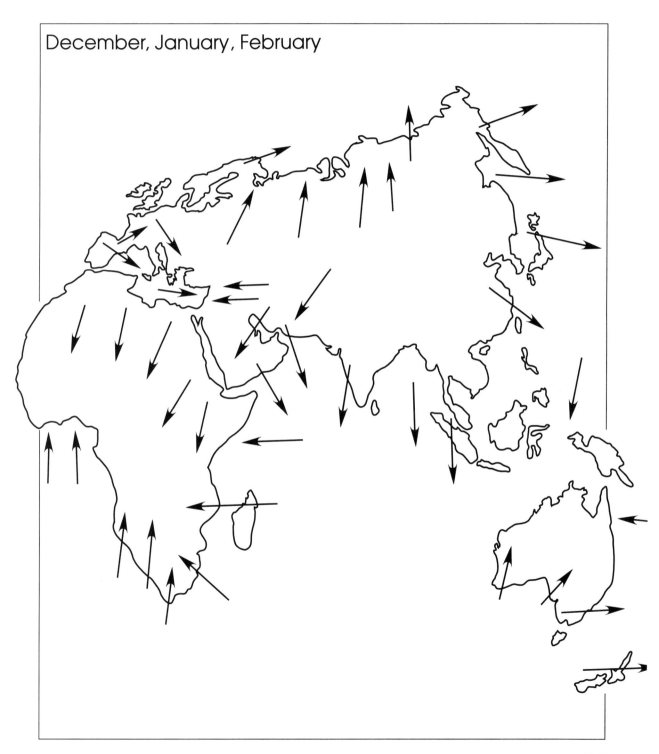

Appendix 3. Weather Tables

3A Temperature Conversion Graph

Centigrade	0	5	10	15	20	25	30	35	40 °C
Fahrenheit	32	41	50	60	68	77	86	95	104 °F

3B Weather Conditions Around the World

Average Daytime Temperature (C)/Average Nighttime Temperature (°C)
Average Monthly Rainfall (mm.)

	JAN	FEB	MAR	APR	MAY	JUN	JUL	AUG	SEP	OCT	NOV	DEC
North America												
Anchorage, Alaska	-7/-15 18	1/-11 20	7/-3 15	12/2 10	17/8 10	19/9 18	18/7 45	14/4 52	6/-2 58	-1/-9 58	-7/-14 28	24
Atlanta, Georgia	11/2 129	12/4 120	16/6 143	22/12 94	25/15 94	30/19 98	31/22 120	30/21 105	28/18 85	23/12 62	15/6 78	11/3 112
Birmingham, Alabama	13/3 124	14/4 118	19/8 147	23/12 132	27/16 97	31/20 114	32/21 127	32/21 94	30/19 72	24/13 57	18/8 78	13/4 108
Columbus, Ohio	3/-5 87	4/-4 72	9/1 79	16/6 74	22/10 84	27/16 88	28/18 93	28/17 83	25/14 62	18/8 68	10/3 72	4/-2 78
Dallas, Texas	13/2 61	16/4 68	19/9 82	25/14 112	28/18 112	32/23 92	33/24 78	34/24 69	31/20 72	26/14 74	29/7 68	14/4 64
Des Moines, Iowa	0/-10 28	1/-9 36	8/-3 45	16/4 72	22/11 108	27/16 132	30/18 82	28/17 90	25/13 98	18/6 63	9/0 34	1/-8 36
Fairbanks, Alaska	-19/-29 24	-5/-20 14	6/-8 20	15/-2 5	12/8 15	22/9 29	18/8 48	12/1 60	2/-8 32	-11/-21 20	18	15
Halifax, Nova Scotia	1/-9 137	-1/-8 109	3/-5 125	8/-1 115	15/4 103	20/9 92	24/13 112	23/12 103	19/9 124	14/5 141	9/0 135	2/-6 144
Los Angeles, California	18/7 80	19/8 72	18/9 64	21/10 23	22/12 8	24/13 3	27/17 0	28/17 0	27/15 3	24/12 14	23/10 28	19/9 64
Miami, Florida	23/16 70	24/15 52	16/17 68	27/19 89	29/23 152	30/23 178	31/24 162	31/24 159	31/23 219	29/22 239	26/19 70	24/17 54
Phoenix, Arizona	18/4 19	21/7 19	24/9 19	28/12 10	33/15 3	38/22 3	40/25 21	38/24 21	36/21 20	30/12 9	23/7 14	19/5 22
Pittsburgh, Penn.	3/-3 70	4/-4 72	9/0 78	16/5 73	22/11 74	26/15 92	29/18 110	28/16 89	24/14 59	18/9 68	11/2 60	5/-2 72
Portland, Maine	0/-9 108	1/-8 98	4/-3 106	10/2 92	16/8 79	22/12 84	24/16 88	23/15 80	20/11 79	13/6 83	7/1 91	1/-6 94
Quebec, Quebec	-8/-17 92	-1/-9 70	62	7/-1 55	25/5 83	22/10 102	25/15 115	23/12 98	18/8 83	11/3 86	2/-3 80	-6/-13 80

264

	JAN	FEB	MAR	APR	MAY	JUN	JUL	AUG	SEP	OCT	NOV	DEC
Salt Lake	2/-8	5/-3	10/0	17/3	23/8	28/12	33/16	32/16	26/9	20/4	9/-2	4/-6
Utah	33	34	45	59	42	23	15	21	18	32	34	33
Saskatoon,	-14/-23		-3/-4	9/-2	17/4	22/9	25/11	23/9	17/3	11/-3	-1/-9	-9/-18
Saskatchewan	24	14	12	23	34	60	65	45	39	23	12	16
St. Louis,	4/-3	6/-2	12/3	18/7	24/13	29/19	32/22	31/21	27/17	20/10	12/3	6/-1
Missouri	54	58	83	96	109	112	86	81	79	76	73	58
Seattle,	7/2	9/4	11/5	14/6	19/8	21/11	22/12	23/12	19/10	15/8	11/5	8/3
Washington	123	98	72	58	46	38	18	20	40	75	125	142
Vancouver,	5/1	7/2	10/3	14/4	19/9	21/11	23/12	23/12	17/9	14/6	9/4	6/2
B.C.	170	130	110	70	60	60	30	30	70	120	170	180
Washington,	6/-2	7/-1	12/2	17/7	24/13	28/17	31/20	29/19	25/15	19/8	13/3	7/-1
D.C.	79	68	89	101	89	108	116	119	96	78	67	76

Central America

	JAN	FEB	MAR	APR	MAY	JUN	JUL	AUG	SEP	OCT	NOV	DEC
Belize	27/19	28/10	29/22	30/23	31/24	31/24	31/24	31/23	30/22	30/22	28/22	27/20
City	140	62	41	58	110	203	160	174	249	310	224	182
Guatemala	23/12	25/12	27/14	28/14	29/15	28/16	26/16	26/16	26/16	24/15	23/14	22/13
City	8	5	15	28	156	276	219	202	240	169	24	5
Havana,	31/20	31/20	32/21	32/22	32/22	33/23	33/34	34/23	34/23	33/23	32/22	31/21
Cuba	30	62	89	157	241	112	68	127	178	175	76	36
Merida,	28/16	29/17	36/20	41/21	20/22	33/23	33/23	33/23	33/23	31/21	29/19	28/18
Mexico	24	20	24	28	80	170	120	130	158	98	34	30
Mexico	19/6	21/6	24/9	25/11	26/12	25/12	23/11	23/11	22/11	21/10	20/8/	19/6
City	10	8	12	20	50	120	160	148	132	53	28	5
San Jose,	24/14	24/13	25/15	26/17	27/17	26/17	26/17	26/16	26/16	25/16	25/16	24/14
Costa Rica	20	8	20	42	220	245	320	249	310	295	140	44

South America

	JAN	FEB	MAR	APR	MAY	JUN	JUL	AUG	SEP	OCT	NOV	DEC
Asuncion,	35/22	34/21	33/21	29/19	25/14	22/13	22/12	26/14	29/16	30/17	32/18	34/21
Paraguay	137	143	111	142	117	73	62	41	67	129	145	156
Autofagasta,	23/16	24/17	28/16	21/14	19/13	18/11	17/11	17/10	17/11	19/13	21/14	22/16
Chile	0	0	0	0	0	3	3	3	0	3	0	0
Bogota,	19/9	19/9	19/10	20/10	19/11	19/11	18/10	18/10	19/10	19/10	19/10	19/10
Columbia	60	60	110	149	111	60	50	59	59	170	120	69
Buenos Aires	29/17	28/16	16/16	23/13	18/8	14/5	14//5	16/6	18/8	21/10	23/13	27/16
Argentina	72	65	112	92	72	75	58	53	87	92	85	98
Caracas,	24/13	25/13	26/14	27/15	27/16	26/17	26/16	26/16	27/17	26/16	25/15	25/14
Venezuela	28	8	18	34	86	110	113	117	103	98	91	46
Georgetown,	29/23	29/23	29/23	29/24	29/24	29/24	29/24	30/34	31/24	30/24	30/24	29/23
Guyana	210	110	180	144	298	289	272	159	90	68	159	278+

	JAN	FEB	MAR	APR	MAY	JUN	JUL	AUG	SEP	OCT	NOV	DEC
Guayaquil, Ecuador	31/22 240	31/22 261	31/22 278	32/22 120	31/21 25	31/20 5	29/19 5	30/18 0	31/19 5	30/20 5	30/20 5	30/20 53
La Paz, Bolivia	17/6 151	17/6 110	17/6 64	18/5 30	18/3 15	17/1 5	17/1 10	17/2 15	18/3 32	18/3 40	19/5 44	18/6 98
Lima, Peru	28/19 5	28/19 0	28/19 0	27/18 0	26/17 5	25/16 5	26/16 5	26/16 10	26/16 10	27/16 5	26/16 0	26/15 0
Manaus, Brazil	31/24 265	31/24 257	31/24 282	31/24 267	31/24 182	32/24 92	32/24 69	33/24 39	33/24 56	33/24 110	32/24 154	32/24 219
Parana, Brazil	32/14 290	32/14 236	32/15 237	32/14 110	33/12 15	33/9 0	33/9 0	34/10 5	35/13 25	34/14 120	33/14 249	33/14 314
Quito, Ecuador	22/8 100	22/8 110	22/82 144	21/8 182	21/8 139	20/7 42	22/7 15	23/7 35	23/7 72	22/7 137	22/7 102	22/8 68
Rio de Janeiro	29/23 129	29/23 131	28/22 142	26/21 110	25/20 76	24/18 55	23/17 42	24/18 43	24/18 59	25/19 78	26/19 99	28/21 132
Trelew, Argentina	27/12 15	25/12 28	20/9 24	28/7 32	13/3 40	8/1 40	8/0 13	12/2 20	14/3 15	20/6 22	22/9 10	24/9 18
Valdivia, Chile	23/11 62	23/11 77	21/9 134	17/8 230	13/6 366	11/6 590	10/5 380	12/4 310	14/5 210	17/7 127	18/8 128	21/10 110

Europe

	JAN	FEB	MAR	APR	MAY	JUN	JUL	AUG	SEP	OCT	NOV	DEC
Athens, Greece	13/6 65	14/8 52	16/9 39	20/11 29	26/16 18	31/20 8	34/23 8	33/23 15	30/19 20	25/15 39	19/13 59	15/8 78
Bordeaux, France	9/2 88	11/3 77	15/5 65	17/6 48	20/9 62	24/12 67	25/14 51	26/14 59	22/12 82	18/9 99	13/5 98	9/3 118
Brussels, Belgium	4/0 65	7/1 65	10/2 58	14/6 65	18/8 57	22/10 72	23/12 105	22/11 88	21/10 63	15/7 83	9/3 74	6/0 76
Bucharest, Romania	1/-7 45	4/-5 27	10/0 27	19/5 56	23/9 76	27/14 113	30/15 54	30/14 39	25/11 41	18/7 29	10/2 29	4/-3 28
Dublin, Ireland	8/1 62	9/2 58	10/3 48	13/4 45	15/6 62	18/9 61	20/11 78	19/10 68	17/9 70	14/5 68	10/4 75	8/3 74
Dubrovnik, Yugoslavia	11/6 141	13/7 127	14/8 98	17/11 72	21/14 54	25/18 23	29/21 32	28/20 44	25/18 99	21/14 176	17/10 205	14/7 166
Edinburgh, Scotland	5/1 53	6/1 41	8/2 41	11/4 44	14/6 57	17/9 44	18/11 79	18/10 72	10/9 59	12/7 62	9/4 59	7/2 57
Hamburg, Germany	2/-2 55	3/-1 49	7/0 44	13/4 54	18/7 54	21/11 62	22/13 82	21/12 89	14/10 62	13/6 61	7/3 57	5/0 55
Helsinki, Finland	-3/-9 54	-4/-9 48	0/-6 34	6/0 38	14/4 44	19/8 52	22/13 68	20/12 68	15/8 69	8/3 68	3/-1 69	0/-5 67
Kiev, Ukrania	-4/-9 61	-2/-8 62	3/-3 50	15/5 59	20/11 45	24/13 92	24/15 92	24/14 30	20/9 34	13/6 57	6/0 62	0/-6 58
Kiruna, Sweden	-2/-7 54	-2/-6 51	1/-5 61	5/-2 45	9/3 44	14/7 64	18/11 57	16/10 84	12/6 92	6/2 89	3/-2 59	-1/-5 57

	JAN	FEB	MAR	APR	MAY	JUN	JUL	AUG	SEP	OCT	NOV	DEC
Lisbon, Portugal	14/8	15/9	17/10	20/12	21/13	25/15	22/17	19/13	17/10	16/9	15/9	14/8
	120	72	110	52	49	28	5	5	28	65	98	113
London, England	6/2	7/3	10/4	13/6	16/8	20/12	21/14	21/13	18/11	14/8	10/5	7/4
	52	48	38	42	49	55	57	47	59	52	63	51
Malaga, Spain	16/10	17/11	18/12	20/13	23/15	25/18	28/20	29/21	26/19	23/17	19/14	17/11
	152	99	110	59	22	3	0	0	24	58	110	129
Milan, Italy,	4/0	8/2	13/5	18/10	23/14	27/17	29/20	28/19	24/16	17/11	10/6	6/2
	48	56	69	81	81	96	59	81	70	119	115	78
Moscow, Russia	-9/-14		0/-8	10/1	19/8	21/11	23/12	22/12	11/7	9/4	3/-3	-5/-9
	40	36	34	36	54	57	78	76	55	48	47	55
Munich, Germany	2/-3	3/-2	8/0	13/4	18/7	21/11	22/13	22/13	19/9	14/5	7/2	3/0
	45	40	32	55	62	69	75	56	51	50	49	47
Naples, Italy	12/3	13/5	15/6	18/9	22/12	26/15	29/18	29/18	26/15	22/12	17/8	13/6
	120	89	72	59	46	28	17	37	66	98	151	142
Oslo, Norway	-2/-7	-1/-7	4/-4	10/1	16/6	20/10	22/13	21/12	16/8	9/3	3/0	0/-4
	48	37	25	45	45	70	84	97	81	75	68	62
Prague, Czech.	9/-12	11/-9	18/-7	23/-1	28/2	31/7	33/9	32/8	29/4	22/-2	10/-9	
	22	24	16	26	45	55	62	61	29	35	22	28
Sofia, Bulgaria	3/-4	4/-2	10/1	16/5	21/10	24/14	27/15	26/16	22/11	19/9	9/3	4/-1
	35	25	44	57	78	68	65	62	41	56	49	50
Stockholm, Sweden	0/-5	0/-5	3/-3	8/1	14/5	19/11	21/14	20/13	15/9	9/5	5/1	2/-2
	45	34	26	33	33	46	59	79	62	48	50	51
Tirana, Albania	13/6	14/6	16/8	19/10	23/13	27/17	30/20	30/19	29/16	23/14	19/11	15/8
	118	108	92	79	56	32	8	24	34	117	189	136
Vienna, Austria	1/-4	3/-3	8/0	15/.6	18/9	23/14	25/15	24/14	20/11	14/7	7/3	3/-1
	38	42	44	46	68	59	87	75	44	55	48	49
Warsaw, Poland	0/-5	0/-6	6/-1	12/3	20/9	22/12	24/15	23/14	19/10	13/5	6/1	2/-3
	31	29	33	28	46	71	98	66	41	39	35	37

North Africa

	JAN	FEB	MAR	APR	MAY	JUN	JUL	AUG	SEP	OCT	NOV	DEC
Algiers, Algeria	15/8	16/9	17/11	19/13	23/16	26/18	28/21	29/23	27/21	24/17	20/13	16/11
	112	84	74	41	46	15	0	5	41	79	130	137
Aswan, Egypt	23/10	25/11	31/14	37/19	39/23	42/26	42/26	41/26	38/24	37/21	31/17	25/12
	0	0	0	0	0	0	0	0	0	0	0	0
Cairo, Egypt	18/8	22/9	24/11	29/14	33/17	35/20	36/21	35/22	31/21	30/18	26/14	20/10
	6	5	5	4	3	0	0	0	0	0	3	6
In Salah, Sahara	20/6	24/6	29/12	34/17	37/21	43/27	45/28	43/27	41/25	34/20	28/12	22/7
	4	3	0	0	0	0	0	3	0	0	5	3
Rabat, Morocco	17/8	18/9	20/10	22/11	24/13	26/16	28/18	28/18	27/17	25/14	20/11	18/9
	66	64	66	45	30	8	0	0	12	50	84	90
Tripoli, Libya	16/8	17/9	18/11	22/14	24/16	27/19	28/22	30/22	29/20	27/18	23/14	10/10
	81	44	30	10	7	3	3	3	10	44	66	98

	JAN	FEB	MAR	APR	MAY	JUN	JUL	AUG	SEP	OCT	NOV	DEC
Tunis, Tunisia	14/6	17/7	18/9	21/11	24/13	30/17	32/21	33/21	31/19	26/15	20/10	16/7
	64	49	41	37	18	5	3	8	27	51	46	61

Eastern and Southern Africa

	JAN	FEB	MAR	APR	MAY	JUN	JUL	AUG	SEP	OCT	NOV	DEC
Addis Ababa, Ethiopia	24/6	24/7	25/9	25/10	25/10	23/10	21/9	21/9	22/9	24/7	23/6	23/5
	10	32	58	74	76	110	210	260	158	15	10	5
Bujumbarra, Burundi	28/18	28/19	28/19	28/19	28/19	29/19	29/19	29/18	30/19	31/20	28/19	28/19
	110	98	126	130	62	79	10	15	37	68	98	125
Cape Town, S. Africa	26/17	26/16	25/14	21/12	20/9	18/8	17/7	18/7	18/10	20/11	23/13	23/14
	15	10	21	45	83	90	93	60	39	31	18	10
Dar'Salaam, Tanzania	30/25	31/25	31/24	30/23	30/23	29/21	28/20	28/18	28/19	29/21	30/22	31/24
	70	70	128	280	172	53	33	25	30	40	82	80
Djibouti	29/24	29/24	30/25	32/26	34/28	37/30	31/30	40/29	36/29	33/26	31/25	29/23
	10	10	30	10	5	0	3	10	10	10	25	10
Dodoma, Tanzania	29/18	29/18	29/18	28/17	27/17	27/14	26/13	27/15	30/15	31/17	31/18	31/18
	150	98	125	67	10	0	0	0	0	3	28	90
Durban, S. Africa	27/21	27/20	27/20	25/15	23/12	22/12	22/13	23/15	24/17	25/18	25/18	26/19
	110	115	125	75	50	30	30	35	70	110	120	120
Francistown, Botswana	30/18	30/18	29/16	18/13	26/10	22/5	23/5	26/7	30/12	32/15	32/18	31/17
	112	82	89	14	3	3	0	0	0	27	58	82
Harare, Zimbabwe	26/16	26/16	26/15	24/13	23/8	21/7	21/7	22/8	25/12	27/14	27/16	27/16
	190	170	120	30	10	3	0	0	10	30	90	150
Huambo, Angola	26/14	26/14	26/14	26/14	25/11	24/8	25/9	27/11	29/12	28/13	26/14	26/14
	220	210	244	160	10	0	0	0	20	137	260	221
Kampala, Uganda	28/18	28/18	27/18	26/17	25/16	25/16	25/16	25/15	27/16	27/17	27/17	27/17
	46	62	133	159	148	72	46	86	91	99	110	85
Khartoum, Sudan	33/15	35/17	38/19	40/23	42/25	41/26	38/25	38/24	38/25	40/24	37/19	33/17
	0	0	0	0	3	7	50	70	15	3	0	0
Lilongwe, Malawi	28/18	27/17	27/16	26/15	25/11	23/8	24/8	25/8	28/13	30/15	29/18	28/18
	208	220	120	44	3	0	0	0	0	0	50	120
Lusaka, Zambia	26/17	26/17	26/17	26/16	25/13	23/10	23/10	24/11	28/16	30/18	29/18	27/17
	220	200	110	26	3	0	0	0	0	10	90	180
Maputo, Mozambique	30/22	30/22	29/20	28/19	27/16	25/13	24/13	25/15	27/16	18/18	29/20	29/21
	130	130	120	50	30	20	15	15	30	50	80	90
Nairobi, Kenya	25/12	26/13	25/14	24/14	23/13	22/12	21/11	21/11	24/11	24/12	23/13	23/12
	45	51	101	206	160	46	14	24	26	53	110	84
Port Sudan, Sudan	27/20	27/20	29/20	32/23	35/25	40/26	41/28	41/28	38/26	34/24	31/24	28/23
	3	3	0	0	0	0	10	5	0	10	40	25
Pretoria, S. Africa	27/16	27/16	26/13	24/10	21/7	18/3	18/3	22/6	24/9	27/13	27/14	28/15
	125	110	115	43	24	19	3	3	22	67	134	130
Windhoek, Namibia	29/17	28/16	27/15	24/13	23/10	20/8	19/7	22/8	25/12	28/15	29/16	31/18
	75	75	80	40	10	0	0	0	3	15	25	53

	JAN	FEB	MAR	APR	MAY	JUN	JUL	AUG	SEP	OCT	NOV	DEC

Central and West Africa

Accra, Ghana	31/24 15	31/24 34	31/24 52	31/24 79	31/24 141	29/23 178	27//20 45	29/21 18	29/22 39	30/22 64	20/22 36	31/22 26
Abidjan, Ivory Coast	31/23 44	31/23 49	32/24 89	32/24 135	32/24 370	30/22 510	28/22 224	28/22 54	29/23 72	31/23 162	31/23 205	31/23 81
Bamako, Mali	33/16 0	37/19 0	29/22 3	29/23 10	39/24 71	35/23 141	32/22 282	31/21 314	32/22 216	34/22 44	34/19 14	33/18 0
Bangui. C.A.F.	32/20 26	34/21 40	33/22 125	33/22 130	33/21 172	31/21 110	29/21 210	29/21 185	31/21 140	31/21 176	31/20 98	32/19 3
Brazzaville, Congo	31/21 140	32/21 124	33/21 187	33/22 189	32/21 124	30/18 5	28/17 0	29/18 0	30/19 42	32/20 143	31/21 238	31/21 205
Dakar, Senegal	27/17 0	27/17 0	27/18 0	27/18 0	29/20 0	31/23 20	31/23 92	31/24 271	32/24 112	32/24 41	31/22 3	27/20 5
Douala, Cameroon	30/23 50	30/23 92	30/23 214	30/23 236	30/23 325	29/22 520	27/22 724	27/22 710	27/22 581	27/22 412	28/23 152	29/23 62
Kisangani, Zaire	31/21 55	31/21 78	31/21 183	31/21 162	31/21 120	30/20 123	29/19 149	28/19 170	31/20 182	31/21 219	31/21 208	31/21 85
Lagos, Nigeria	31/23 40	32/24 57	32/26 100	32/25 115	31/23 215	28/23 336	28/23 150	28/23 59	28/23 214	29/31 222	31/24 79	31/23 42
Liberville, Gabon	31/23 250	31/23 260	31/23 330	31/23 350	30/22 240	29/21 15	28/20 5	30/21 20	30/22 100	30/22 330	31/23 370	31/22 250
N'djamena, Chad	34/15 0	36/17 0	41/21 0	42/34 3	40/26 15	38/24 52	33/22 165	31/22 310	33/22 101	36/21 28	36/18 0	33/15 0
Nouakchott, Mauritana	29/14 0	31/15 3	32/17 0	32/18 0	34/21 0	33/23 3	32/23 15	32/24 114	34/24 24	33/22 10	32/19 3	28/13 0
Niamey, Niger	34/15 0	38/18 0	41/23 3	42/25 10	41/27 30	38/26 80	34/23 140	32/22 198	34/23 99	37/23 20	38/20 0	34/15 0

Middle East

Aden. Yemen	28/22 3	28/33 0	30/24 3	32/25 0	33/25 0	37/29 0	37/28 3	35/28 0	35/28 0	33/23 0	30/23 5	29/23 5
Baghdad, Iraq	16/5 24	18/6 26	21/9 29	28/14 12	35/20 3	41/23 0	43/24 0	43/24 0	40/21 0	33/16 3	25/11 15	18/6 25
Beirut, Lebanon	16/11 190	17/11 175	18/12 89	21/14 58	25/18 22	28/21 3	31/23 0	32/24 0	20/22 3	27/20 34	23/16 136	18/13 179
Ismir, Turkey	13/4 104	14/5 98	17/6 72	21/9 39	25/13 27	30/17 15	33/22 5	32/21 3	29/17 15	24/13 54	19/9 87	14/6 124
Jerusalem	13/5 124	13/5 128	17/8 62	23/10 28	27/14 3	29/16 0	31/16 0	32/18 0	29/17 0	27/15 8	21/11 66	15/6 82
Kuwait	16/9 24	18/12 23	22/15 26	28/20 3	34/24 0	37/27 0	40/30 0	40/30 0	38/27 0	33/22 3	24/17 12	18/12 23

	JAN	FEB	MAR	APR	MAY	JUN	JUL	AUG	SEP	OCT	NOV	DEC
Nicosia, Cyprus	14/5 75	15/6 36	19/7 28	24/10 24	29/14 20	34/18 8	37/21 0	36/20 0	33/18 8	28/14 28	22/10 37	17/7 72
Riyadh, Saudi Arabia	21/8 3	24/9 15	28/14 23	32/18 24	38/23 8	42/25 0	42/26 0	42/25 0	37/22 0	34/16 0	30/13 0	21/9 0
Tehran, Iran	6/-3 46	9/0 34	15/4 42	22/9 38	28/14 18	34/20 3	37/23 3	36/22 0	32/17 3	24/13 8	17/7 21	11/1 29
Tibilisi, Georgia	7/0 15	9/1 15	13/3 30	17/8 62	24/12 78	28/17 55	31/20 47	30/19 47	26/15 42	20/9 30	14/5 30	9/1 18

Asia

	JAN	FEB	MAR	APR	MAY	JUN	JUL	AUG	SEP	OCT	NOV	DEC
Bankok, Thailand	32/21 5	33/22 25	34/23 35	35/24 62	34/25 175	33/24 176	32/24 169	32/24 179	32/24 305	31/23 233	31/22 62	30/21 5
Beijing, China	1/-9 3	4/-8 5	11/0 8	21/6 15	26/12 34	31/18 68	31/21 254	30/20 158	26/14 62	20/6 15	9/-1 8	3/-8 3
Bombay, India	27/17 0	28/18 0	30/23 0	32/24 0	33/26 20	33/26 500	30/24 600	29/24 350	29/24 250	32/24 50	32/22 10	30/20 0
Chungking, China	9/5 15	12/7 22	17/10 41	23/16 89	27/20 145	29/22 179	34/24 137	35/24 112	28/22 163	22/15 121	16/12 49	13/8 22
Colombo, Sri Lanka	31/22 90	31/22 67	31/23 145	32/24 232	31/25 144	29/25 226	29/25 145	29/25 121	29/24 175	29/24 356	29/23 331	29/22 146
Dacca, Bangladesh	25/12 15	27/14 32	33/16 59	35/22 113	34/25 189	32/26 332	31/25 423	31/25 297	30/24 247	30/24 172	29/18 43	26/13 3
Delhi, India	21/6 25	24/9 21	31/15 15	36/19 8	41/26 15	40/27 67	36/27 175	35/26 156	34/24 120	33/18 8	29/12 0	23/8 8
Hyderbad, India	28/15 8	31/18 8	35/21 15	37/23 31	40/27 31	35/25 114	31/23 146	31/22 147	31/22 162	31/21 58	30/17 24	29/15 8
HoChiMinh, Vietnam	32/21 10	33/22 10	34/23 12	35/24 55	34/24 205	33/23 305	31/23 260	31/24 269	31/23 310	31/23 265	31/23 119	31/22 45
Irkutsk, Siberia	-16/-26 13		-4/-18 10	6/-17 8	13/0 25	20/7 62	21/10 88	20/9 69	14/2 47	5/-5 18	-10/-20 10	10
Islamabad, Pakistan	16/2 64	19/5 64	24/10 80	31/15 42	37/21 22	39/34 58	36/24 230	34/24 260	34/22 88	31/15 18	28/9 15	20/3 20
Jakarta, Java	29/23 290	29/23 280	30/24 222	31/24 157	31/23 104	31/23 87	31/23 57	31/23 52	31/23 71	30/23 98	30/23 125	29/22 210
Kabul, Afghanistan	2/-7 29	4/-5 41	12/2 87	19/6 114	26/10 15	30/13 5	33/16 3	33/15 3	29/11 0	23/6 15	17/2 24	8/-2 14
Katmandu, Nepal	17/2 0	18/3 0	25/6 0	27/12 5	30/16 10	30/18 30	29/20 75	29/20 50	28/19 25	27/14 5	23/7 5	19/3 0
Kwanchow. China	19/13 34	17/13 41	19/15 65	24/19 123	27/22 267	29/25 359	30/26 376	31/26 356	29/24 223	27/22 123	23/18 32	20/15 26
Lhasa, Tibet	7/-9 0	9/-7 10	12/-1 10	16/1 5	18/5 22	24/9 61	23/9 113	22/9 76	21/7 69	16/0 10	13/-4 5	9/-9 0

	JAN	FEB	MAR	APR	MAY	JUN	JUL	AUG	SEP	OCT	NOV	DEC
Manila, Philipp.	30/21 24	31/21 15	33/22 15	34/23 35	34/24 136	36/24 266	32/24 410	31/24 425	31/23 360	31/23 187	31/22 145	30/21 76
Phnom Penh, Kampuchea	30/20 8	32/22 8	34/23 35	34/24 75	35/24 135	34/24 160	33/24 175	32/24 150	31/24 225	30/24 270	30/23 110	30/22 40
Rangoon, Burma	31/17 3	33/19 3	35/22 10	36/24 50	33/25 322	30/24 428	29/24 609	29/24 534	30/24 402	30/24 176	31/23 68	31/20 8
Sararinda, Borneo	28/22 214	29/23 222	30/23 189	30/23 204	29/23 223	29/22 186	29/23 176	29/23 157	29/23 134	29/23 129	29/23 178	29/23 210
Seoul, S. Korea,	0/-9 31	3/-6 22	8/-1 35	17/5 78	22/11 78	27/15 130	28/20 380	31/22 265	27/15 120	20/7 52	11/0 48	3/-7 29
Singapore	32/22 164	32/22 221	33/23 276	33/23 267	33/23 234	33/23 121	33/23 98	32/23 45	32/22 221	32/22 267	32/22 254	32/22 201
Tokyo, Japan	8/-1 48	9/0 73	12/3 103	17/7 135	22/12 140	24/17 175	29/20 144	30/22 149	27/18 220	20/13 213	16/6 99	11/0 58
Ulanbatar Mongolia	-12/-22 15	0/-10 8	15/2 10	21/8 35	25/12 24	27/14 47	27/13 22	21/8 27	10/0 18	0/-10 41	-8/-13 41	8

Australasia

	JAN	FEB	MAR	APR	MAY	JUN	JUL	AUG	SEP	OCT	NOV	DEC
Darwin, Australia	32/25 362	32/25 322	32/25 262	33/25 110	33/24 10	33/23 0	32/22 0	31/20 5	33/23 15	34/25 60	34/25 140	33/26 236
Hobart, Tasmania	22/12 45	22/12 34	20/10 47	17/9 47	14/7 47	12/4 52	11/3 49	13/5 44	15/6 49	17/8 56	19/9 62	21/11 57
Melbourne, Australia	26/14 47	26/14 47	24/13 57	21/11 57	17/8 50	14/6 55	13/6 47	14/6 49	17/8 55	19/9 65	21/11 56	24/12 58
Port Moresby, New Guinea	32/24 184	31/24 186	31/24 165	30/24 110	30/23 66	29/23 33	28/23 25	28/23 15	29/23 20	29/24 35	30/24 49	31/24 110
Perth, Australia	29/17 8	29/17 8	26/16 20	24/14 45	21/12 132	18/9 175	17/9 180	17/9 144	19/11 87	21/12 55	24/14 20	26/16 15
Wellington, New Zealand	21/13 80	21/13 80	19/12 78	17/11 92	13/8 110	12/7 115	11/6 137	12/7 120	14/8 87	16/9 99	17/11 85	19/12 86

Appendix 4. Useful Addresses

Algeria

Office National Algérien
Touristique
54 Rue Ali Haddad
El Mouradia, Algiers

Argentina

Direccion General de Turismo
Calle Suipacha 1111, 21 p.
1368 Buenos Aires

Australia

Australian Tourism Commission
Box 73
Melbourne, Vic. 3004

Bicycle Institute of New South
Wales
GPO Box 272
Sydney N.S.W. 2001

Youth Hostel Association
60 Mary Street
Surry Hills, N.S.W. 2010

Austria

Jugend Informationszentrum
Dambockgasse,1
1170 Wien 17

Bangladesh

National Tourist Organization
233 Airport Road
Tejgaon, Dhaka 15

Belgium

Centre Infor Jeunes
27 Rue Marche aux Herbes
1000 Bruxelles

Royale Lingue Vélocipédique
Belge
49 Avenue du Globe
1190 Bruxelles

Fiets Overleg Vlaanderen
Eglatierlaan 41
2020 Antwerpen

Benin

Office National du Tourisme
B.P. 89
Porto-Novo

Bolivia

Instituto Boliviano de Turismo
Edif. Herrmann, 4 p.
Plaza Venezuela
Casilla 1868, La Paz

Botswana

Tourism Division
Ministry of Commerce and
Industry
Private Bag 0047, Gaborone

Bulgaria

Automobil and Touring Club
Rue Sv. Sofia 6
Sofia

Brazil

Centro Brazileiro de Informacáo
Turistica
Rio de Janeiro, RJ

Cameroon

Delegation Generale au Tourisme
B.P. 266
Yaoundi

Canada

Canadian Cycling Association
1600 James Naismith Dr.
Gloucester, Ont. K1B 5N4

Canadian Government Office of
Tourism
235 Queen Street
Ottawa, Ont. K1A OH5

Surveys and Mapping Branch
Department of Energy, Mines and
Resources
Ottawa, Ont. K1A OE9

Central African Republic

Office National du Tourisme
B.P. 655
Banguti

Chile

Servicio Nacional de Turismo
Calle Catedral 1165, 3 y 4 p.
Casilia 14082, Santiago

Congo

Direction Generale du Tourisme
B.P 456
Brazzaville

Cuba

Empresa de Turismo National
Calle 23 No 156
Vedado, Apdo 6560
Havana

Czechoslovakia

Czechoslovak Cycling Federation
Velodrom, Nad Trebesinem III
1000 Praha 10

Denmark

Dansk Cyklist Forbund
Avedor Traervej 15
2650 Hvidovre

Youth Information Center
Radhusstraede, 13
1466 København

Ecuador

Dirección Nacional de Turismo
Reina Victoria 5144
Roca, Quito

England and Scotland

Britsh Cycling Federation
70 Brompton Road
London SW3 1EX

Cyclists' Touring Club
69 Meadrow
Godalming, Surrey GU7 3HS

Scottish Youth Association
7 Glebe Crescent
Stirling, Scotland 5K8 2AJ

British Youth Hostels Assocation
Trevelyan House
8 St. Stephens Hill
St. Albans, Hertfordshire AL1 2DY
or
14 Southhampton St.
London WC2E 7HY

Egypt

Egyptian Government Tourist
Office
630 5th Ave.
New York NY 10111

Ethiopia

Ethiopian Tourism Commission
Box 2183
Addis Ababa

Finland

Suomi Touring Club
Unioninkatu 45H
Helsinki 17

Matkailum Edistamiskeskus
Asemapaallikonkatu 12b
00520 Helsinki

France

Féderation Française De
Cyclotourisme
8 Rue Jean Marie Tego
75013 Paris

Féderation Française des Usagers
de la Bicyclette
4 rue Brulee
F-67000 Strasbourg

Féderation Unie des Auberges de
Jeuness
6, Rue Mesnil
75116 Paris

Touring Club de France
65 Avenue de la Grande-Armee
Paris 75016

Germany

Allgemeiner Deutscher Fahrrad
Club
Postfach 107744
Bremen 2800

Ghana

Ghana Tourist Board
State House Complex, 6th floor,
bay 2
Box 3106
Accra

Holland

ANWB Royal Dutch Touring Club
Wassenaarseweg 220
Den Haag

ENFB, Echte Nederlandse
Fietesers Bond
Postbus
Woerden

Nederlandse Rijwiel Toer Unie
Postbus 76
Zoetermeer

Bureau Voor Internationale
Jongeren Kontakten
Prof. Tupstraat 2
1018 HA Amsterdam

India

Department of Tourism
Government of India
Pariament Street
New Delhi 110001

Indonesia

Dewan Parivisata Indonesia
81 Jalan Kramat Raya
Jakarta

Ireland

Federation of Irish Cyclists
Halston Street
Dublin 7

Irish Youth Hostels Association
39 Mountoy Square
Dublin 1

Northern Ireland

Youth Hostel Association
23 Bedford St.
Belfast BT2 7FE, Northern Ireland

Israel

Israel Cycling Association
45 Katznelson Street
Givatayim 53216

Italy

Bici e Dintorni
Corso Reg. Margher 52
10152 Torino

Italian Cycling Center
2117 Green Street
Philadelphia PA 19130

Touring Club Italiano
Corso Italia 10
Milano

Ivory Coast

Ministere du Tourisme
BP V77
Abidjan

Japan

Japan National Tourist
Organization
Tokyo Kotsu Kaiken Bldg.
2-10-1, Yurako-cho, Chiyoda-ku
Tokyo

Youth Hostels, Inc.
Hoken Kaikan, 1-2
Sadohara-cho, Ichigaya
Shinjuku-ku, Tokyo

Jordan

Ministry of Tourism
Box 224
Amman

Malaysia

Tourist Development Corporation
17th and 18th floors
Wisma MP1

Mali

Societé Malienne d'Exploitation
des Ressources Touristiques
Place de la Republique
BP 222
Bamako

Mauritania

Societé Mauritanienne de Tourisme
BP 552
Nouakchott

Mexico

Secretaría de Tourismo
Avda Pat. Masaryk 172, 3 p.
11587 Mexico DF

Morocco

Moroccan National Tourist Office
20 East 46th Street
New York NY 10017

Nepal

Department of Tourism
HM Government of Nepal
Tripureswar, Kathmandu

New Zealand

New Zealand Cyclists
Box 5890
Aukland

Tourist and Publicity Department
Private Bag
Wellington

Nigeria

Nigerian Tourist Board
Takawa Balewa Square Complex
Box 2944
Lagos

Norway

Norway Cycling
Maridalsveinen 60
N-0458 Oslo 4

Pakistan

Pakistan Tourist Development
Corporation
House #2 St. 61, F-7/4
Islamabad

Paraguay

Dirección General de Turismo
Ministerio de Obras Publicas y
Comunicaciones
Oliva y Alberdi
Asunción

Philippines

Philippine Tourism Authority
4/F Legaspi Towers
300 Roxas Blvd.
Manila

Poland

Polorbis Tourist Office
500 5th Avenue
New York, NY 10110

Portugal

Poruguese Cicloturismo
Ave. Miguel Bombarda 147 2 D
1000 Lisboa

Romania

Romanian National Tourist Office
573 3rd Avenue
New York, NY 10016

South Africa

South African Tourism Board
Menlyn Park Office Block
Menlyn Drive and Atterbury Road
Menlyn 0081

Spain

Amics de la Bici
Apartat de Correus 10012
08080 Barcelona

Pedal Libre
Calle Campomanes 13
28013 Madrid

Sudan

Public Corporation of Tourism
Box 7104
Khartoum

Sweden

Svenska Turisforeningen
Stureplan 2
Stockholm 7

Switzerland

Touring Club Suisse
Rue Pierre-Fatio 9
1211 Geneva

Cartel Suisse des Associations de
Jeunesse
Fathausgasse 47
3000 Bern 7

Taiwan

Taiwan Visitors Association
5th Floor, 111 Mincharan East Rd.
Taipei

Tanzania

Tanzanian Tourist Corporation
Box 2485
Dar es Salaam

Thailand

Tourism Authority of Thailand
4f Ratchadamnern Nok Ave.
Bangkok 10100
or 5 World Trade Center
New York NY 10048

Turkey

Ministry of Culture and Tourism
Gazi Mustafa Kemal Bulvari 33
Demirtepe, Ankara

Uganda

Uganda Tourism Development
Corporation
Box 7211
Kampala

U.S.A.

American Youth Hostels
Box 37613
Washington DC 20013

Bicycle Frederation of America
1818 R Street NW
Washington DC 20009

Bikecentennial
Box 8308
Missoula MT 59807

East Coast Bicycle Congress
626 South 4th Street
Philadelphia, PA 19141

League of American Wheelmen
6707 Whitestone Rd. #209
Baltimore MD 21207

Michelin Guides and Maps
Box 188
Roslyn Heights, NY 11577

National Off-Road Bicycle
Association
Box 1901
Chandler AZ 85244

U.S. Geological Survey (maps)
Distribution Section
Federal Center
Denver, CO 80225
or
1200 South Eads St.
Arlington VA 22202

U.S. Canadian Map Serivce Bureau
Midwest Distribution Center
Box 249
Neenah, WI 54956

Women's Cycling Network
Box 73
Harvard, IL 60033

Venezuela

Departmento de Turismo
Palacio de Miraflores
Caracas

Zaire

Office National du Tourisme
Immeuble de la Rwindi
Box 9502
Kinshasa

Zimbabwe

Zimbabwe Tourist Office
1270 Avenue of the Americas
New York NY 10020

International

Council for International
Educational Exchange
205 East 42nd Street
New York NY 10017

World Alliance of Young Men's
and Women's Christian
Assocations
37 Quai Wilson
1201 Geneva, Switzerland

National Campers and Hikers
Association
7172 Transit Road
Buffalo, NY 14221

**Some Commercial U.S.-based
Bicycle Touring Organizations**

All Adventure Travel
Box 4307
Boulder CO 80306

American Youth Hostels
Dept. 806
Box 37613
Washington DC 20013

American Wilderness Experience
Box 1486
Boulder CO 80306

Asian Pacific Adventures
336 Westminister Ave
Los Angeles CA 90020

Australian Bicycle Events
Box 1108
Tallahassee FL 32302

Backroads Bicycle Touring
Box 1626-RB
San Leandro CA 94577

Bicycle Adventure Club
2369 Loring Street
San Diego CA 92109

Bicycle Africa
4247 135th Pl SE
Bellevue VA 98006

Bicycle Detours
Box 44078
Tuscon, AZ 85733

Bike Quest
Box 332-B
Brookdale CA 95007

Boojum Expeditions
2625 Garnet Ave.
San Diego, CA 92109

Breaking Away Bicycle Tours
1142 Manhattan Ave #253
Manhattan Beach, CA 90266

Butterfield & Robinson
70 Bond St.
Toronto, Ont. M5B 1X3

China Passage
168 State Street
Teaneck NJ 07666

Country Cycling Tours
140 W. 83rd St.
New York NY 10024

Cycle America, Inc.
Box 29
Northfield MN 55057

Cycle Tours
2007 39th St.
Des Moines IA 50310

CycleVentures
R.R. #2
Cumberland, Ontario
KOA 1SO

Easy Rider Tours
Box 1384
Arlington MA 02174

Excursions Extraordinaires
Box 3493
Eugene OR 97403

Euro-Bike Tours
Box 40
DeKalb IL 60115

Four Seasons Cycling
Box 203
Williamsburg VA 23187

Journey Associates
1030 West Southern Ave.
Mesa AZ 85210

Open Road Tours
1601 Summit Dr.
Haymarket VA 22069

Ten-Speed Tours
7013 Haskell Ave. #203
Van Nuys CA 91406

Vermont Country Cyclers
Box 145
Waterbury Center
Vermont 05677

WomanTrek
Box 20643
Seattle WA 98102

Bibliography

A. Bicycle Adventures

Nick and Richard Crane. *Bicycles up Kilimanjaro* (Interbook. 1985) Adventure travelers who also wrote *Journey to the Center of the Earth* (Bantam, 1987) about their ride through Central Asia, and *Atlas Biker* (Oxford Illustrated Press, 1990), about mountain biking down Morocco's Atlas mountains.

David Duncan, *Pedaling to the Ends of the Earth* (Simon and Schuster, 1985). Three Americans who traveled through Europe, North Africa, and Asia.

Anna and Howard Green, *On a Bicycle Made for Two* (Hodder & Stoughton, 1990). Relates a 6000-mile tandem trek to Nepal.

Dervla Murphy, Full Tilt (John Murray, 1965; Arrow, 1987 Describes a trek from England to India.

Anne Mustoe, *Bike Ride: 12,000 Miles Around the World* (Virgin 1991). Adventures of a spirited 54-year-old woman alone.

Kameel Nasr, *The World Up Close* (Mills & Sanderson, 1990) Bicycle adventure on five continents.

Barbara Savage, *Miles from Nowhere* (Mountaineers, 1985. Account of an around-the-world trek. The author was killed in a bicycle accident a few miles from her home after the adventure.

Bettina Selby, *Riding to Jerusalem* (Sidgwick & Jackson, 1985) This is her third bicycle travel book, following Riding the Mountains Down (Trafalger, 1980), which relates her journey from Karachi to Kathmandu, and Riding the Desert Trail (Sphere, 1989), about her North African adventure. She traveled alone.

Miranda Spitteler, *Four Corners World Bike Ride* (Oxford Illustrated Press, 1989). Describes four teams of tourists on four continents.

Thomas Stevens, *Around the World on a Penny Farthing* (Seven Palms/Century, reprinted 1988). The first adventure cyclist, who started on his 50-inch machine in 1884.

Virginia Urrutia, *Two Wheels & a Taxi: A Slightly Daft Adventure in the Andes* (Mountaineers, 1988]. No one would guess that the author was 70 years old.

Robert Winning, *Bicycling Across America* (Wilderness Press, 1991).

B. The Americas

The Complete Guide to America's National Parks by the National Park Foundation (Prentice Hall, 1992). One of several works focusing on the U.S. and Canadian parks popular with cyclists.

Paul Glassman, *Guatemala Guide* (Champlain, 1990). Detailed and useful for explore ing the country1 but not geared to cycling.

Scott Graham, *Adventure Travel in Latin America* [Wilderness Press, 1990). It1s hard to get useful literature for touring Latin America. This one is mostly for backpackers.

Karen and Gary Hawkins, *Bicycle Touring in the Western United States* (Pantheon, 1982). Gives suggestions for roads that avoid the dense traffic. There are hundreds of other guides to specific regions in the U.S. and Canada.

David Stanley. *Alaska-Yukon Handbook* (Moon Publications, 1984). Very useful for cyclists.

Lonely Planet guides. They produce a guidebook for most countries, as well as thick guides for all of central and South America. These provide city information but do not describe road conditions. Their guide to Costa Rica is adequate for cyclists.

C. Europe

Nicholas Crane, *Cycling in Europe* (Pan Books, 1984). Detailed country by country description, but no routes.

Jeremy Evans, *Off-Road Adventure Cycling: 50 Routes in England for the Mountain Bike* (Crowood, 1990).

Bob Hunter, *Cycle Touring in France* (Frederick Muller, 1984), and Britain by Bicycle (Weidenfeld & Nicolson, 1985). Gives suggestions for 20 tours in each country.

Illustrated Guide to Britain, Automobile Association (Drive Publications, 1985). This detailed guide with copious color photos would be useful for cycling backroads.

Susi Madron, *Cycling in France* (George Philip, 1988). Several easy tours throughout the country.

Robin Neillands, *Cycle Touring in France* (Oxford Illustrated Press, 1989). Twenty tours and good information.

Barry Ricketts, *The Mountain Biking Handbook* (Arena Press, 1988) Detailed information on ATBs and some tours in England.

Jerry H. Simpson, Jr., *Cycling France* (Bicycle Books, 1992). Gives general information and detailed tours.

Nadine Slavinski, *Cycling Europe* (Bicycle Books 1992). The best overall guide to Europe, particularly for budget travel.

Karen and Terry Whitehill, *Europe by Bike* (Mountaineers, 1987) Describes, day-by-day, 18 different routes.

Les Woodland, *Get Away by Bike* (Viking Penguin, 1990 Provides general touring information and specifics on Europe.

D. Africa

Kathleen Bennett, *Cycling Kenya* (Bicycle Books, 193'=2). Invaluable for getting around that country.

Simon Glen, *Sahara Handbook* (Hunter Publishing, 1987). covers necessary information with useful clarity.

Jim Hudgens and Richard Trillo, *West Africa, the Rough Guide* (Harrap-Columbus, 1990). A 1200-page work providing detailed information on each country. Rough Guide produce books for many countries around the world. These are not bicycling guides, but they do provide useful, accurate information.

Bob Swain and Paul Snyder, *Through Africa: The overlanders' Guide* (Bradt, 1991). This book gives special consideration to cycling and should be read by prospective African cyclists.

Zimbabwe, Botswana & Namibia: Travel Survival Kit (Lonely Planet, 1992). Since roads in this area are few, this guide would be adequate for travelers to those countries.

E. Asia and Australia

Tom Brosnahan, *Turkey: a Travel Survival Kit* (Lonely Planet, 1987). Many people cycle through Turkey, and this guide is good for hotels and attractions, not so much for roads.

Michael Buckley, *Cycling to Xian and Others Excursions* (Crazyhorse Press, 1988). A personal 4000 mile story, but should be ready by those contemplating cycling in China.

Simon Calder, *Soviet Union & Eastern Europe Survival Kit* (Vacation Work, 1989). This is already old; new guides are being commissioned, but information will have to be updated frequently.

Bill Dalton, *Indonesia Handbook* (Moon Publications, 1988). The most useful to bicycle tourists, although not a cycling guide.

Malcolm Gordon, *Outback Australia at Cost* (Little Hill Press, 1989). Details excursions to remote areas that can be made by train, camel, and bicycle.

Leigh Hemmings, *Bicycle Touring in Australia* (Mountaineers, 1991). The first bicycle guide to the entire country, though there are many guides to specific areas available locally.

Suzanne Lee, *Bicycling Japan: A Touring Handbook* (Zievid Press, 1991). Gives road conditions and route suggestions.

Lonely Planet Guides: Since there are no good guides for specific roads in Asia, Lonely Planet country guides, and especially South-East Asia on a Shoestring and central Asia on a Shoestring, are about the most useful.

Brian Schwartz, *China: Off the Beaten Track* (China guides, 1985). There are many china guidebooks; this gives some details that would be useful to cyclists. Consider also Nagel's 1500 page guide, China.

F. General Bicycle Books

Richard Ballantine, *Richard's New Bicycle Book* (Ballantine Books/ Pan Books). Good guide for understanding bicycles.

Bicycle Magazine's Cycling for Fitness and Endurance (Rodale Press, 1990). Gives tips for improving performance.

Raymond Bridge, *Bike Touring: The Sierra Club Guide to Outings on Wheels*, (Sierra, 1979). Was a good guide when it first came out, but other books have replaced it.

Fred DeLong, *DeLong's Guide to Bicycles and Bicycling* (Chilton, 1987). Technical information.

Dick Marr, *Bicycle Gearing* (Mountaineers, 1989). For touring and racing, with many charts.

Tony Oliver, *Touring Bikes: A Practical Guide* (Crowood Press, 1990). Technical but understandable.

Rob Van der Plas, *Bicycle Technology* (Bicycle Books, 1991). All of Van der Plas' books, including *The Bicycle Touring Manual*, *Roadside Bicycle Repairs*, *The Bicycle Repair Book*, and *The Mountain Bike Book*, are the most practical and helpful.

Carlton Reid, *Adventure Mountain Biking* (Crowood Press, 1990). Strong on techniques and equipment.

Susan Weaver, *A Woman's Guide to Cycling* (Ten Speed Press/Kingswood Press, 1990). Practical advice for women.

Index

Other Books by Bicycle Books

We issue about four new titles each year. The following list is up to date at the time of going to press. If you want more details, you may order our full-color catalog from the address below or by calling 1-800-468-8233.

Title	Author	US price
The Mountain Bike Book	Rob van der Plas	$12.95
The Bicycle Repair Book	Rob van der Plas	$9.95
The Bicycle Touring Manual	Rob van der Plas	$14.95
Roadside Bicycle Repairs	Rob van der Plas	$4.95
Major Taylor (hardcover)	Andrew Ritchie	$19.95
Bicycling Fuel	Richard Rafoth	$9.95
In High Gear	Samuel Abt	$10.95
Mountain Bike Maintenance	Rob van der Plas	$9.95
Mountain Bike Maint. and Repair	John Stevenson	$22.50
Mountain Bike Racing (hardcover)	Gould and Burney	$22.50
The Bicycle Fitness Book	Rob van der Plas	$7.95
The Bicycle Commuting Book	Rob van der Plas	$7.95
The New Bike Book	Jim Langley	$4.95
Tour of the Forest Bike Race	H.E.Thomson	$9.95
Bicycle Technology	Rob van der Plas	$16.95
Tour de France (hardcover)	Samuel Abt	$22.95
Tour de France (softcover)	Samuel Abt	$12.95
All Terrain Biking	Jim Zarka	$7.95
Mountain Bike Magic	Rob van der Plas	$14.95
The High Performance Heart	Maffetone & Mantell	$9.95
Cycling Kenya	Kathleen Bennett	$12.95
Cycling France	Jerry Simpson, Jr.	$12.95
Cycling Europe	Nadine Slavinski	$12.95
The Backroads of Holland	Helen Colijn	$12.95
Bicycle Touring International	Kameel Nasr	$18.95

When it comes to buying books, support your local book shop!

To obtain a copy of our current catalog, including full descriptions of all our books, please send your name and address to:

Bicycle Books, Inc.
PO Box 2038
Mill Valley CA 94942
or to the national distributor listed on the back cover if you live in Canada or the UK.

We encourage our readers to buy their books at a book or bike shop. All our titles are available from our own book trade distributor, as well as from the major book trade distributors Ingram and Baker & Taylor. In addition, many bicycle and outdoor sport shops carry our most popular books.

If your local shop is not willing to order the books you want, you can order directly from us. In that case, please include the price of the book plus postage and handling ($2.50 for the first book, $1.00 for each additional book), as well as sales tax for California mailing addresses. When ordering from Bicycle Books, prepayment or credit card number and expiration date are required. We'll gladly fill your order, but we'd prefer you try the book shop first.